Politics

of

Liberal

Education

Post-Contemporary

Interventions

Series Editors

Stanley Fish and

Fredric Jameson

The Politics of Liberal Education

Darryl J. Gless and
Barbara Herrnstein Smith, Editors

Duke University Press   Durham and London

The text of this book was originally published
without the present introduction or index and
without the essays by Stanley Fish and Francis Oakley
as Volume 89, No. 1 (Winter 1990) of the *South
Atlantic Quarterly*.
© 1992 Duke University Press
All rights reserved
Printed in the United States of America
on acid-free paper ∞
Library of Congress Cataloging-in-Publication Data
appear on the last printed page of this book.
Second printing in paperback, 1992

Contents

Acknowledgments

Most of the essays printed here first appeared in the Winter 1990 issue of the *South Atlantic Quarterly*, where they received the expert editorial attentions of the journal's managing editor, Melissa Lentricchia, and her assistant, Emily White. A number of other people at both the University of North Carolina, Chapel Hill, and Duke University contributed substantially to the success, logistic and otherwise, of the conference from which this book derives. Special acknowledgment is owed to Robert A. Allen, H. Keith H. Brodie, Richard Dienst, Jackie Gray, J. Lee Greene, Phillip Griffiths, Paul Hardin, Fredric Jameson, Sharon Landesmann, Frank Lentricchia, Marlin Price, Candice Ward, and Richard A. White.

The

Politics

of

Liberal

Education

Introduction: The Public, the Press, and the Professors

The essays collected in this volume, with two exceptions, are versions of papers presented at a conference, "Liberal Arts Education in the Late Twentieth Century: Emerging Conditions, Responsive Practices," held in 1988 at Duke University and the University of North Carolina.[1] The occasion and motive for the conference were explained in a letter sent to proposed speakers by its organizers (a committee of faculty members from both universities, cochaired by the present editors). The letter, which conveys something of the spirit of the subsequent event, read in part as follows: "In view of the recent eruption of reports in the national press of an alleged 'attack on the classics' and 'fall of standards' in American education, and in view also of the increasingly strenuous criticism of liberal arts teaching—and teachers—by, among others, officials in the Department of Education and the National Endowment for the Humanities, we believe that concerned members of the academic community are eager for occasions to explore these issues responsibly and to discuss them with each other and with the public."

Since the conference was designed to respond to attacks on current humanities teaching and curricular reforms, it is not surprising that most participants defended current educational practices and attempted to explain and justify such reforms, current or proposed. Contrary to subsequent reports in the national press, however, conservative perspectives were well represented both on the platform and among audience members, and participants included outspoken proponents of various aspects of educational tradition. The phrase "cultural left," used wryly by one of the speakers and repeated, also with some irony, by a second, was seized upon by an attending journalist and has now become an easy label. Irony, an occupational habit of philosophers and English teachers, fares very poorly under conditions of public controversy.

Neither political uniformity nor political diversity per se was sought by the conference organizers. What was sought, rather, was a group of informed, interested, and articulate educators in a variety of fields—classics, education, history, literature, and philosophy, among others—who could illuminate the issues from the perspectives of both their special disciplines and their individual experiences as teachers. (As the list of contributors to this volume attests, they were and are, by most measures, a distinguished group of scholars and teachers.) "Politics" as generally understood, moreover, was not the sole or even central theme of the conference. In accord with the announced title of the event, participants were invited to discuss the changing conditions (especially social and technological) to which educational practices were responding, the broader historical and intellectual contexts of contemporary curricular reforms, the formation and revision of literary canons both currently and as a general question, and the politics—local and national, disciplinary and professional—of the ongoing educational controversies.

The array of specific topics to which they directed their attention—as represented by the contributions to this volume—is a telling portrait of the group and index of the moment: the development of "canons" in the ancient world and of the humanities in the modern one; the drama of the revision of "Western culture" requirements at Stanford University; the critical reception of African-American writing; the educational implications of political movements, such as feminism, and of social pathologies, such as homophobia; the cultural and intellectual implications of the electronic media; the dubious claims made for "cultural literacy"; the dubious idea of a single, common culture; the possibility of a critical "reading" of television drama; the possibility of more politically enlightening and intellectually engaging pedagogies; and public perceptions and misperceptions of academic controversies. The presentations—always lively, often witty, sometimes elegant, sometimes biting—were, of course, of topical interest and are, we believe, of continuing intellectual significance as well.

"Contrary to reports in the national press. . . ." As suggested above and as readers of this volume will find increasingly evident, that *contrariety* is a running theme of these essays: their initiating motive, constant accompaniment, and continuing caveat. Indeed, media exploitation—determined misrepresentation as well as extensive publicity—has been a considerable factor in all the controversies examined here. Important issues certainly abound in the contemporary debates over education, and much discussion and reporting of them in the press have been conscientious. The controversies have also been accompanied and inflamed, however, by a remarkable series of cross-citing and mutually puffing newspaper articles, magazine stories, and topical books, duly peppered with selective statistics, evocatively illustrated by menacing photos, and obviously produced by and for persons remote from the scenes of the alleged crimes.

The initial reports of educational chaos were evidently of considerable interest to the American public ("strikes a responsive chord" was the phrase in play: tracing the notes of that chord would require an extensive psycho-political-historical analysis). Not altogether coincidentally, one suspects, there has now arisen a whole army of defenders and exposers of higher education, many of whom, while championing Reason and Intellectual Standards, appear more intent on providing occasions for public outrage and targets for private malice than in securing either accuracy or illumination. The educational problems of the nation are extensive and complex. Demons are always easier to fashion than solutions. And someone is always ready to take advantage of a communal anxiety by producing a communal scapegoat.

Can the distortions be untwisted? Not, it appears, too readily. Certain types of messages are especially hard to put across the public media, and they are just the types—long on concepts, short on personalities; long on analyses, short on punch lines; long on new, challenging ideas, short on familiar, confirming ones—that teachers and scholars characteristically send their students and each other via other channels (e.g., in classrooms, in specialized journals, and at professional conferences). On the other hand, certain sorts of messages go especially well across the public media: vivid, dramatic, particular, newsy at the level of information, not so newsy at the level of ideas. And, of course, these are just the sorts of messages that journalists, by profession, and public officials, by necessity, are most practiced at sending. It is not surprising that, in the race for the public ear, professors tend to come in last.

Of related significance here is the widespread conviction, especially common among journalists, that the first type of message should be more like the second or, in other words, that the way to reform humanities education is to make professors sound more like journalists. There is a corresponding conviction, especially common among professors, that the trouble with the public media is that its reporting does not resemble more closely the articles in academic journals, and that journalists would do better to write more like professors. The more general problem, it appears, is a failure to recognize that the constraints on each type of transmission—that is, liberal arts scholarship and public journalism, even at their best—are inevitably as different as their respective objectives. Such cross-purposes may be comical or, at worst, exasperating under ordinary circumstances. Currently, they aggravate other—often ideological—conflicts between academics and members of the press.

Contributing to the difficulty of disentangling disinformation here is the fact that when messages of the first type (conceptual, abstract, challenging, unfamiliar, and so forth) are reported in the public media, they routinely become indistinguishable from the second type: witness the astonishing ongoing transformation of virtually the entirety of twentieth-century thought along with what is specifically referred to as "theory" into the "blather" and "gobbledygook" that they are simultaneously charged with being. To be sure, not all the aberrations of transmission originate in the public media. The more radical and arcane developments of twentieth-century thought have not been digested wholesale within the universities, either; and the same processes that become so dramatic when a hundred-page treatise becomes a one-phrase print-bit or quarter-minute sound-bite (that is, abbreviation, domestication, personalizing, and all-around mangling) are duplicated in the journalistic writings and public pronouncements of a good number of professors also.

Crisscrossing the educational controversies at every level are conflicts of a more obviously political kind, including ongoing struggles for status among haves, have-nots, and used-to-haves within various communities, including academic departments and disciplines, professions and governmental bodies, and, to be sure, political organizations and parties in the strict sense. As is often the case in such conflicts, all sides claim to represent the common good and to be moved by a disinterested concern for truth and reason, and all parties charge their adversaries with representing special interests and being moved primarily by the wish to gain or retain personal advantages. These claims are often transparently hypocritical but may also be sincere enough; people tend, on the whole, to regard their own motives charitably and the motives of their adversaries uncharitably. Moreover, the charges are, on all sides, *sometimes* true enough—how often, exactly when, and how significantly, are, of course, issues themselves. We return to this last point later but would stress here that (as is also the case in all such conflicts) there are other ways to tell the stories that are being told. The contributors to this volume do not and could not provide full rebuttals to distorted accounts of contemporary educational practices and the motives for recent reforms; but they do offer perspectives on these controversies that are rather different from those most commonly represented in the media.[2]

The educational offenses supposedly being exposed in best-selling campus-rakers—"abandonment of the classics," "scrapping of standards," "politicizing of the classroom," and so forth—are, for the most part, things that are not happening at all or things that are happening in ways, and for reasons, very different from those reported. It is simply not true, for example, that the classics are no longer being taught. The teaching of literature is, of course, changing. It would be more remarkable if, at Duke, Stanford, and other allegedly outlaw universities, exactly the same poems, novels, and essays were now being studied—and in exactly the same ways—as in, say, 1950. There is, however, no large-scale disavowal of master truths or discarding of masterpieces. As has been repeatedly stated and documented, nothing in higher education has been more stable over the past forty years than the curriculum of departments of English—except, perhaps, the periodic table of elements in departments of chemistry. Across the nation, in Durham and Palo Alto as in Cambridge and Chapel Hill, teachers still assign, explicate, and celebrate works by those still-honored writers whose portraits still adorn department halls and office walls.

But, of course, even the table of elements—durable icon of Fact, Truth, and Law that it is—is not altogether what it was in our youth, if that was forty years ago. And, true enough, contemporary fiction, Western (in both senses) films, and writings by women and minority authors are being studied and taught where they were not studied and taught before. These developments, however, do not reflect or require blithe disregard for appropriate standards. Nor can they be reduced to the desire by new faces in the academy to see counterparts of themselves on its shelves of Great Books. Self-representation and proportional representation are sometimes sought, but they are not the crucial objectives involved. Moreover, even where such objectives (or "demands") are explicitly named, their satisfaction is not the crucial mechanism of canon revision. The issue is central but easily muddled.

Many public critics of the academy and, more understandably, most members of their public audiences have little idea of what occurs in contemporary classrooms, including what it means—or ever meant—to "teach" literature. It does not mean—and never did or could mean—simply assigning and celebrating classic texts. Nor, by the same token, does the "teaching" of a film or a work of popular fiction mean simply assigning and celebrating *it*—"side by side with Homer and Shakespeare," as the recurrent image of outrage has it. On the contrary, what is often represented to the public as the "traditional" way to teach literature has probably never been practiced in any intellectually respectable college or university anywhere. What the educational investigative reporters have apparently not detected is that humanities teaching, by definition and indeed tradition, must attempt to meet a number of significant but diverse educational objectives. What they have also not detected and certainly not appreciated is that the societal and institutional conditions under which teachers now attempt to fulfill those objectives are very different from what they were forty years ago.

Most teachers of literature, now as before, see their primary task as enabling their students to read literature—*some* literature, *any* literature—with interest and understanding and to appreciate its power to reflect and convey beliefs, to make what is alien recognizable, to illuminate what is familiar, to articulate elusive but important feelings, and to give scope to imaginative play and intellectual speculation. That is quite a tall order, but that is not all. For, in addition, humanities teachers typically see the study of literature as an occasion to explore an important range of topics that their students, many of whom will never take another humanities course in their lives, may have no other occasion to study. When and where else, for example, would an engineering major be taught anything about the operations of metaphor or the workings—for good and for bad—of rhetoric more generally? When and where else would an accounting major have a chance to learn something about the cultural history of her own region, not to mention more distant places? When and where else would a chemistry major have a chance to engage and discuss certain recurrent metaphysical, ethical, or political themes in Western, not to mention non-Western, thought? The answer is: very likely never and nowhere else. But what are the implications of this answer?

One implication, well known to all humanities teachers who take seriously their responsibilities to the students actually in front of them (as distinct from their recollections or fantasies of students elsewhere or in some previous era), is that they must be exceptionally canny and resourceful in designing their courses and in selecting readings for them. Not *all* the worthy objectives of contemporary humanities education can be served by the study of *only* the classic authors. Those authors—Homer, Dante, Milton, Shakespeare—are unique, and much of what they do they do uniquely. They do not do everything uniquely, however, and there are some worthy things that they do not do at all—which is not only why canons keep expanding but also why writers keep writing. Nor is it obvious that knowing as many classic authors as possible should be, per se, an absolute educational priority; and, where it is or has been an absolute priority, one may well ask what that "knowing" consists of and at the expense of what other valuable enlightenments.

It is commonly said that, with only a limited amount of time available, only the best writings should be studied. That, in our view, is correct. The question is: given the enormous store of literature, the traditional and otherwise desirable educational objectives indicated above, and any set of specific students, conditions, and institutional constraints, which writings *are* "the best"? The point made over and over by the contributors to this volume is that the answer to that question is not self-evident, cannot be determined in the abstract, and is not always the same.

═════

What about those allegedly lowered standards? Is it not true that, as a columnist recently put it, just when so many women and African-Americans are being hired, everyone is reading books by "writers nobody ever heard of before"? The question, with its factually false premises and naive (not to mention self-revealing) imputations, is recurrent. What is false is the idea that no one heard of these authors (presumably women and African-Americans) before. What is naive (and self-revealing) is the suggestion that "affirmative action"—in the now commonly insinuated sense of an otherwise unjustifiable action performed only to meet externally imposed racial and sexual criteria—is responsible for both the hirings and the readings.

Authors such as Charlotte Perkins Gilman, Frederick Douglass, and Zora Neale Hurston, whose names may not be known to most columnists or to many of their readers, are well known (and have been for some time) to most scholars, teachers, and critics—and to a large number of general readers—of American literature. Moreover, in the view of many of these readers, the works of such authors exhibit, in generous supply, not only the virtues said to be among the "purely literary standards" now "downgraded" by professors of English ("grace of style, vigor of prose, and originality of expression," as another columnist puts it), but also certain other qualities not commonly found either on standard lists of "standards" or in the works of most other widely taught and studied authors: for example, subtle insight into and strong evocation of the lives of women and African-Americans.

The point is not that everyone now recognizes that the works of Gilman, Douglass, and Hurston do, after all, possess those virtues—the purely literary ones—per se. The point is that their works evidently did not exhibit those virtues to certain *other* readers in the past, or, perhaps, decisively exhibited *other* qualities that were, for such readers, rather disquieting and, as they might have put it themselves, intensely *un*interesting: for example, the qualities noted above as being *additional* virtues for many contemporary readers, namely, subtle insight into and strong evocation of the lives of women and African-Americans. Two further points are crucial here. One is that, while the two groups of readers indicated above—past and contemporary—obviously have had significantly different tastes and interests, *both* groups have included people who, by reason of their positions in the academic and/or literary worlds (e.g., respected scholars and critics, teachers at "standard-setting" colleges and universities, and reviewers for major literary and intellectual journals), have been—not individually, but in concert and cumulatively—influential enough to make the names of certain authors household words in those worlds. The second point is that, both now and in the past, the authors or works thus promoted would have been the ones which those readers, given their particular tastes and interests, found especially appealing and which, given what they assumed (correctly or not) were more broadly shared tastes and intellectual or educational interests, they judged especially important to study and teach. For it is this way that literary works become what we call "canonical": *this* way, and not by their satisfaction of "purely literary standards" or by "affirmative action."

═══════

What, finally, *is* the "politics of liberal education"—and should there be any? Depending on their own broader values, concerns, and allegiances, the individual contributors to this volume would probably answer that question differently. But this very fact—that one's views on educational issues are affected by one's broader values, concerns, and allegiances—would have to figure in their answers. For this reason, the inevitable reply to the charge that humanities education has been "politicized" is that it has always been political. This is not to say that education is "indoctrination" or that advocacy in the classroom is never an abuse of authority. It is to say, however, that no community can transmit skills and information—to its children or to anyone else—without also transmitting, wittingly or otherwise, and for better or for worse, its own prevailing beliefs and attitudes (or, to use the much abused term, "ideologies"). What is new about American education in this regard is not its political character as such; what is new is the wide range of interests and perspectives now in play, the increased sharpness of their divergence from each other, and, consequently, the more numerous occasions for collisions among them. "Politics" or "ideology" is always part of education, but an invisible part so long as everyone agrees—or appears to.

———

As was noted above, multiple conflicts at many levels crisscross and exacerbate the current educational controversies. Also exacerbating them, most significantly but not exclusively in the public media, are determined conflations of what is most reasonable with what is least reasonable. Descriptions of ongoing educational reforms that could be seen by many members of the public as understandable and desirable are disingenuously combined with reports of "demands" that are bound to seem outrageous and dangerous and that may in fact be absurd or, from other or broader perspectives, unjust and undesirable. For here, as in all large-scale social movements and changings of institutional guards or generations, there are always enough individual episodes of folly, arrogance, and opportunism, always enough individual memories of loss, injury, and humiliation, to give the exaggerations plausibility and to keep the anxious fantasies alive. Where irresponsible conflation is the offense and danger, the defense and response must be careful differentiation, that is, the always arduous, never glamorous—and, in the midst of battles, often thankless—task of recognizing and indicating differences: here, crucial differences in the operation and upshot of specific educational proposals, practices, and policies. The results of such efforts—carefully framed analyses, critical comparisons and assessments—must compete with more vivid and seductive polarizations and demonologies, by allies as well as adversaries. The only alternative, however, is to accept the triumph of such polarizations and demonologies, at considerable loss and cost for all concerned.

=====

A final word. Various groups of people in this nation—and, to be sure, probably in every other nation in the world—have been subjected, and still are subjected, to extensive political, legal, and otherwise institutionalized biases that limit and damage their lives. The observation hardly needs documenting, or so one would have thought. Such matters do apparently need simple stating, however, in the face of currently powerful reactions against the political, legal, and other social reforms of the last decades. It has been said that social revolutions, often in precise proportion to the violence of the oppressions that engendered them, risk repeating that violence in reverse. That may be so. Lash follows lash, backlash follows lash *and* backlash. The script—inscribed in one version over twenty centuries ago by an Athenian playwright—seems as durable as any classic text or law of nature. Like the table of elements cited above, however, perhaps it, too, can be revised.

B. H. S.
Durham, April 1991

Notes

1   The exceptions are the essays by Stanley Fish and Francis Oakley. Professor Fish participated in the conference but did not present a formal paper at that time. The contribution by President Oakley was originally a public lecture delivered at the National Humanities Center in Research Triangle Park, North Carolina.

2   We do not respond here to the numerous misrepresentations and oversimplifications of individual contributors' papers that appeared in immediate newspaper accounts of the conference or to similar distortions that have been produced and perpetuated in subsequently published commentary on these essays. It is hoped that, with the publication of this volume, a broader group of readers will have the opportunity to judge the conference proceedings for themselves.

Mary Louise Pratt

Humanities for the Future: Reflections on the Western Culture Debate at Stanford

SWM, 38, 5' 10", N/S, Stanford scientist, average-looking, a bit eccentric, blindingly brilliant, phenomenally funny, amazingly humble, likes jogging, bicycling, all things done with racquet-like instruments, movies, literature and most aspects of western civilization, but most interested in a reasonably attractive and intelligent 25–45 PA female capable of being interested in me. Send photo & brief description of your life, liberty and pursuits of happiness. Box 65C.

This singles ad appeared late last summer in the personals column of a local weekly serving the communities of Palo Alto, California, and neighboring Stanford University. Apart from its intriguing characterization of the "Stanford scientist," I quote it here to suggest the extent to which Stanford's long and intense debate over its Western culture curriculum last year permeated local life. In the semiotics of representation and identity, "Western civilization" remains a constant and intensely meaningful point of reference.

The debate which took place at Stanford during the winter of 1988 and the resulting reform of the Western culture requirement received a great deal of national attention, largely due to the involvement of then Secretary of Education William Bennett, who chose to use the Stanford case as a platform to advocate his views, quite literally making a federal case out of it. Perhaps because of Bennett's own partisanship, the account of the Stanford debate in the national press had a shape somewhat different from the local experience. As other institutions face similar struggles, fuller accounts of the workings of change at Stanford may be helpful. At the same time, there is an urgent need to formulate the concerns that so unexpectedly made freshman book lists an object of wide public concern. What nerves had been touched?

Histories of Western culture curricula in the United States point to the Western civilization course instituted at Columbia University in 1919 as a main antecedent for such courses all over the country. One recent account, however, notes that the Columbia course had a direct antecedent of its own, a War Issues course instituted in 1918 at various universities, including Columbia. Its aim was "to educate recently conscripted American soldiers about to fight in France . . . to introduce [them] to the European heritage in whose defense they were soon to risk their lives."[1] A new tie to Europe was constituted in relation to a national imperative.

Current struggles over Western culture curricula—both challenges to them and reactionary attempts to reassert them—also emerge from urgently felt national imperatives. Among these is an imperative to reimagine cultural and civic identity in the United States in the wake of vast changes produced by the decline of its global hegemony, the rapid internationalization of capital and industry, the immigrant implosion of the "third world" onto the "first," and the democratization of American institutions and political processes that occurred in the two decades prior to 1980. The question can be posed in Pierre Bourdieu's sometimes helpful language: What is to count as "cultural capital" in a culturally plural nation and a globalized human world? How will that capital be constructed and deployed, how will people

be asked to identify with it? How might the United States project itself into the future as a cultural and political entity? In the words (a
few of which I've emphasized) of one speaker in the Stanford debate:

> The character of U.S. society is changing. More and more North
> Americans insist on affirming the specificity of their class, eth-
> nicity, gender, region, race, or sexual orientation, rather than
> melting into the homogenizing pot. They see such affirmations as
> *intrinsic to their citizenship*. Culture, literature, and the academy
> have been important sites for these affirmations: it will be neither
> productive nor comfortable to commit ourselves only to resisting
> these developments, rather than engaging with them.

Having acquiesced to change, by what visions will United Statesians
be guided into a future where they and their society will be different
from what they are now? What is the United States trying to become?
What are the options?

The world is full of multicultural, multi-ethnic, multilingual nations, so there are plenty of models around. Indeed, Bloom, Bennett,
Bellow, and the rest (known by now in some quarters as the Killer B's)
are advocating one of them: to create a narrowly specific cultural
capital that will be the normative *referent* for everyone, but will
remain the *property* of a small and powerful caste that is linguis-
tically and ethnically unified. It is this caste that is referred to by
the "we" in Saul Bellow's astoundingly racist remark that "when the
Zulus have a Tolstoy, *we* will read him." Few doubt that behind the
Bennett-Bloom program is a desire to close not the American mind,
but the American university, to all but a narrow and highly uniform
elite with no commitment to either multiculturalism or educational
democracy. Thus while the Killer B's (plus a C—Lynne Cheney, the
Bennett mouthpiece now heading the National Endowment for the
Humanities) depict themselves as returning to the orthodoxies of
yesteryear, their project must not be reduced to nostalgia or conservatism. Neither of these explain the blanket contempt they express
for the country's universities. They are fueled not by reverence for
the past, but by an aggressive desire to lay hold of the present and
future. The B's act as they do not because they are unaware of the cultural and demographic diversification underway in the country; they

are utterly aware. That is what they are trying to shape; that is why they are seeking, and using, national offices and founding national foundations.

Many citizens are attracted to Bloom's and Bennett's pronouncements, on the other hand, out of fairly unreflected attachments to the past (including their own college experience), and simply have trouble seeing how good books could possibly do any harm. Many people are perfectly ready for change but remain deeply anxious about where it is all supposed to be heading. Other visions of the cultural and educational future in the United States, then, are likely to generate as much interest as the Killer B's', if they can be effectively introduced into the national discussion. The attention drawn by Bloom's intellectually deplorable *Closing of the American Mind* and Bennett's intellectually more deplorable "To Reclaim a Legacy" most directly reflects not levels of enthusiasm for their programs (though much enthusiasm does exist), but levels of anxiety that have developed around the issue of national cultural identity. Even among the many people ready for change, one seems to hear voices asking, "If I give up white supremacy, who am I? Am I still American? Am I still white? If I give up homophobia, who am I? Am I the same as gay? If I give up misogyny, am I still a man? a woman? an American? If I learn Spanish, does it make me Mexican? What ties me to these gays, these feminists, these Salvadorans, these Vietnamese, these Navaho, these white people?" And perhaps more acutely, "What ties them to me?" The sooner answers to these questions are attempted, the better. What, indeed, would it mean to adopt the "non-hierarchical, intercultural perspective on the study of culture and the West" called for by one Stanford humanist (a classicist, at that)? What can cultural citizenship and identity be in a radically plural society enmeshed in relentlessly globalizing relations? Can there be transnational national culture? Can it be good?

Alongside the understandable apprehensions such questions generate (especially late in a century), it should be possible to create some excitement and curiosity. After all, this could become, perhaps has become, a fabulously energetic and revealing cultural experiment. It has tremendous imaginative appeal. Does the United States not badly need to revitalize its image and understanding of itself? Is there not much to be learned about the fluid global cultureways that bring the music of Soweto into living rooms across the United States, and make *The Cosby Show* the most popular TV program in South Africa? Is there not much to be learned about the past by rereading it in the light of contemporary intercultural understanding?

Stanford adopted its first Western civilization course in 1935, and, like many other universities, abolished it around 1970. Efforts to restore a requirement began around 1975 on the part of a group of senior faculty in literature, classics, and history. By 1978 a two-year pilot program had been approved and in 1980 a new year-long required course began for all incoming students. It consisted of several tracks corresponding roughly to different departments and schools, and sharing a core reading list that became the focus of the controversy. It is interesting to note that the notorious reading list was not part of the original proposal for the requirement. The list evolved during the pilot program out of desire to guarantee a "common intellectual experience," a phrase that acquired great importance in the subsequent debate without acquiring any greater specificity of meaning. Here is the much-discussed list:

ANCIENT WORLD

Required:
Hebrew Bible, Genesis
Plato, *Republic*, major portions
  of books 1–7
Homer, major selections from
  Iliad, *Odyssey*, or both
At least one Greek tragedy
New Testament, selections
  including a gospel

Strongly recommended:
Thucydides
Aristotle, *Nicomachean Ethics*,
  Politics
Cicero
Virgil, *Aeneid*
Tacitus

MEDIEVAL AND RENAISSANCE

Required:

Augustine, *Confessions*, 1–9
Dante, *Inferno*
More, *Utopia*
Machiavelli, *The Prince*
Luther, *Christian Liberty*
Galileo, *The Starry Messenger*,
   The Assayer

Strongly recommended:

Boethius, *Consolation of Philosophy*
Aquinas, some selection which
   illustrates the structure of
   a Thomistic question
A Shakespearean tragedy
Cervantes, *Don Quixote*
Descartes, *Discourse on Method*,
   Meditations
Hobbes, *Leviathan*
Locke, *Second Treatise of Civil
   Government*

MODERN

Required:

Voltaire, *Candide*
Marx and Engels, *Communist
   Manifesto*
Freud, *Outline of
   Psychoanalysis*,
   *Civilization and Its
   Discontents*
Darwin, *Selections*

Strongly recommended:

Rousseau, *Social Contract*,
   Confessions, *Emile*
Hume, *Enquiries*, *Dialogues on
   Natural Religion*
Goethe, *Faust*, *Sorrows of Young
   Werther*
Nineteenth-century novel
Mill, *Essay on Liberty*,
   The Subjection of Women
Nietzsche, *Genealogy of Morals*,
   Beyond Good and Evil

Participants in developing the course say that in its specifics the list was not intended to be written in stone. It represented a series of compromises rather painfully hammered out by a committee, inevitably through some of the crudest kind of horse-trading—Catholics for Protestants, poets for scientists, Italians for Germans. In the end, ironically, the difficulty of negotiating the list was one source of its permanence: the process had been so painful and so lacking in intellectual integrity that no one expressed the slightest desire to repeat it.

In any case, regardless of its specific content, the list did the job of shaping the requirement in, for many people, unnecessarily narrow ways. Indeed, its extreme narrowness clearly contributed to the breakdown of the program at Stanford. Most conspicuously, the list installed a specific historical paradigm: one quarter for ancient world, one for medieval-renaissance, and one for the past five hundred years. Implicit in the sequence was the canonical narrative of origins deriving the present from classical Greece via the Italian Renaissance and the Franco-German Enlightenment, a narrative that begins and ends with European lettered high culture. (Where is America?) Clearly, teachers of the course could question that implicit narrative, and some did. But to do so in a consistent or structured way involved teaching against the grain of the syllabus, an extremely difficult pedagogical task that often confused students more than it empowered them.

Second, the list not only lays down a Eurocentric paradigm, but also embodies a very restricted sense of Europe. France and even England are barely represented in the required readings; Iberia, Eastern Europe, and Scandinavia not at all. Only "high" culture is represented, an exclusion that has long been under challenge not just by the Black Students' Union, but by whole schools of mainstream literary and historical scholarship. One thinks of the scholars at Princeton's Center for European Studies, or the Berkeley-based new historicism, movements that are in no way radical or critical of the West, but which refuse to give "high" culture or belles lettres a monopoly on cultural understanding. Many Stanford scholars were troubled by the fact that the course organized itself around authors and orthodoxies rather than around problematics or issues, and that it therefore took *as* orthodoxies matters that were actually under serious debate in their fields. Translated into practice, this amounted to a structure of exclusion of faculty who took other perfectly legitimate approaches to culture and to the West, as well as of faculty who worked in non-European literatures and cultures. "For some scholars," said one colleague, "to see a book or an entire cultural tradition as if it were a self-contained whole is like listening to only one side of a phone conversation. For these scholars there is no place in the current program."

Third, the list implicitly suggests a monumentalist attitude to the texts as great works whose interest and value were sui generis. Again, teachers were of course not forbidden to adopt a critical attitude, but to do so required teaching from the negative position of a counter-discourse or a heresy. What you couldn't do was embark positively on a different project or way of thinking, even one that was equally celebratory and equally Eurocentric. An attempt was made to set up a critical track, a course titled "Conflict and Change in Western Culture." In many ways this course was extremely successful, but its founders were constantly hampered by the structure of center and periphery into which they were locked. To bring in other texts was always to bring in "Other" texts. In the end, this structure of otherness comprises, depending on your perspective, the main *obstacle to* or the main *bulwark against* relational approaches to culture. "The *notion* of a core list," argued one teacher in the history track,

> is inherently flawed, regardless of what kinds of works it includes or excludes. It is flawed because such a list undermines the critical stance that we wish students to take toward the materials they read. . . . A course with such readings creates two sets of books, those privileged by being on the list and those not worthy of inclusion. Regardless of the good intentions of those who create such lists, the students have not viewed and will not view these separate categories as equal.

The asymmetry can be exemplified by a remark made in support of retaining the core list. Referring to the autobiography of the West African Olaudah Equiano, published in England in the late eighteenth century, one English scholar argued that students "who have studied Genesis, Aquinas, and Rousseau have a good chance of understanding with some precision what the ex-slave Olaudah Equiano meant when he spoke of 'that first natural right of mankind . . . independency.'" The remark, true enough in a way, easily invites some troubling inferences. Would one want to suggest that students who have *not* studied Genesis, Aquinas, and Rousseau have *no* chance of understanding Equiano? That Equiano himself would not have understood liberty without his European education? Neither inference is true in the slightest. There are plenty of readings that can serve to illuminate Equiano to American students, and these certainly include Rousseau, Aquinas, and Genesis. As for Equiano himself, no slave ever needed

Rousseau or anybody else to know the difference between freedom and slavery, though a slave might find Rousseau helpful (as Equiano did) in attempting to argue matters with the enslavers. It is not from Europeans that enslaved peoples have learned how to construct cultures that conserve a sense of humanity, meaningful life, and an abiding vision of freedom in the face of the West's relentless imperial expansion. Indeed, it is essential to reverse the direction of inference and note that students who have read Equiano have a good chance of understanding what Rousseau meant in talking about human rights and equality. From there follows the question many find deeply but unnecessarily disturbing: To what extent was Rousseau influenced indirectly by the African slaves, whose fearsome rebellions and unquenchable demands for change echoed constantly back to Europe from the colonial frontier? From an intercultural perspective, the initial statement about Equiano taken by itself reproduces a monumentalist cultural hierarchy that is historically as well as morally distortive.

Many critics felt that the Western culture program set a tone for the humanities as a whole at Stanford, in the words of one Latin Americanist, making "second-class citizens out of faculty whose work focuses on non-European literatures, on noncanonical writers, on European literatures not included in the core, or on the West in dialogue with other parts of the world." In terms of faculty, in the years the Western culture program was in place, classics outgrew all the departments of modern languages and literatures; a Europeanist comparative literature department was founded; the English department continued to boast four medievalists while African, African-American, and Caribbean literatures in English were represented by a single half-time faculty member (whose tenure was hotly contested), and so-called "Commonwealth" literature not at all. The curriculum in French continued to include not a single course in Franco-African or even Quebecois literature. The number of Chicano faculty remained the same in 1988 as it was in 1972. A new humanities center, on the other hand, did assert a broader range, successfully seeking out interdisciplinary scholars and grants to fund minority and third world fellows.

The opposition to the Western culture curriculum that eventually coalesced at Stanford was there pretty much from the beginning. In the planning stages, it turned out, no fewer than seven other proposals for a culture requirement had been made and set aside. Several of these involved intercultural perspectives and heavily non-European materials. Right from the start many faculty in relevant fields chose not to participate in the course, including what was described as a near boycott by minority, women, and younger faculty. Then a beginning assistant professor, I recall vividly being asked to teach a section in one of the tracks. When I objected to the absence of the Iberian world and the Americas from the core list, I was told I might be invited to give a lecture on things written in Spanish since *Don Quixote*, "if I thought there was anything worth talking about." But really, the senior historian said, the advantage of the assignment was that it would help me avoid getting caught in a "Hispanic rut."

The fact that the course excluded or marginalized the work of many of the university's own humanities faculty made it a good deal more expensive than anticipated. Several hundred thousand dollars a year were needed to pay instructors on short-term contracts, most of them recent Ph.D.'s in the humanities. Many of these teachers did not share the monumentalist project, and they too became an impetus for change, as they introduced other materials and persectives in their sections. By the time the reform was proposed, the core list was widely tampered with and no longer enforced. Some people were teaching against the grain—but the grain was still very much there. Organized student advocacy of reform was a consistent and essential component throughout the three-year process. Student momentum began to coalesce during Rainbow Coalition activity for the 1984 election, and through the intense anti-apartheid activity of 1985–86. A coalition of student groups, including the Black Students' Union, the Movimiento Estudiantil Chicano de Aztlan (MEChA), the Stanford American Indian Organization, the Asian American Student Association, and Students United for Democracy in Education formed to exert continuous pressure on the reform process, from within and without.

The chronology of the reform process ran roughly as follows:

(1) In the spring of 1986 the dean of undergraduate studies, a European historian and the first woman to hold the position, appointed a task force to review the Western culture requirement and produce recommendations for the faculty senate's Committee on Undergraduate Studies. The task force consisted of three undergraduate students, two senior historians (one Europeanist and one African-Americanist), a senior philosopher (who had helped draft the original requirement), a senior woman classicist (who had taught in the "critical" track of the course), a senior Chicano administrator, and one of the lecturers in the program.

(2) Throughout the 1986–87 academic year the task force met regularly, speaking with all the relevant parties and anyone else who wished to address them. In the spring of 1987 they released an interim report calling for a reconception and restructuring of the requirement. This trial balloon provoked a great deal of discussion and response that was quite polarized.

(3) In the late autumn of 1987, believing it had the support of all relevant parties, the task force released a revised report and recommendations to the Committee on Undergraduate Studies. The report argued (in passages later deleted) that "courses that do not acknowledge in some degree both the cultural diversity of Europe and the even greater diversity of our present American society have increasingly come to seem intellectually inadequate"; such courses, moreover, "have been open to the charge of being socially irresponsible, however unintentionally and inadvertently, for they seem to perpetuate racist and sexist stereotypes and to reinforce notions of cultural superiority that are wounding to some and dangerous to all in a world of such evident diversity." The report recommended a modified requirement called Culture/Ideas/Values (CIV) structured around a series of ground rules rather than a core list. Four instructional objectives were proposed which can be summarized as follows: increasing understanding of cultural diversity and interaction within the United States and elsewhere; engaging students with works that have intellectual importance "by virtue of the ideas they express, their mode of expression, or their influence"; developing critical thinking; and increasing skills in reading, reasoning, arguing, and analyzing texts. Requirements for social, geographical, and historical diversity would mean courses designed to "confront issues relating to class, ethnicity,

race, religion, gender, and sexual orientation; to include the study of works by women, minorities, and persons of color"; to study works from at least one European and at least one non-European culture in their own historical and cultural context; and to involve at least six to eight centuries of historical depth.

(4) In January of 1988 the new recommendations headed for the floor of the faculty senate with committee approval. At this juncture, opponents of the reform surprised many by introducing counterlegislation which retained the status quo but added one woman and one black writer to the core list for the third quarter of the course. This polarizing move set the stage for the debate that went on through the winter and into the spring. The faculty senate at Stanford is an elected body of fifty-five faculty members which inevitably includes a high proportion of senior scholars and former administrators. Given Stanford's composition, the senate is dominated numerically by faculty from the sciences and professional schools. Advocates of the reform were unprepared for a floor fight in the senate, most of whose members had not been educated as to the stakes and the issues. Senators were prone to support the familiar status quo. On the other hand, the election of this particular senate had involved, for the first time, a small effort to promote women candidates. Though this was not done with the Western culture debate in mind, the four women elected each made crucial contributions on behalf of the reform.

It would be absurd to summarize the untold hours of meetings, statement writing and reading, corridor talk, cynical maneuvering, and brutal negotiating sessions that followed. Despite the Machiavellian dimensions, two decisions in particular gave the process a democratic character that lends credence to the outcome. First, the weekly faculty/staff newspaper announced that it would print all statements on the matter that it received, from any person. An extraordinary number and range of people responded, making this newspaper the main medium for the community debate. Within the senate, it was likewise decided that anyone who signed up to make a statement would be permitted to do so, whether or not they were a member of the senate, and again many people responded, including student representatives. Thus, within the local taboos on, say, openly racist or openly Marxist language, a fairly full range of views was expressed, with deep conviction and eloquence on all sides. (The scientists, one should note, showed no reservations about expressing themselves on the matter, though it proved extremely difficult to communicate the issues to them.) The five senate meetings on the subject were opened to anyone who requested visitor status, though visitors could not participate. As a result, senate meetings uncannily reproduced the very core-periphery structure that was under debate. In a large round amphitheater, the senators, overwhelmingly senior white men, sat in the middle while up around the outside were gathered the women faculty, the minority faculty, the students, the black and Chicano administrators, all the "other Americans" not authorized to speak, but speaking powerfully through their bodily presence. There we were on the margins, we said, but *we were in the room*, and something had to be constructed that came to grips with that fact.

Perhaps the biggest surprise for naive observers like myself as we listened and read was what some of us came to call the "willful ignorance" factor. It was saddening to hear academics saying please don't make me read anything new, I refuse to agree there are things I am ignorant of that are important and worthwhile. "Does that make me a racist?" one old friend and colleague asked. What would Aretha Franklin reply, I wondered. At the same time, especially given the rantings of the official right, it is important to affirm the thoughtfulness and intellectual quality of the discussion that took place at Stanford, and to give you some examples. It was, for example, George Will and not an academic colleague who, amazingly, called for courses that "affirm this fact: America is predominantly a product of the Western tradition and is predominantly good because that tradition is good." It was William F. Buckley, and not a Stanford professor, who displayed his ignorance by declaring that "from Homer to the nineteenth century no great book has emerged from any non-European source." Below I offer some excerpts from what Stanford faculty and students did say, for and against the reform (the quotations are taken from statements published in the campus newspaper):

CON: Education is an exercise of modesty, a process whereby we give up some of ourselves to gain an understanding of that which is *not* ourselves, an understanding of things still shaping us. It's a kind of surrender; we learn that some things are superior in consequence to us, even to our particular gender, to our particular ethnic heritage, to all the parochialisms to which we are subject. Then the apparent foreignness of the past, its record of people seemingly *unlike* ourselves, becomes much less foreign and those people much less strange and irrelevant.

PRO: The famous texts of the past cannot continue to live for us if we simply place them on a pedestal and teach our students to worship them. Only if we see them as engaged with the stuff of history, both of the times in which they were written and of those later times, can we give a continuing life to these texts and to our cultural tradition as a whole. Only if we understand how the idea of a Western culture took shape in differing ways over the centuries and how it defined itself in relation to other forms of culture, can we justify giving it the prime consideration . . . to our students.

CON: As a historian of the United States I would be the last person to deny the ethnic, racial, and cultural complexity of American society. But, from the same perspective, I find it puzzling, if not troubling, to learn that some of the dominant and influential ideas in modern America are to be seen [in the new legislation] as originating outside the West. Few historians of the United States believe that the culture of this country has been seriously influenced by ideas from Africa, China, Japan or indigenous North America. . . . There is no direct connection between the dominant ideas and institutions in American culture and the cultures of Africa or Eastern Asia. [The roots of American culture], if one is talking about ideas and institutions, are derived overwhelmingly from Europe. To contend otherwise, I think would cause American historians to scratch their heads in amazement.

PRO: A "liberal education" for our time should expand beyond the culture-bound, basically colonialist, horizon that relies, albeit subtly, on the myth of the cultural superiority of the "West" (an ill-defined entity, in any event, whose borders are ludicrously artificial). . . . Does the new, integrated vision of Area One entail our teaching the Greek Hermes and Prometheus alongside the North American Indian Coyote or the West African Anansi and Legba as paradigms of trickster heroes, or Japanese Noh alongside Greek drama or Indian philosophy alongside Plato? If the answer is yes, so much the better.

PRO: I was never taught in Western Culture the fact that the Khemetic or "Egyptian" Book of the Dead contained many of the dialectic principles attributed to Greece, but was written three thousand years earlier, or the fact that Socrates, Herodotus, Pythagoras, and Solon studied in Egypt and acknowledged that much of their knowledge of astronomy, geometry, medicine, and building came from the African civilizations in and around Egypt. . . . I was never told that algebra came from Moslem Arabs, or numbers from India. I was never informed when it was found that the "very dark and wooly haired" Moors in Spain preserved, expanded, and reintroduced the classical knowledge that the Greeks had collected, which led to the "renaissance." . . . I read the Bible without knowing St. Augustine looked black like me, that the ten commandments were almost direct copies from the 147 negative confessions of Egyptian initiates, or that many of the words of Solomon came from the black pharaoh Amen-En-Eope. I didn't learn that Toussaint L'Ouverture's defeat of Napoleon in Haiti directly influenced the French Revolution or that the Iroquois Indians in America had a representative democracy which served as a model for the American system. . . . I'm damned if my children have to go to a school that preaches diversity, then refuses to practice its own values because it was scared.

═════

In the end, the reform legislation was passed, with some substantial amendments. One, for instance, required courses to "include treatment of ancient and medieval cultures"; another required faculty teaching in the program to agree each spring on a set of "common elements" which all tracks would share the following year. The latter amendment, which finally broke the deadlock, is a very big loophole. It leaves open the unlikely possibility of faculty agreeing to restore the entire core list, or of the whole battle being fought over in miniature every spring. At the moment, it seems more likely that the parties will learn to understand each other better through this compulsory conversation. The actual consequences of the reform remain uncertain, however. With only minor alterations, the standard Great Books course *can* continue to exist at Stanford, and nobody is being required to reeducate him or herself. You can certainly talk about gender without challenging sexism, or race without challenging racism, or class without challenging classism. On the other hand, a space has been made for much greater change by those who desire it. Tracks constructed around other understandings of culture and broader perspectives on the West are now possible. Their existence and survival depends, however, on the presence of sufficient faculty to teach them, and the hiring and tenuring of such faculty is not possible without the acquiescence of those who opposed the reform. It is no accident that the final amendment passed by the senate deleted a phrase calling for the recruitment of minority faculty to teach in the new program. In the larger national picture, it seems fair to say that the new program puts Stanford in the vanguard of the rear guard, for other schools have long since left our modest reform behind. (Write, for example, for the catalog of Oglala College in Pine Ridge, South Dakota.)

Three faculty have jointly prepared a course according to the new guidelines. It is a course called Europe and the Americas which studies the European, African, and native American strands of American cultures, and the history of their interaction in the Americas. Canonical European texts retain a place in the course, but rather than forming its center of gravity, they simply coexist with American, Caribbean, Spanish-American, native-American and Anglo-American materials. "The complex interactions of colonialism, slavery, migration and immigration," says the course's preamble, "have produced on this side of the Atlantic societies that are highly diverse in origin, and in many cases multicultural and syncretic. European traditions play a prominent and indeed decisive role in these societies, *though by no means the same roles they play in Europe.*" At times the course adopts a comparative perspective—Haitian Vodun and Greek Dionysus are brought together, for instance, in a section on religious syncretism and ecstatic cults; a section on representations of the self juxtaposes the extroverted, historicized self-representation of a Navaho oral history with the confessional modes of St. Augustine and Freud. Historical dialogues are pursued—the legacy of Shakespeare's *The Tempest* in Aimé Césaire's *A Tempest*, José Enrique Rodó's *Ariel*, and Roberto Fernández Retamar's *Calibán* are examined; the give-and-take between European enlightenment discourse on human rights, American independence movements, abolitionism, and slave rebellions is considered; indigenous traditions are traced, from the ancient Mayan *Popul Vuh*, for instance, to the contemporary *testimonio* by Guatemalan indigenous activist Rigoberta Menchu, or from the pre-Colombian Inca state to the Spanish conquest (through Andean eyes) to the great Andean rebellions of the 1780s to the contemporary Quechua poetry of José María Arguedas. Terms like creolization, transculturation, and syncretism are used to develop an approach to culture that is relational and at the same time recognizes the internal fullness and integrity of particular moments and formations.

Approaches to culture and to United States culture such as those this course adopts are widespread in higher education, but are scarcely to be found in official discourse on education, nor in the national media's depictions of the curricular controversy. Partisans of reform have so far had little success at getting across in the public discourse the modes of understanding against which the monumentalist approach seems narrow and impoverished. Few people reading Bloom or Bennett, even those critical of them, can bring to bear a picture of what nonhierarchical, relational approaches to culture are or what people stand to gain from learning them. Stanford's scientists, in being asked to vote for reform, had little idea of what they were voting *for*. How could they not fall back on the common sense of the man in the personals ad I quoted at the beginning who simply likes most aspects of Western civilization? (As the West Texan is supposed to have said against daylight saving time, "If central time was good enough for Jesus Christ, it's good enough for me!") When then Secretary Bennett and Stanford President Donald Kennedy debated the issue on the *MacNeil/Lehrer Report*, neither party possessed a clear picture of alternative visions of culture, the West, or the United States. Bennett knew only vaguely what he was opposing, and Kennedy what he was defending. Lehrer also seemed to be groping for an unknown. And yet, one goes on to wonder, why should the discussion remain in the hands of those three people, a remarkably uniform group? Where are the voices of those who have the most fundamental, bodily stakes in efforts for change? For the moment, those voices are not authorized to speak for "us" all, the way Bennett, Kennedy, and Lehrer can. When they are, change will have occurred.

=====

The final amendments-to-the-amendments on the Stanford reform were resolved in the last week of May 1988. In the days that followed, a series of local events suggested with unexpected clarity the need for the experiment Stanford had embarked on. A student was expelled from his dormitory after a year of disruptive activity directed especially toward a gay resident assistant, culminating in an assault on the resident and the vandalizing of the dormitory lounge. The following evening, ten fraternity brothers, in defense of the expelled student's freedom of speech, staged a silent vigil at midnight outside the dormitory lounge wearing masks and carrying candles, a gesture that seemed to deliberately invoke the customs of the Ku Klux Klan. The reactions of black students who assembled at the site ranged from terror to outrage, and the action was treated by the university as a serious racial and homophobic incident. The ten demonstrators, however, claimed complete ignorance of the associations their vigil invoked. They did not know, they said, that masks and candles at midnight had any connotations—it is just what they thought a vigil was. The following day a group of sorority women, as part of a rush ritual, performed a mock "Indian dance" around a fountain which happened to stand in the doorway of the native American student center. Asked to stop, they refused, later saying they did not intend to offend, or see the dance as offensive. It was just a tradition.

Many people did not believe these students' pleas of ignorance. But either way, the call for educational change was reinforced. If it is possible for young adults to leave the American educational system ignorant of the history of race relations in the United States (not part of standard Western culture curricula), then something needs to change. And if a person who knows the history of race relations and their symbolizations feels free to reenact racist rituals of mockery or intimidation, something needs to change. At the same time, blame must be placed where it belongs. In pleading ignorance, the students were following the example of many of the country's own leaders, for whom ignorance had become an acceptable standard of public life. Throughout their high school and college years these students had looked to a president who consistently showed himself to be both ignorant and utterly comfortable with his ignorance. (The Stanford incidents coincided with Reagan's extraordinary remarks in Moscow about the "coddling" of native Americans.) For many of us exhausted by conflict that spring, these discouraging incidents reminded us of what we were fighting for.

A week later a less weighty event drew local attention, when two California students turned up as the two finalists in the National Spelling Bee. Their names were Rageshree Ramachandran, an Indian-born American from Fair Oaks (who won), and Victor C. Wang, a Chinese American from Camarillo (who came in second). Nothing could have suggested more clearly the multicultural, multiethnic future taking shape on the West Coast. The final words in the spelling bee, the report noted, were these: buddleia (from an Englishman's surname), araucaria (from South American indigenous language), mhometer (from a German electrician's surname, spelled backwards), ovoviviparous (from Latin), caoutchouc (from another South American indigenous language, via French), stertorous (from Latin), and elegiacal (from Greek). "Who makes up these words?" asked Victor Wang as he went down to defeat on "stertorous." Good question, Victor. And as you head on up the educational ladder, I hope you find a system that will give you an honest and imaginative answer.

Notes

1   See Gilbert Allardyce, "The Rise and Fall of the Western Civilization Course," *American Historical Review* 87 (1982): 695–743, cited by Herbert Lindenberger in his admirable essay, "On the Sacrality of Reading Lists: The Western Culture Debate at Stanford University," to appear in the British journal *Comparative Criticism*, Fall 1989.

Richard A. Lanham

The Extraordinary Convergence: Democracy, Technology, Theory, and the University Curriculum

On a mid-September weekend in 1988, a number of scholars met at Duke University and the University of North Carolina (Chapel Hill) for another session of the oldest class in American education, the Seminar on the Future of the Liberal Arts. Our class had, over the decades, featured many distinguished seminarians but a repetitive syllabus: Does the center of liberal education lie in methods or texts? If methods, intuitive or empirical? If texts, ancient or modern? In an age of specialization, how specialized should liberal education be? Should it have a core curriculum common to everyone and, if so, what kind? How democratic can liberal education become without trivializing itself? What, if anything, is a liberal education good for? And finally, why, if we have such a dynamite product, is it often so hard to sell?

This discussion began (if such deep matters can be said to begin) with the Yale Faculty Report of 1828. President Jeremiah Day and his colleagues addressed all these issues, and their answers don't differ much from ours.

They argued that students should know a lot, as E. D. Hirsch has recently recommended,[1] and that they should think a lot, as the Association of American Colleges panel has recently urged.[2] President Day's group stressed the final responsibility of each student for his own education, as did a subsequent Yale panel in 1972.[3] Day's committee argued that a liberal education should not be specialized or preprofessional but broad and humane, and these expansive sentiments have found echo in the Rockefeller Commission's Report of 1980, where we read that "the essence of the humanities is a spirit or an attitude toward humanity."[4] The 1828 group argued that a core curriculum is essential; so have many since, from John Erskine's great books course at Columbia in 1920 and its descendents at Chicago, Yale, and elsewhere, to recent pronouncements by former Education Secretary William Bennett and the *Wall Street Journal*. And just as Yale in 1828 thought the proper time to move students from general education into their favorite special subject was the junior year, so do we.[5] Like us, they were concerned to democratize access to higher education, and sought to encompass this, as do we, by raising admissions standards. And of course they debated the canon, their Ancients and Moderns differing in language, but not in argument, from ours.

The best of our curricular historians, Frederick Rudolph, has some harsh words for the 1828 patriarchs: "They embraced the uses of the past, but they withdrew from the uncertainties of the future. . . . Their respect for quality, for standards, for certain enduring definitions of human worth, was class bound. They were blinded to much that was insistent and already out of control in American life."[6] Just so. But here we were debating the same issues 160 years later. Why hadn't we found some answers? Had nothing changed in this endless debate?

I think three things have changed. Three new conditions, or clusters of conditions, have emerged—social, technological, and theoretical—and their convergence suggests a new kind of "core" for the liberal arts, a new responsive practice.

The social pressures are the easiest to summarize. First, the radical democratization of higher learning. In the early nineteenth century only one or two in a hundred Americans attended college, and they were almost all male, white, leisure-class native English speakers;

now half do, and they are often none of these. This change has been a gradual one, of course, but the quantitative change has now become a qualitative one. American minorities hitherto excluded from higher education have demanded access to it, and a new influx of immigrants has joined them. The immigrants who created modern America came in successive waves that left time for assimilation, and they came into an agrarian and then into an industrial society. Today's immigrants come from dozens of cultures and languages all at once, and into an information society which rewards linguistic competence more than willing hands. Over six hundred thousand immigrants came to this country in 1987—probably more than to all the other countries in the world put together.[7] And we have more in prospect: "In industrial countries the population is growing slowly and aging rapidly; in developing countries—China excepted—the population is growing fast enough to double in less than a generation and 40% of the people are under age 15."[8] If we want to use that youthful energy, then large-scale immigration, and the linguistic and cultural adjustments which it brings with it, will be with us for a long time to come. Liberal arts education has been built on the word, and in America on the English word as spoken by middle-class white native speakers. We have thought of ourselves, up to now, as a monolingual country and have always, after each wave of immigration, become one again, notoriously so in fact. That monolinguicity has now been destabilized. We will have to rethink our whole enterprise. If we grow into bilinguicity—English and Spanish—as well we may, that will present its own particular problems in the university, as it has for some time done in the schools. It may also present its own unique opportunities, as Greek and Latin once did working against each other in classical culture. If you want a numerical marker for this change, here's one from the place where I earn my living: last autumn, for the first time, undergraduate enrollment in the University of California at Berkeley and at Los Angeles was more than 50 percent nonwhite.

To this situation, add a further complication. These new immigration patterns, permitting for the first time substantial entrance from non-Western lands, have brought to America a new citizenry for whom the "Western Tradition" that informs our traditional humanities curriculum is totally alien. Judeo-Christian culture stands now

subject to a polite but puzzled reappraisal. And other, very different reappraisals of the liberal arts are being made from very different
points of view by women and by blacks.

This linguistic and cultural revolution will force an answer to a
major question that has been on our agenda since 1828: How can we
democratize the liberal arts without trivializing them? Up to now,
our answer has been the 1828 Yale answer: don't really democratize
them; it can't be done; proceed as we always have—what else can
we do, eternal verities being our principal product?—and let all these
"nontraditional" students learn our ways as best they can. But political and economic pressures have become too insistent for this. We are
now required to find really new ways to widen access to the liberal
arts without trivializing them.

The second social pressure is for systematic public accountability.
Since government, whether federal, state, or local, increasingly pays
for our labors (and those of our students—last year the federal government spent 13 billion dollars on student loans), it demands an
accountability which Arnoldian Sweetness and Light have not formerly been asked to supply. We face a really new, more searching
and quantitative invigilation. We claim to teach culture, civic virtue,
and advanced symbolic processing. When asked to prove it, we have
always begged the question: of course we are vitally important, even
though, since we do what we do "for its own sake," we can't tell you
why. But the issue is now being forced. George Steiner has been pressing it for years, to our polite embarrassment, juxtaposing the preten-
sions of Western culture to the 100 million people that culture has
slaughtered in the twentieth century. And now the government, with
less elegance and learning, is asking the same question: if the liberal
arts do supply these needful qualities, as you claim, let's have some
proof; show us some statistics. If you can't or won't comply, then
resources now given to you will go elsewhere.

The liberal arts, like higher education as a whole, have operated
heretofore on our version of the "General Motors Rule" ("What's
good for General Motors is good for the country"). What's good for
the arts must be good for the country. To doubt this only proves you
a philistine. Now we are asked, shocking though it be, to do some
cost accounting. We shouldn't be surprised at this. Every other sector

of American professional life is being held accountable in new and detailed ways for its practices. Why not us? With our customary GM complacency and with a conception of costs that would disgrace a falafel stand, we will find this required accounting more than an incidental bureaucratic aggravation. It will force us to rethink the heart of our enterprise, to provide at last a straight answer to another central question we have been dodging since 1828: What are the liberal arts good for?

Third, educational sequence. Students now often come older to the university, often attend in broken times more than one institution, take more than four years to graduate, and more of them work and work more. This fragmented, discontinuous pattern is now more norm than exception. To it we may add the conceptual dislocations they feel hourly as they change classes from one disciplinary universe to another. Yet our undergraduate curricular thinking continues to assume the four-year, upper and lower division linear sequence and ignores the conceptual bewilderment it imposes on students. This assumption blinds us to the only kind of core curriculum—a third key item left over from the 1828 agenda—possible today.

None of these social pressures—democratization, accountability, or educational sequence—is unprecedented, but surely we must reckon their intensity and combined force as something really new. The second emergent condition I'll consider, the pressures of electronic digital technology on the liberal arts, is in itself truly a new thing under the sun.

Let's begin with the codex book. It has provided the technological base for the liberal arts since the fourth century, and a fortiori since the invention of printing. Eric Havelock, in his brilliant papers on the Greek alphabet,[9] argued that an alphabet which could underpin genuine literacy had to be so simple and easy to learn that it could be fully internalized in early youth and ignored thereafter. It had to become so transparent to the user that the world of thought it carried would come to seem just out there, unintermediated, a referential reality. That "Havelock Compact" was enshrined in the printed book. Its typography was ideally, to use a famous phrase, as transparent as a crystal goblet.[10] Its linear flow was not, except incidentally, interrupted by iconographic information. Above all its text was definitive, unchangeable. This definitive fixed text has stood at the center of humanism, of liberal arts education, since the Renaissance. It defines the Great Books curriculum and its passively adoring audience. The definitive great text communicates directly, in Arnold's words, "what is excellent in itself, and the absolute beauty and fitness of things." It works, that is, as a cultural communion wafer. We have only to receive to be saved. If this seems a preposterous caricature, just read Allan Bloom's recently popular book, where the whole of liberal education is reduced to just this, a series of Platonic communion wafers with Guess Who as the serving priest.[11]

When you reproduce a written text on an electronic screen, as we are now doing everywhere in our society, this whole structure collapses. A text repainted sixty times a second on phosphor is a very different cultural artifact—even if it is the same text—from a text printed once and for all on paper. First of all, the electronic word breaks the Havelock Compact. That transparent surface which guarantees the identity and stability of the conceptual life becomes opaque and volatile, dynamic not static. The machine upon which I project this essay can, with a few keystrokes, metamorphose the typographic surface, put it into continual play. The electronic word smashes the crystal goblet. I can make my typography allegorical, play it off against sense. I can bring to bear the whole repertoire of iconographic imagery—it is increasingly available in cataloged software libraries, like rhetorical topoi. I can, that is, alter the whole alphabetic/iconographic ratio which has underwritten our traditional idea of the higher literacy. The pixeled word vaporizes Arnold's touchstones and the whole conception of the liberal arts as a museum of eternal masterpieces and verities—our conception—which is built upon it.

And the reader has been as transformed as the text. The electronic reader, unlike the passive reader whom Arnold took over from the newly silent Victorian public audience, need no longer be content with breathless admiration. Instead of sifting a dubious classic as Arnold recommends, he can fix it up. Interactive computer fiction, where the reader enters the narrative and chooses its direction, mixes critic and creator in ways which leave not only fiction, but the whole of literary criticism, never the same again. An interactive fiction can take virtually an unlimited number of forms. It is a protean, growing, changing thing. Its "original" form is an electronic code which is far more like a genetic code than a fixed literary text, a Great Book which a Great Critic can nail to the wall once and for all. In the pixeled literary work there is, as Stewart Brand has said about digitized film, no "final cut." Our whole critical apparatus, built as it is on final cuts, on beginnings, middles, endings, and the structures which depend therefrom—whether they yield an ideal form and meaning or forever prohibit one—has to be rethought.

Imagine a student brought up on computers, brought up interacting with text, moving it around, playing games with it, illustrating and animating it. Now let her follow Arnold's advice and sift a dubious classic like, say, *Love's Labor's Lost.* Imagine her charting the rhetorical figures, displaying them in a special type, and then diagraming them, and cataloging them, and then, using a cheap program now available, making hypertext animations of how they work. She'll use another program now on the market to make her own production, plotting out action, sight lines, costumes, etc. And then use a voice program to suggest how certain lines should be read. Or she can compile her own edition, splicing in illustrations of chirographia from the contemporary manuals. Or make it into a film. Or simply mess around with it in the irreverent way undergraduates always have, mustaching the Mona Lisa just for the hell of it.

All of these machinations upon greatness are pedagogical techniques which open literary texts to people whose talents are not intrinsically "literary," people who want, in all kinds of intuitive ways, to operate upon experience rather than passively receive it. Codex books limit the wisdom of the Great Books to students who are Great Readers—as, of course, all of us who debate curricular matters were and are. Electronic text blows that limitation wide open. It offers new ways to democratize the arts, of just the sort society is asking us to provide. If groups of people newly come to the world of liberal learning cannot unpack the Silenus box of wisdom with the tools they bring, maybe we can redesign the box electronically, so the tools they have, the talents they already possess, will suffice. We need not necessarily compromise the wisdom therein.

I don't think that the Great Books, the classical tradition now defended with such Luddite determination, will suffer by electronic presentation. Just the opposite, in fact. (And, we might reflect, because they are mostly in the public domain, the Great Books will be the first to be digitized.) We have, ever since the Newtonian Interlude banished rhetoric, sifted out the rhetorical ingredient from our classical texts. Yet all these texts, the Greek and Roman ones entirely, the Medieval and Renaissance ones in Christian partnership, were created out of a rhetorical tradition and can be understood only in light of it. We have had such a hard time selling the Great Books partly because we have systematically travestied their greatness, strained out—both in commentary and in translation—half of what makes them great. They weave their spell out of the ancient quarrel between the philosophers and the rhetoricians, and we have cut that quarrel in half and broken the spell. Here, as so often, the humanities have *created* the "humanities crisis" they have spent the last century maundering on about. The bit-mapped, graphics-based personal computer—and in this essay I can only present, not defend this contention—is intrinsically a rhetorical device. In its memory storage and retrieval, in its fundamental dynamic interactivity, in the basic dramatic rehearsal reality it creates, in the way game and play are built into its motival structure, it expresses the rhetorical tradition in the same way that the codex book embodies the philosophical tradition. Its oscillation between reader and writer reintroduces the oscillation between literate and oral coordinates which stands at the center of classical Western literature. The electronic word will allow us to teach the classical canon with more understanding and zest than ever before. We don't need to worry about its impending destruction, or deconstruction. Western lit is in no danger from Westerns. They are both going interactive.

Indeed, by devising new ways to unlock the Western tradition for *nontraditional* students, we may find out more about what that wisdom finally is and does, begin to answer that other pressing question, what are the arts and letters really good for? Up to now, the liberal arts have always, when pressed, been able to define their essence by appealing to their expressive means. Literary scholars read books and write them. Musicians compose music and play it. Artists paint pictures. Taking away this physical definition of the liberal arts—

defining them by pointing to the physical objects they create, or that create them—compels the arts to define their essence in a new way.

The powers of digital technology both to teach nontraditional students and to document how they learn are being explored in a world the academic liberal arts have ignored, the world of applied learning technologies developed for business, government, and the military. The developers of these interactive laser-disk "texts" and computer-managed instructional programs, because they do not share our commitment to the codex book, and because they must document the success of their efforts, have approached digital pedagogy without crippling preconceptions. They are redefining what a textbook is, among other things, and completely renegotiating the traditional ratio of alphabetic to iconographic information upon which it has been based. Their logos has become bistable and it is a fascinating thing to watch.

They capitalize on another democratizing insight traditional humanists have ignored. When the arts are digitized, as they now have all been, they become radically interchangeable. A single digital code can be expressed in either sight or sound. Even the most traditional musicians are coming to see that the whole basis for the creation, notation, and performance of music has become digitized. It is not simply that notation and printing, the notoriously expensive bottleneck in that art, is now almost a do-it-yourself affair. Musical instruments themselves have been transformed. The clavier keyboard is now a unitary input device for all kinds of musical output. One digital "horn" creates the sounds of a whole wind ensemble. Visual and musical signals are routinely translated into and out of one another for sampling and editing. If you sit down to a weighted-action electronic keyboard, you confront not only the familiar eighty-eight in white and black, but wave forms graphically displayed, a library of sounds on disk, and a computer to play, and play with, them. Such instruments, and such a manner of composition and performance, call upon talents quite different from those demanded when our mothers cajoled us into doing our Czerny exercises. The neural mix seems almost totally new, in fact. One cheap and widely available program allows anyone, with no training whatsoever, to compose music by drawing with a mouse and then translating the sketch into its musical equivalent. (No, the music thus produced isn't horrid.) Digital synthesizers and samplers allow sounds to be created and edited as visual patterns. Musicians can even choose, as a keystroke performance parameter, which temperament they wish to observe, from conventional equal temperament to the just intonation of Harry Partch. Digitization has rendered the whole world of music-making infinitely more accessible than it was, accessible to people who before had not the talent or the resources to make music and hear how it sounds.

The metamorphic pressures on painting are equally Ovidian. Just as pixeling a written text onto an electronic screen radically destabilizes and volatilizes it, so painting on an electronic screen launches the image into an existence which is fundamentally *in potentu*. Electronic painting exists to be transformed by the viewer. The image you see is but one readout of a digital code which can produce hundreds more. Apply a contrast enhancement program and you have a different picture; a Fourier transform and you get yet another. The Arnoldian ideal of fixed perfection simply dissolves. Again, as with literature, the whole supporting structure of criticism must be re-computed.

This digital revolution offers the most extraordinary opportunities to *teach* the arts in new ways, from kindergarten to graduate school. The criticism/creation dichotomy becomes in such a world automatically a dynamic oscillation; you simply cannot be a critic without being in turn a creator. This oscillation prompts a new kind of teaching in which intuitive skills and conceptual reasoning can reinforce one another directly. The digital interchangeability of the arts through a common code—that old Platonic dream that everything returns to mathematics—allows us to translate one range of human talents into another. Our whole sense of how teaching *in* the arts, and *about* the arts, ought to proceed is metamorphosed, again with truly Ovidian intensity and insouciance, by this convertibility. Academic humanists, so far as I can see, have hardly begun to think about these opportunities, but they will help us answer the social pressures of the time.

Digitization of the arts radically democratizes them. The woman who wrote the program which translates a drawing into music did so because she wanted to open up musical composition to people who had no training in or talent for it, but loved it nevertheless. Digitization makes all the arts fundamentally interactive, opens them up potentially to the whole range of talents which humankind possesses. The people who developed the personal computer considered it a device of radical democratization from its inception. It was a way to open levels of symbolic transformation, and the work and information which went with them, to people hitherto shut out from this world. Such democratization is a perfect instance of the new thinking that society is demanding of the liberal arts.

I have remarked in passing that digitizing the arts requires a new criticism of them. We have it already, of course, in the postmodern aesthetic. The fit is so close that one might call the personal computer the ultimate postmodern work of art. The Italian Futurists at the beginning of the century attacked the codex book and its conventional typography, and in their "Teatro di Varietà" bullied the silent Victorian audience into interactivity. Duchamp and Stella exhibited, or tried to exhibit, their famous urinal in order to move the definition of art from the masterpiece to the beholder. John Cage opened music-making to everyone by converting everything into a potential musical instrument. The repetition and variation of motifs drawn from a treasure house of standard forms, a routine postmodern rhetorical tactic from Andy Warhol to Charles Moore, is also what the electronic arts do with ridiculous ease. Electronic interactive fiction finds rehearsals in printed postmodern fiction.

One of the computer's most powerful gifts of interactivity is the power to change scale. It has absolutely altered one boundary-condition of the visual arts, put scaling into continual dynamic play as a choice for beholder as well as creator. Scaling is an analytic as well as creative tool of extraordinary power, and available to anyone "reading" images on a graphics computer. You just click in the zoom box. You find it everywhere in the postmodern arts, from Oldenburg's great hundred-foot baseball bat in Chicago and Rosenquist's gigantic billboard paintings, to the music of Philip Glass. Robert Wilson's dramas are extended experiments in the time scaling of rhetorical gesture, in the revelations of very very slow motion. Everywhere such experiments strive to make us aware of how scale determines the world we live in, and gives us an extraordinary power to domesticate it, live in it comfortably. (This lesson also seems to be taught by the fractal geometry of chaos theory, to take an example from beyond the great Art/Science divide.) When you stand back staring at Oldenburg's baseball bat, for example, viewing it against the skyscrapers of the Loop, the huge and impersonal scale of the buildings seems to become humanized by another scale, the playful one of a gigantic baseball diamond sized up to fit the bat and making human sense even of the grandiose Sears building. Scale change has always been an implicit lesson in the arts. Oldenburg's bat, besides being a critical observation of that fact, radically democratizes this crucial artistic decision. Anyone can look at that bat and see the gigantic human ballfield it holographs onto the cityscape. Again, a major element in the liberal arts has been factored out of the masterpiece aesthetic and radically democratized, and has found a direct digital counterpart.

The most powerful influence of the computer on modern thinking, I would argue, is not statistical or scientific but humanistic. Rhetorical, in fact. Just as the rhetorical practice of declamation put dramatic rehearsal at the center of classical thought, the computer has put modeling at the center of ours. It is difficult to overestimate the influence of this across-the-board dramaticality in the world of contemporary affairs. And again we find a counterpart in the whole range of postmodern art which constitutes itself from self-conscious happenings.

Let me select just one example to illustrate my thesis that both electronic technology and the postmodern aesthetic that prophesied its coming address directly the questions first formulated by the 1828 Yale committee: How do we democratize art without trivializing it? How do you factor out the powers of the masterpiece and make them available to an untrained audience? If the liberal arts teach citizenship, how can they do it for every citizen?

In 1976, Christo Javacheff built a twenty-four-mile canvas curtain in northern California. It was called "Running Fence" and ran from Petaluma to the sea. As with all of Christo's works, the "work" involved not only building the fence itself but, through hearings and publicity and subsequent films and publications, turning into self-conscious art the four years of arrangements and permits and bureaucratic wrangling needed to legalize such a structure, and all the engineering efforts needed to design and build it, and the civic efforts needed to control and comfort the crowds who would view it. He converted American industrial enterprise, that is, into a gigantic happening, a live civics lesson. It was not intended to allegorize the deficiencies of bureaucracy and thus reform them, but only to make people see large-scale human organization in a clearer and more self-conscious way, as having its own form, justification, and even beauty. It made its art up out of politics. But to act in, and thus to "appreciate" "Running Fence," no one needed a credential in connoisseurship. They had only to be what they were, do what they did to earn their living and play their social roles—but to look at all this in a new way, to look *at* it rather than *through* it. Christo was creating the kind of pedagogical technique society now requires of the liberal arts, a new liberating art which could offer art's defamiliarizing power to a wider audience. It was not intended to be immortal (like all Christo's work, it was soon taken down) but to teach the opposite lesson, a reverence for transitory, *mortal* enterprise. The "Running Fence" was also extraordinarily beautiful, because the beauty was needed to teach the whole lesson, show the dynamic relation between beauty and purpose which Christo has given his career to illustrating.

I have been edging sideways toward the third of my three emergent conditions. To it I have despairingly—like an outfielder throwing his glove at a ball soaring overhead into the stands—given the name of "theory." The ball I'm throwing my glove at represents, if I have drawn its many parts together correctly, the revival of the classical system of education, the rhetorical paideia, of an applied rather than a pure, an interactive rather than a passive, conception of the liberal arts. This system of education prevailed in the West from the Greeks onward, until it was set aside by Newtonian science. It is now returning, but in so many guises and in so many areas of our intellectual landscape that one almost despairs of bringing it to a central focus. It includes precisely the emergent social conditions I have been describing, as well as the postmodern digital aesthetic which is replying to them. Indeed, rhetoric itself may be viewed, like them, as an attempt to democratize genius for those not gifted with it, by nature or society, to explore how far contrivance might supplement talent. Thus a fit between the rhetorical paideia and the social and technological conditions that are helping to revive it makes intrinsic sense. It is not simply an accident. This revival of our traditional paideia includes those parts of contemporary literary criticism and cultural studies which have rediscovered that all arguments are constructed with a purpose, to serve an interest—a rediscovery symbolized for me by that wonderful moment at the end of Terry Eagleton's theory book[12] when, after having surveyed the whole brave new world of literary theory, he pauses and reflects that, "Gosh, folks, maybe we might as well just call it 'Rhetoric.'" It departs, as does so much current thinking, knowingly or not, from Kenneth Burke's revival of the *Theatrum Mundi* metaphor for study of the arts and letters. It includes that part of behavioral biology which has, after our Boasian period of radical culturalism, resupplied us with a human nature, one not genetically determined but not infinitely flexible either. This biological recalcitrance offers to the modern rhetorical paideia that needful area of firm extralingual reference, so despaired of by the hard-line deconstructionist, which Aristotle's theory of character types and human seasonality supplied to classical rhetoric. And of course it includes a great deal more. Taken together—wrapped up into that ball soaring above this essay's outstretched glove—these theoretical efforts to make sense of our time amount, as the revival of rhetoric should, to a curricular revolution, a new didacticism. I have come to call it experimental humanism.

Rhetoric persuades by taking for its engine our evolutionary heritage as primates—our need for pure play and competitive hierarchy—and slipstreaming behind them some act in the practical world. Here, I suppose, lies the main bone of contention over which the philosophers and the rhetoricians have been fighting all these twenty-five hundred years. The philosophers believe that human motive is purpose-driven, and play and game derivative functions; the rhetoricians—forced to get results in the world of affairs—have always inverted this pattern. Sensible use, commonsensical reason, took charge, when these rarities could take charge, because the evolutionary deities of game and play, or the politicians and rhetoricians who manipulate them, had prepared the way.

We now find ourselves in yet another rehearsal of this ancient quarrel between the philosophers and the rhetoricians. We pit sacred texts against topical ones, ultimately meaningful ones against ultimately meaningless ones, Plato against Isocrates, finally—you can fill in the other contrasted pairs of proper names yourself—pitting Almighty God against what one eminent theorist has called "the pleasures of the bottomless." The history of Western thought suggests that if we wait until this dispute is resolved before devising a responsive liberal arts curriculum, we shall wait a right good while. But Western education has never had the leisure to wait. The great historian of classical education Henri Marrou argued that, in this historic quarrel, although Plato won the battle, Rhetoric won the war, actually formed the curriculum. I must differ with this profound scholar. The rhetorical paideia did not resolve this struggle, or simply teach the rhetorical side of it, but built the debate into Western education as its central operating principle. Rhetoric as a theory has proved so exasperating and unsatisfactory precisely because it oscillated from one worldview to the other. Rhetorical man was a dramatic game-player but he was always claiming that the ground he presently stood upon was more than a stage. Rhetoric's central decorum enshrined just this bistable oscillation: the great art of art was the art of hiding art, but you had better start out with some art to hide. In behavior, you should always be sincere, whether you mean it or not. This root self-contradiction, as Baldesare Castiglione saw when he gave it the Renaissance name *sprezzatura*, causes trouble only when you take it out of time. *In* time, as a perpetual oscillation, it works fine. It is, as George Herbert Mead rediscovered at the beginning of this century, how we constitute human social reality. Generations of thinkers have bemused themselves, as we do today, by taking the oscillation out of time, stopping it to point out how immiscible the two ingredients are, how moral and formal judgments can never mix. This is how Peter Ramus, in the middle of the sixteenth century, started our humanities crisis. The rhetorical paideia which is now returning puts the oscillation back into time, handles the problem the Renaissance way. It is that oscillation which experimental humanism, with its often outrageous didactic, seeks to reanimate. It thus represents not a nihilistic repudiation of the Western intellectual tradition but a self-conscious return to it.

The primary social pressure on the liberal arts—this at least has not changed—has always been a deep hunger for secular wisdom, for some cybernetic control of the forces that threaten to destroy us. This is what the rhetorical paideia, in the bistable form which I have described, has always tried to supply. Such a system of education does not deny our need for absolutes; it seeks to domesticate and control that need. In its fundamental oscillation, the rhetorical paideia is deeply irenic, would keep the peace by preventing us from filtering the self-interest and self-consciousness out of our most profoundly disinterested convictions and then committing atrocities in their name. It would control purpose, as Gregory Bateson counseled in his famous article on the Treaty of Versailles, by showing us its roots in play and game.[13] A rhetorical education reminds us of the inevitable circumstantiality of all human judgment, but shows us how we can control and offset that circumstantiality. G. B. Kerferd remarks, in his recent book on the Greek Sophists, that it is not two-sided argument per se which distinguishes rhetorical education but the insistence that the *same person* take both sides, first one then the other.[14] Civility requires the acceptance of imposture. That necessary lesson in toleration and self-understanding stands at the center of civic education in a secular democracy. It is the lesson that Americans are asking us once again to teach them. How, using the technological and theoretical resources we have just been pondering, might we do so? What would a liberal arts curriculum responsive to such emergent conditions look like? Let me briefly sketch a possible pattern.

It would depart, as I see it, from a reversal of the basic structural polarity of the undergraduate curriculum. The fundamental structure of undergraduate education has been the separation between the first two years and the last, the upper and lower divisions. Ever since the upper division coalesced around the disciplinary major, it has predominated. The lower division has languished, a low-rent dumping ground without a rationale of its own. If I am correct that the convergence of social, technological, and theoretical emergent conditions constitutes a return to the classical rhetorical paideia, then this fundamental dominance is about to reverse itself. Rhetoric has always been a *general* theory. That is its whole reason for being. It is centripetal, not centrifugal. It draws all subjects into its political and social center rather than spinning them out into separate, apolitical integers, as the modern curriculum has done. Rhetoric's natural home is the lower division not the upper. If we are in the midst of a fundamental change from specialized inquiry to general systemic thinking, then the felt seriousness of the curriculum will shift from the upper division to the lower.

Our educational history is littered with the corpses of lower division programs. Because the lower division occupied a central position as climax of secondary preparation and necessary basis for the major, its conceptual vacuum has proved chronically painful, and we have filled it with one program after another, but never with real success. These usually Edenic programs have seldom outlasted their original visionary creators and they have rarely proved popular either with students or teachers. Both always knew that the "serious" world lay in specialized inquiry and hastened to join it. Such general programs in the liberal arts have failed because they have been, for the last hundred years and more, working against the general intellectual orientation of higher education, an orientation built upon the reductive specialized inquiry inspired by Newtonian science and the complexities of the modern world. In that scheme of things no core curriculum could be found because none, by design, could exist. Because that orientation is now changing, we may be able to build a lower division program which, since it no longer stands at variance with the felt center of its time, will endure.

The structure for such a program is already in place and funded —the *infra dig* freshman composition program. We need only expand from that base. The low esteem accorded to freshman comp by the humanist establishment bears directly upon our agenda: the way we have trivialized the teaching of composition is exactly the way we have trivialized the liberal arts themselves. We teach comp only as the art of transparent expression of pure, apolitical, extrahuman truth. We remove the rhetoric, the human interest, from it. As with our typography, the ideal is a crystal goblet. The utopian world implied by this Edenic view of human communication is precisely the world of unchanging and nonnegotiable secular truths that Thomas More enshrined in his *Utopia* and that the liberal arts have used as a lodestone ever since. In it, the basic rhetorical impulses of competition and play are outlawed in favor of plain Edenic purpose. Style gives way to an insubstantial something we have learned to call "substance." Thus the liberal arts deny their own reason for being. They conceive themselves as teaching a utopian, Socratic lesson about the primacy of substance over style, and yet their own substance, their words and sounds and shapes, are denied and repudiated by just such primacy. The liberal arts have for four hundred years been trying to pull the rug out from under their own feet, and more often than not, they have succeeded; the liberal arts have made their own problems. That crucial oscillation between play and purpose which constitutes their creative center has been taken out of time and shut down. No wonder we academic humanists have a hard time explaining what we do.

Rhetorical education works in the opposite way. Stylistic decorum measures how we look alternately *at* and *through* a text (or a painting), first accept it as referential and then refer it to a reality beyond. This same measurement is then mapped onto behavior as a social decorum. Every stylistic balance models a social one. Thus, in the rhetorical scheme of things, formal and moral judgments, though immiscible, are held in manageable alternation. Such a system of education spins out of its center in bistable decorum a stylistic-behavioral allegory. Here is where we must look if we are to answer that longstanding question about what the arts are good for, about how moral and formal truths can be related in human life. This bistable conceptual core, and its lessons, ought to stand at the center of the composition course, as they should at the center of the liberal arts more largely conceived.

The logical course to follow such a composition course builds upon the digital interchangeability of the arts. It should develop what for the first time we now can develop, a genuine rhetoric of the arts, a general discussion of their means and ends. Such a discussion will not distinguish between the fine and applied arts, because digitization has intermixed them beyond recall. It will assume the digital presentation of the arts as a second norm and contrast its dynamic genius with masterpieces of fixed presentation, thus reflecting the oral/literate axis around which the Western liberal arts have always circled. Such a course should provide students of the humanities with a general framework within which they can locate all their further work in the liberal arts—and, I should say, not only in the liberal arts. It will embody, that is, a genuine core for this core curriculum.

The third course in such a sequence would seek to teach the discipline of two-sided argument I have just described. Here is the real way to open the American mind: to show it that democratic government requires allegiance to genuine two-sided argument, to the psychological and social discipline required when you learn to speak on both sides of any question, put yourself in your opponent's shoes. This discipline is no mystery; it forms the secular basis of individual tolerance and humane understanding. And, obviously enough, it enfranchises our public system of justice, of a trial by jury in which competing dramatic reenactments are staged and one is determined to be referential, and in case law becomes so. This moment of determination, when the contingent becomes the absolute, is the moment of just that oscillation we have found again and again in the emergent conditions we now face; the oscillation from a "reality" to the circumstances which have created it and back again.

We can study it in an infinity of manifestations, theoretical and historical. Surely, for example, it is the pivotal oscillation of English constitutional history, where the monarchy, that needful absolute, has had to be repeatedly reinvented and reabsolutized by the most preposterous myths, only to be repeatedly compromised and qualified by good sense or violence. And we have, in the legislative and executive branches, built this same oscillation into the center of our own American constitution. If you want to teach citizenship in American democracy, you don't build your educational system on Hirsch's collection of canonical facts, or Bennett's collection of canonical texts —or on Allan Bloom's collection of rancid Platonic pieties either. You build it, as the educational system that was invented to sustain democracy built it in the first place, upon this essential bistable alternation between the contingent and the absolute. The only true absolute, in such a secular democratic education, is the obligation to keep that oscillation going, preserving a bistable core for the Western tradition which is not timeless but forever in time. The ways to do this are as infinite as the particular courses such a curriculum would create, but the center remains the same.

Such a sequence, such a new core curriculum in language, the arts, and democratic politics, is do-able right now. It needs no further study. The electronic technology needed is for sale in the market-place, and cheap. Is, in fact, pixelating around looking for its natural home. The administrative structure is there. We could do it right now.

How would it affect the upper division of specialized inquiry? Our thinking about the core curriculum has been based on the conventional upper-division, lower-division separation, the linear four-year progression, and the common faculty, which were assumed by the Yale Report of 1828. Because times are different now, that whole *way of thinking* will no longer work. We need a new *conception* of a "core" for the whole four years. Let me borrow one from an original book by the architect Robert Venturi and his associates, called *Learning from Las Vegas*. Venturi took his Yale seminar out to Vegas for a design exercise. From the ordinary judgmental point of view of a modern city planner, there was only one ideal solution: level the place and start over. Just as, for Hutchins and his associates at Chicago, and "core" curriculum planners ever since, there was only one solution to the marketplace curriculum: abolish it and establish a whole new, ordered, linear sequence in its place. Ideally, a St. John's College, four years of lockstep courses teaching the classics just the way the classics, by Zeus, used to be taught. Venturi suggested, instead, that the seminar suspend judgment and look at Las Vegas, since it consisted largely of signs, as a system of signs. What did it do? How did it do it? Could a semiotic compass of some sort be devised to find one's way around in such a world? Perhaps, having mapped it, to enjoy it?

From such thinking emerged the whole eclectic aesthetic of post-modern architecture. This aesthetic sought not to tear the city down and "renew" it but to teach us how to see it and—at our own pace and in our own way, by ourselves and in small groups—to mend it. It taught this lesson by designing eclectic buildings as self-consciously didactic exercises in how to look at the stylistic repertoire found in American cities. I suggest we use this interactive aesthetic, based on beholder as well as beheld, as an educational pattern.

Imagine the lower-division sequence I have sketched as just such a building, a continually remodeled and adaptive self-conscious work of art. The sequence ought to provide for an undergraduate a way to see the educational city as it is, a curricular compass to navigate in the academic marketplace and construct a personal order there. We are not going to change, probably we *should* not change, the way disciplinary inquiry proceeds or teaches. Humankind is naturally specialist. But we can set up an *integrative* pattern with which specialization can alternate, a lower-division program which can help students find their way in the specialized lands through which they must voyage. Here, too, a lowly structure lies ready to hand as a place to begin, the "Writing across the Curriculum" courses so common now in American universities. Such courses can examine the "rhetoric" of the specialized disciplines, show students the boundary conditions within which these "absolute" disciplinary truths are created, map them on a basic rhetoric of the arts and sciences. Renew, that is, the vital oscillation between absolute and contingent which disciplinary specialization has all but shut down.

Such a pattern of courses, such a new "core curriculum," would once again put the lower division and the upper division into fruitful oscillation, bring this dead administrative sequence back into time, into a generative bistability that reflects its theoretical premise. Our present disciplinary structure, as Gerald Graff's superb new history, *Professing Literature*, makes clear, is built upon defusing conflict by putting the opposing parties, if they bicker long enough, into separate departments so they no longer have to talk to each other. Built upon, that is, shutting down just the oscillation central to the liberal arts. We must start it going again, and if we cannot do so in the separate disciplines, we can show our students how to do it for themselves. If art can lie in the beholder, why not the liberal arts curriculum which studies it?

Such a lower-division program ought to be organized not as an academic department but as an "intrapreneuring" unit, a quasi-independent division that pioneers changes in a large bureaucracy. It should, for a start, experiment with different patterns and terms of faculty hiring. If all our theoretical thinking blurs the distinction between critic and creator, perhaps our hiring policies should follow suit. Not all the creative thinking in the liberal arts is taking place in university seminars. The fundamental intellectual contracts for the next century—between word and image, between page and screen, between goods and information, between high and low art, between the society's need for symbolic processing and who is to supply that need—are all, in fact, being negotiated off-campus. It might be a good idea for us to get to know the people doing the negotiating, maybe even hire one or two of them.

This intrapreneuring unit also should experiment with new administrative patterns. If our present labor practices in the liberal arts are a scandal—and they are—the poverty of our organizational thinking is even worse. Along with enrichment of this thinking should go—another first—some real cost accounting. And such a program might train a new kind of academic administrator as well, one whose skills at refereeing the career game are complemented by a larger strategic vision.

And, finally, it should foster *systemic* thinking. Education by discipline provides every discouragement possible, for both student and teacher, to any kind of systemic thinking. The massive bureaucratization of learning which has taken place in America since World War II has intensified this discouragement. To try to take a large view of *anything* is automatically suspect. Implicit in the argument of this essay, and in every development in the arts I've alluded to, is a return to systemic thinking for liberal education. The classical rhetorical paideia was the original training in systemic thinking. It considered liberal arts education as a system, from early childhood to the forum and law court. We must recover that systemic view and the responsibilities that go with it. We now can see the whole infrastructure of literacy upon which the liberal arts depend as a social construct; there is nothing inevitable about it and we can no longer depend on middle-class customs to sustain it. The intrapreneuring lower division ought to think of this whole system as within its charge. It will have, for openers, the world of electronic "text" and "textbook" to redefine and recreate, and the liberal arts curriculum with it. The arts and letters cannot be taught by means of a technology that stands at variance with the technology which creates and sustains the general literacy of its society. To make sure such a technological gap does not open ought to be an essential charge to this new academic unit.

Such an endeavor contravenes what many feel to be the true center of the liberal arts—their "purity," their distance in time and place from the ordinary world of human work and pleasure. But the "humanities crisis" which has been our routine cry for a century and more is one we have manufactured ourselves by just this distancing ourselves from the world. Claim to be above the struggle, specialize in "values" which others have to embody, and then wonder why the world sets you aside. Implicit in such a revolution in the liberal arts as I have tried to describe is a return to a systemic and systematic involvement in the social purposes of our time.

I began by asking whether anything new has appeared on our agenda. Obviously I think something has. The extraordinary convergence of social, technological, and theoretical pressures indicates this beyond dispute. We have until now considered these pressures as problems, threats to our traditional essence. I suggest that we view them, instead, as telling us what that essence really is, and how we might embody it in answerable practices which will bring our students, all of them, up to the height of our times.

If my analysis of these three emergent conditions is correct, our times could hold for the liberal arts just the centrality which we have so long sought. This centrality won't be given to us; we shall have to create it. We can do this. But we cannot do it by ignoring everything new and exciting and promising that has happened to the liberal arts in the twentieth century—as does, to instance an egregious example, the clone of the 1828 Yale Report which the National Endowment for the Humanities issued on the eve of the conference which occasioned this essay.[15] We should not lose heart because the current public conversation about the liberal arts has been so ignorant, shortsighted, and pedagogically sterile. The long-term march of events, the extraordinary convergence, is there for anyone with the eyes to see it—and it ought to fill us with excitement, with hope, and with resolution.

Notes

1   E. D. Hirsch, Jr., *Cultural Literacy: What Every American Needs to Know* (Boston, 1987).
2   Association of American Colleges, *Integrity in the College Curriculum: A Report to the Academic Community* (Washington, D.C., 1985).

3 Robert A. Dahl, *Report of the Study Group on Yale College* (1972).

4 Commission on the Humanities, *The Humanities in American Life* (Berkeley, 1980), 3.

5 *American Higher Education, a Documentary History*, ed. Richard Hofstadter and Wilson Smith (Chicago, 1961), 1: 284.

6 Frederick Rudolph, *Curriculum: A History of the American Undergraduate Course of Study since 1636* (San Francisco, 1977), 75.

7 *Wall Street Journal*, 6 June 1988.

8 Ibid.

9 Eric Havelock, *The Literate Revolution in Greece and Its Cultural Consequences* (Princeton, 1982), especially chaps. 3–6.

10 Beatrice Warde, *The Crystal Goblet: Sixteen Essays on Typography* (Cleveland, 1956), 11ff.

11 Allan Bloom, *The Closing of the American Mind: How Higher Education Has Failed Democracy and Impoverished the Souls of Today's Students* (New York, 1987).

12 Terry Eagleton, *Literary Theory: An Introduction* (Minneapolis, 1983).

13 Gregory Bateson, *Steps to an Ecology of Mind* (New York, 1972), 469ff.

14 G. B. Kerferd, *The Sophistic Movement* (Cambridge, 1981), 84ff.

15 Lynne V. Cheney, *Humanities in America: A Report to the President, the Congress, and the American People* (Washington, D.C., 1988).

Gerald Graff

Teach the Conflicts

To teach or not to teach the great books? High culture or popular culture? Classics or commercials? Western lit or Westerns as lit? Open canons or closed American minds? *King Lear* or *King Kong*? Rimbaud or *Rambo*? Plato or Puzo? These are just a few of the conflicts that divide the educational world today.

In recent writings, I have been proposing a solution to these conflicts that I think is both practical and democratic: *teach them*.[1] My argument is that the most educationally effective way to deal with present conflicts over education and culture is to teach the conflicts themselves. And not just teach the conflicts in separate classrooms, but structure them into the curriculum, using them to give the curriculum the coherence that it badly lacks.

Not that we should spurn consensus when it proves possible to get it. But when it does not, we should recognize that such conflicts are here to stay and start looking for ways to make them educationally productive. We should use the "dissensus" (in Sacvan Bercovitch's useful term) to make education more coherent and interesting to students than it is now.[2]

=======

The mistake of traditional educational thinking has been to assume that schools and colleges have to *resolve* disagreements in order to teach effectively, that without a consensus on what to teach and why, the curriculum will be chaotic, confused, and without direction. This reasoning is seductive to those outside the university and to many inside. It has inspired a great revival of a philosophy of education I call "educational fundamentalism," which urges the reorganization of the curriculum around a "common culture" based on unitary truths and values.

Unfortunately, the educational fundamentalists fail to confront the question of whose common culture it is to be. Educational fundamentalists look back fondly to a past when there was still enough consensus over the content of higher education that this question did not have to arise. They conveniently ignore the fact that that past consensus was made possible only by the narrow and exclusive social base from which educators and educated then were drawn. It is not too hard to get a consensus if you start by excluding most Jews, blacks, immigrants, women, and others who figure to make trouble.

Then too, even this delimited consensus had already become fragile as early as the 1870s when the modern university first began to take shape. And the great economic and demographic changes of the twentieth century, which have made higher education increasingly available to wider social strata, have knocked the stuffing out of what was left of that earlier consensus. These changes have greatly expanded the range of cultures, subcultures, and traditions that are in a position to demand representation in the curriculum. At the same time, the so-called knowledge explosion and the increasingly self-critical impulse within the disciplines have so diversified the ways of thinking about academic subjects that the conventionally accepted definitions of many fields and departments have been called into question.

Thus, at the moment when, outside the university, a single shared cultural tradition has been giving way to competing traditions, inside the university the premises of knowledge and taste have been coming under redefinition and revision. Put these developments together and you begin to see why the claim that reforming education requires a consensus on what should be taught is a prescription for paralysis.

The most conspicuous symptom of this paralysis is the "cafeteria-counter" curriculum, which almost everyone now finds inadequate. This amorphous curriculum is a product of that democratic expansion of traditions and perspectives I just described. It has come about by a process of accretion, trade-offs, and "Let's Make a Deal" games, as the curriculum has been stretched to accommodate the many new subjects, methods, interests, and minority cultures that have clamored for representation. The attempt to please everybody has led to a curriculum that now pleases nobody.

Educational fundamentalists seem to me right in arguing that the cafeteria-counter curriculum has become so incoherent that for most students it is a downright obstacle to learning. But the only alternative the fundamentalists can envisage is for everyone to agree on a common curricular content, a content that they, the fundamentalists, will be happy to prescribe. If you ask the fundamentalists why we should choose their version of curricular coherence over competing versions, they reply that theirs is not one "version" among others but an embodiment of universal values, transcending mere "special interests."

The striking parallel between this defense of a common culture against educational "special interests" and the recent campaign rhetoric of the Republican party does not seem accidental. The same problem arises in both contexts: Who gets to determine which values are deemed "common" and "universal" and which merely "special"? To this question the fundamentalists have no answer except to take the offensive and accuse the questioner of "relativism," a tactic which may be polemically effective but is not a useful response to the situation. The problem the fundamentalists never bother to face is that the supposedly universal values they are promoting could be institutionalized in the curriculum only by shoving them down dissenters' throats.

A sensible alternative to fundamentalism, it seems to me, would be to concede its view that the curriculum is badly in need of coherence, but to reject its prescription for supplying that coherence.

Instead of trying to superimpose coherence from above, we should try to locate the principle of coherence in the cultural conversation itself in all its contentiousness. This would mean starting with what we already have, drawing on the potential coherence that is latent in the academic-intellectual conversation but that the disconnection of departments and courses has always obscured. "Starting with what we already have" would mean using recent conflicts over texts, canons, traditions, and ideologies—and the rich history of these conflicts—to make the curriculum less disconnected and help students make sense of their studies.

Something like this, I think, is part of the implicit rationale of the new programs in "cultural studies" that are now in the trial stage at Syracuse, Carnegie Mellon, and other universities. It is also part of the rationale of the current attempts to revise the canon that have aroused public controversy at Stanford, Duke, and elsewhere. Contrary to the impression one would get from many of the recent journalistic accounts of these episodes, the point of the attempt to alter the canon is not to scrap the classics and substitute "Westerns as lit" for "Western lit," or to declare, "Say goodnight, Socrates," as ill-informed news reports have recently complained. The point is not to get rid of the classics but to teach the classics in relation to the challenges being posed to them. It is not, in other words, a question of substituting *Rambo* for Rimbaud so much as putting highbrow and lowbrow traditions back into the dialogical relation in which they have actually existed in our cultural history.

By studying high and low culture in juxtaposition, students would have a chance to understand how the hierarchy of "high" and "low" was constructed to begin with, and with what social, cultural, and literary consequences. I doubt this would lead to that erasure of all hierarchies that traditionalists fear, but it would clarify the nature and sources of these hierarchies, and would open up a debate over the relation between social and artistic value that has too long been brushed aside or allowed to fall between the cracks that separate literary study from history and social thought. In the long run, such a challenge can only be good for the classics, which have been damaged more by their admirers' worshipful isolation of them (putting the classics on a pedestal) than by anything their radical debunkers have said against them. The best way to kill the classics has always been to protect them from competing traditions and hostile criticism.

Of course to advocate "teaching the conflicts" is to go against one of the sacred taboos of pedagogy, which is that students should be exposed to the *results* of their elders' conflicts, but not to the conflicts themselves. In this respect, the university is rather like a family in which the parents hide their conflicts from the children. The analogy may be uncomfortably paternalistic, but so are the infantilizing effects of the conflict evasion that I am describing. Students have a way of sensing the battles being hidden from them—they are not ignorant of what is going on—but what they do not get is the opportunity to become active, informed participants in those battles rather than passive objects of them.

Consider our most familiar image of the college, graphically depicted in the photographs of virtually every catalog: an oasis of pastoral serenity, removed from everything that is conflictual and dissonant in adult urban experience. Small, intimate groups of students and professors gather under shady trees on the smooth, sloping campus green. The professors are a benevolent lot, formidably learned and strict, of course, if colorfully ineffectual in the real practical world. For like ministers of the church, they presumably live removed from the harsh demands of commercial getting and spending that "real people" must reluctantly graduate into after their college days are over.

It is just this otherworldliness that makes the professors' lessons so valuable in retrospect (however often one may have slept through them at the time). These lessons exemplify that realm of "values" that the commercial and industrial world has so little respect for. These values are implicit in every college subject, but above all in the humanities, a dim appreciation for which the professors somehow manage to instill despite the best efforts of one's youthful hedonism and anti-intellectualism to resist it.

What is interesting is the emotional hold of this sentimental image of college life even though we know perfectly well that it is false. Just as we know that the kindly minister of New England myth has now become—in prominent instances anyway—the televangelist on the take (and on the make), we know that the benevolent Mr. Chips of benign memory no longer exists, if he ever did.

To remind ourselves of the reality we need only return to the college catalog again, shifting our attention this time from the pictures of pastoral harmony to the dissonant contents. Here are vocational programs jostling with cultural and humanistic ones; hard sciences with soft culture; Ph.D. research professionalism with undergraduate general education; the technocratic rationality of degree requirements and parking regulations with the Platonic rationality of truth and wisdom. But most clashing of all are the juxtapositions represented by the lists of departments and courses: here is traditional culture coexisting with subversive critique. Aristotle and Aquinas are being taught at the same time as a course on Freud, Marx, and Nietzsche down the corridor. Samuel Johnson is expounded in the same classroom as Samuel Beckett an hour later, while the critical theories of Sidney and Arnold are aired in the same time slot as those of Derrida, Kristeva, and Jameson. These and innumerable other juxtapositions abound right before our eyes, yet they are not foregrounded, either in the catalog or in the students' experience. In fact, we are trained not to *see* them as having any possible dialogue with one another except the private dialogue each student may or may not construct inside his or her head. We are certainly not trained to think of these juxtapositions as something we could *do* something with within the curriculum structure.

But it is no use waxing moralistic over the situation I am describing. The pattern of conflict evasion is there whether anybody consciously intends it or not, for it is a function of structure and ideology, not of individual preference or temperament. To be more specific, it is a by-product of a model of education in which students "cover" a series of fields in separation from one another and thus rarely become aware of the conflicts and convergences which created those fields in the past and relate them in the present. A curriculum composed of disconnected courses masks the implicit conversation the courses are always in, and apart from which their subject matter is virtually unintelligible.

Which suggests an important point about teaching the conflicts:

that it is difficult to do it all by yourself. For this reason, I doubt that significant changes can result from even the most radical transformations in individual teaching practices alone. Yet it is the individual classroom we have tended to focus on in educational reform discussions, a fact that our very use of the expression "the classroom" betrays. Equating pedagogy with what happens in "the classroom" involves a confusion of education with *teaching*. Every educational problem is reduced to a question about what an isolated teacher will do in an isolated course, and we are discouraged from thinking of courses as a system, whose relations (or nonrelations) limit what individual teachers can accomplish.

It is interesting that whereas we academics have long been used to thinking skeptically about the concept of the "department," we rarely direct the same skepticism at the concept of the "course." Whereas departments presumably represent bureaucracy and mechanization, courses represent a pastoral alternative to bureaucracy and mechanization. For traditionalist and radical teachers alike, one's course constitutes a refuge from the vulgarization of organized systems, and for the junior faculty from the panoptic gaze of authority. Yet the isolationism of the course is a product of the same institutional dynamic as the isolationism of the department.

A truly structural approach to education would consider the ways avoidance of conflict is built into the very organization of courses themselves, however much individual instructors may emphasize conflict within the privacy of their own courses. Conflict avoidance is built into the familiar "add-on" principle of departmental and curricular change: by this principle, whenever a new and challenging idea or method arises, it is assimilated into the university by the device of *adding* another unit to the existing aggregate. The result is that established departments and factions do not have to confront the challenge of the new idea or even notice its existence.[3] We should not undervalue the benefits of the add-on method in making possible the impressive diversity that we now take for granted in the better-endowed universities. But we should also see that these benefits are paid for at the cost of making public discussion unnecessary.

The add-on principle has determined not just the shape of departments but of the curriculum as well, creating the cafeteria-counter model that is so widely deplored today. As new subjects and view-points are added to the aggregate, the curriculum becomes a geological overlay of ideologies, many of which contradict one another, but since they coexist in separation the contradictions are not experienced by students *as* contradictions. A situation in which contradictions fester without any public outlet is clearly a dangerous one: it enables antagonisms to be repressed until they reach a breaking point, when they erupt in hatreds that can no longer be hidden from view—usually in appointments and tenure meetings.

Yet such an acrimonious situation offers an opportunity if we can begin to see conflicts as a potential basis for new departmental and curricular arrangements rather than merely a chronic cause of paralysis. I stress conflict not because I *like* it as a good in itself or because I ascribe some magic virtue to it, but because it is *there* in our situation, and unless it is dealt with will continue to undermine productive action. Conflict often defines the way we are related to one another (though it is not the only way), and unless students see teachers in relation to one another they will be unable to make sense of the diversity they are exposed to.

═════

To all this it will be objected that the recent controversies over the canon and the methods of studying literature are of primarily professional interest—suitable enough for the specialized graduate seminar, perhaps, but hardly for undergraduate teaching where the primary concern must be just to read the books and get the students to read them. Given world enough and time (so this objection runs), teachers might have the luxury to engage students in esoteric disputes over theory. But when crunch time comes, as it always does, our main responsibility is to teach *Paradise Lost*. To do less would be to waste precious time on diluted content instead of serving the most nourishing fare.

Allan Bloom speaks for such objectors in *The Closing of the American Mind*, when he says that "a liberal education means reading certain generally recognized classic texts, just reading them, letting them dictate what the questions are and the method of approaching them—not forcing them into categories we make up, not treating them as historical products, but trying to read them as their authors wished them to be read."[4] Instead of letting the texts themselves dictate the questions we ask about them, Bloom complains, today's professors engage in "endless debates about methods—among Freudian criticism, Marxist criticism, New Criticism, Structuralism and Deconstructionism, and many others—all of which have in common the premise that what Plato or Dante said about reality is unimportant."[5]

What could be more obvious and sound than the idea of "just reading" the great texts with one's students? But as Richard Rorty has objected, we always "read books with questions in mind—not questions dictated by the books, but questions we have previously, if vaguely formulated." Rorty grants that interpreters are obliged "to give authors a run for their money," respecting "an author's way of talking and thinking, trying to put ourselves in her shoes." But he points out that "it is not clear how we can avoid forcing books into 'categories we make up.' "[6]

One need go no further than Bloom's statements here for an illustration of Rorty's point. When Bloom invokes Plato and Dante to deplore the practices of current teachers, he is *not* letting Plato and Dante dictate the agenda, but is putting them into categories that he, Allan Bloom, has "made up." What did Plato and Dante know of Freud, Marx, postmodern relativism, contemporary professors of literature, and other targets of Bloom's polemic? In using Plato and Dante to attack current targets, Bloom is not reading those writers as they wished to be read, but *applying* them to a context they did not and could not have anticipated.

Urging us to cut out the nonsense and get back to "just" reading good books evades what is centrally at issue in the conflict over the canon: What does it mean to "read" a text? What does it mean to call a book "great"? As theorists from Stanley Fish to Jacques Derrida to Mary Louise Pratt have been arguing, reading always takes place in a context of interests, and those interests vary from reader to reader and culture to culture; therefore, what it means to read a given book is not self-evident but is always potentially open to interpretive controversy. No text, however eloquent, interprets and teaches itself, for even the most scrupulous attention to the author's intentions (the stage of "putting ourselves in the author's shoes" to which Rorty refers) must be selective, and what is selected for attention will reflect the values of our own time.

Then too, the practice of "just" reading the classics in a contextual vacuum would not have come under so much recent fire if it had not failed so disastrously as a pedagogical approach. What has to be challenged is the habit of thinking of the contexts of texts as an agent that *interferes* with reading rather than a necessary aspect of reading. We would not be experiencing the present turmoil if it were not that mere exposure to great works, even under the guidance of the best teachers, singularly failed to make large numbers of students able and eager to read the great works with interest. There is reason to think that a curriculum that would clarify rather than obscure the conflicting theoretical and interpretive frameworks to which students are exposed would do more to make texts interesting to students than teaching those texts as monuments of eternal verities.

It is not true that recent theoretical controversies are merely narrowly professional and esoteric, or for that matter that they are even particularly recent. To be sure, these controversies often seem narrow and pedantic, but this has less to do with anything intrinsically obscure about theoretical controversy than with the fact that, as it is now organized, the university makes *all* general issues seem obscure, including the issues of the traditional culture. Aristotle's *Poetics* is not in any way more clear or less jargon-ridden than the works of Barthes or Foucault, and students have as much trouble with it as with recent theory. If the conflicts of the humanities seem obscure or beside the point to laypeople, this is neither because these conflicts are intrinsically obscure or because laypeople are incapable of taking an interest in them. It has more to do with the fact that laypeople never see those conflicts in circumstances that might make them intelligible. In this respect, the much-lamented disconnection of the humanities from the world outside the university is a function of the disconnected state of the humanities in relation to themselves. Naturally, the humanities are going to look esoteric and overspecialized if you experience them only as a set of disjunctive monologues.

If current theory were really as esoteric and irrelevant as it is said to be, nobody would be so alarmed by it. The real fear, one suspects, is that the import of current theory will become all *too* clear to students and laypeople. The deeper source of the reaction against the changes going on in the humanities comes from the recognition that these changes aim to make politics a central category.

When I said earlier that what it means to call a book "great" is one of the things the current humanities conflict is about, I was referring to the argument of recent theorists that preferences of taste, culture, and canon reflect nationalist, racist, and sexist ideologies. Serious objections can be made to some of the answers now being given to the question of the politics of canon formation (I have made some myself), but the *question* is a legitimate one. Nor is it "relativism" to recognize that standards which were formerly taken for granted among the educated are now controversial, and have to be defended by argument against rival positions. Here, I am afraid, is what really enrages middlebrow critics about the changes now taking place in the teaching of literature: whereas these critics could once assume that their view of what constitutes proper literature and criticism would automatically be the official one, they now have to *argue for* their view like everybody else. Whereas their type of person once got to define what counts as "literary culture," that type now has to contend with groups that think differently. Here is a side of the picture that the media coverage of the controversy over the humanities has failed to bring out. It is in the interests of all ideological factions on the current scene to recognize that there are legitimate reasons for disagreement about what is to be taught in universities and how it is to be taught, and that rival positions cannot always be reduced to a clear distinction between trendy irrationalism and sound common sense.

=====

How, then, could teaching the conflicts actually be done? First off, we should be wary of the idea that there is some one way to proceed that will work for every type of institution. Faculties would best start not by casting about for a master plan, but by taking inventory of their local resources (while continuing to ask where those resources are deficient in relation to the larger culture and the profession) and then asking what instructive conflicts and convergences are present in those resources and how these could be dramatized in ways that would engage students. The most direct tactic is the team-taught introductory lecture course, versions of which have long had success. A good solution to the controversy over the Western civilization course at Stanford, for example, would be to require a course on the issues involved ("Canons in Conflict," or "Western Civilization and Its Discontents," or even "The Canon Conflict at Stanford"), assigning a selection of Western and non-Western texts. The point would be neither to deify nor to debunk Western culture, but to put it into relation to the forces challenging it.

Where team teaching proves too expensive, or fails to arouse students from passive spectatorship, faculty might try a "teacher-swapping" tactic, in which they periodically take one another's classes. The point is to create situations in which teachers become contexts for one another to play off of, helping one another rather than working at cross-purposes or in isolation.[7]

But perhaps the most promising idea is to import something of the atmosphere of conferences like this one into the everyday pattern of study. For faculty members, such conferences have already become a substitute for the continuing intellectual community that fails to exist at the home campus. This suggests that the conference principle could be used to create some of that continuing community if we started using it to connect courses. It is sadly symptomatic of current academic life that undergraduates are rarely encouraged to attend our conferences, for things happen at conferences that do not and cannot happen when teachers remain imprisoned in "the classroom." Conferences make symbolic *drama* out of intellectual culture that courses by themselves fail to do. By putting courses into dialogue, they create an academic public sphere.

Imagine, then, that six weeks into the term, instead of meeting as usual as separate courses, the course on Rimbaud and modern French poetry and the course on *Rambo* and current popular film meet for a joint conference. (I learned after writing this essay that the literary echo of the name "Rambo" was not simply fortuitous.) The preparation could be modest—agreement on one or two common texts—for the aim would be to discover what connections and contrasts emerge across high and low culture and then what can be made of them. Students could take various roles in the conference, from giving some or all the papers in it, to writing papers about it afterwards, to planning and organizing the program. Anyone who has ever run an academic conference will have found that the experience makes one think about the categories of intellectual classification in a surprisingly challenging way.

Myriad possibilities for such multicourse conferences are already richly suggested in the course description booklet for any given semester. One need only read through the descriptions of any humanities department's courses to see numerous possibilities for structured exchanges that are being wasted. Prior agreement between instructors to teach common texts, if only to make it possible to expose their different ways of reading and contextualizing them, would enable many kinds of clarifying cross-discussion to take place that cannot do so now. The texts themselves could be varied from semester to semester to suit diverse interests.

Of course if things happen at conferences that cannot happen in "the classroom," the reverse is also true. Spectacle, drama, and gossip can be hindrances as well as helps, and conference fatigue and burnout are distinct dangers. But there is no need to scrap the existing structure in order to infuse it with other structures.

But other objections will be made: Would not teaching the conflicts require too radical a change in the way we think about education to be a realistic proposal? In my view, what is needed is not a change in the way we think about education so much as a recognition of the fact that our thinking already changed long ago, as it had to in response to the vast changes forced on education by mass-education. But the departmental structure and the curriculum have never been fully reshaped to accord with this recognition. They have been prisoners of the add-on method of assimilating innovation, which arises when it is assumed that the only way to structure conflicting values and methods is to keep them separate.

But again, a better way to adapt to change and conflict would be to forget about superimposing "higher" values on the curriculum than those already contained in it and try to get more out of the mixed bag that we already have in academic culture by clarifying its relations to itself and therefore to the larger culture. What would then happen is not fully predictable or controllable. But it would not have to be if the end is not to indoctrinate students but to interest them in joining the academic conversation.

Of course, if you think education should or has to be indoctrination, you will find this conception of the goal woefully inadequate, not to say insidious. Educational fundamentalists will object that "the mixed bag that we already have" is contaminated by degraded professionalism, pedantry, and populism. On the other side, some educational radicals will object that the bag is not mixed enough, but is still limited by class, race, and gender exclusion. Other radicals will object that too mixed a bag cannot be an effective instrument of revolution.

Speaking as a leftist, I too find it tempting to try to turn the curriculum into an instrument of social transformation. But I doubt whether the curriculum (as opposed to my particular courses) can or should become an extension of the politics of the left. The question not addressed by proponents of "the pedagogy of the oppressed" such as Paulo Freire and Henry Giroux is what is to be done with those constituencies which do not happen to agree with them that social transformation is the primary goal of education. Such proposals seem to presuppose a school or department in which such dissenters do not exist. In so far as it is to provide a general model, no educational proposal is worth much that has no strategy for dealing with disagreement. No proposal will work that fails to make a place for those who will inevitably resist any single philosophy, leftist, rightist, or centrist. In a democratic culture, planning a curriculum inevitably means organizing ideas and approaches that you often do not like very much.

My argument should not be confused with "pluralism," for its point is to sharpen conflicts and bring them out in the open, not mush them over in the pluralistic compromise we now have. Of course if what we mean by "pluralism" is the assumption that in a democratic culture a plurality of methods, values, theories, and viewpoints has to be tolerated, then it is hard to think of any alternative to pluralism except a dogmatism that wants its voice to be the only one in the discussion.

But which voices *will* be in the conversation and which ones will be excluded? Isn't the concept of a culture or curriculum as a "conversation" just a familiar liberal myth, that all social groups begin from an equal starting point, when we know that access to the conversation in the first place is asymmetrically stacked in favor of some groups over others? It is true that any institutional conversation will have had to constitute itself by the initial exclusion or marginalization of some groups and viewpoints. But relative to the American university of thirty or forty years ago, the present-day American university has become far less culturally and intellectually exclusionary (it could not have become such a political battleground if it was not). So to "teach the conflicts" in 1990 means something very different from what it would have meant in 1940 or 1950, much less in 1900, when academic culture was far less demographically and politically representative. Then, too, if some groups are necessarily excluded or marginalized by any system of organization, a system that foregrounds conflicts figures to give the more arbitrary exclusions and marginalizations a better chance than they now have of coming to light and becoming an explicit theme of intellectual discussion.

Nor should my proposal be confused with *disputation* or with getting hostile factions "talking to one another"—which is just one possible means among many. The important thing is not that professors talk to one another (though this may sometimes be productive), but that students get a sense of what is at issue in the cultural controversies they have a stake in. *How* this happens is another question—the most effective means will differ from one local situation to the next.

Since it is common academic folklore that college professors are a notoriously contentious group, the idea of drawing educational dividends from this contentiousness should not seem completely outlandish. Then too, the current generation of younger academics, which grew up during the 1960s, tends to be more at home than its elders with openly expressed conflict and communal discussion, and more impatient with traditional academic and bureaucratic evasions. It is no accident that the word "interdisciplinary" is now one of the honorifics in the professional vocabulary; that "conversation," "dialogue," and "rhetoric" have become models of thinking across the disciplines; and that those associated with these terms—Kenneth

Burke, Richard Rorty, Jacques Derrida, Mikhail Bakhtin, and Jürgen Habermas—have become household names. For some time now, gentility, managerialism, and positivist fact gathering for its own sake have been on the defensive, and there is a discernible longing for intellectual community.

This attitude marks a large-scale shift in the way academic culture conceives knowledge and inquiry, which explains why it collides so sharply with the lay culture and with the older forms of academic culture. As the disciplines have moved away from the positivism of the nineteenth century, knowledge has come increasingly to be visualized not as a unified structure, a pyramid of building blocks, but as a set of social practices, a conversation. Whether this spells the death of the concept of the disciplines as a "body of knowledge" is still very much open to debate—the kind of debate that I have been recommending we put in the forefront of education. But we do not necessarily have to reject the body-of-knowledge conception of the disciplines to see that even in the harder sciences the "body" has been so fractured that it no longer appears as a unified organism.

What makes me most optimistic about the prospects of "teaching the conflicts" as a new curricular model is my conviction that there is no other way. The very intensity of our recent conflicts vividly illustrates that traditional consensus thinking on education has broken down and is unlikely to be made whole again. The only alternative is to agree to disagree.

Notes

1 See my *Professing Literature: An Institutional History* (Chicago, 1987), and the following essays: "Taking Cover in Coverage," *Profession 86* (1986): 41–45; "What Should We Be Teaching—When There Is No 'We'?" *Yale Journal of Criticism* 1 (Summer 1987): 189–211; "Conflicts Over the Curriculum Are Here to Stay; They Should Be Made Educationally Productive," *Chronicle of Higher Education*, 17 February 1988, A48; "Teach the Debate about What Books Are In or Out," *Christian Science Monitor*, 22 April 1988, B6–7; and "Teach the Conflicts: An Alternative to Educational Fundamentalism," in *Literature, Language, and Politics*, ed. Betty Jean Craige (Athens, Ga., 1988), 99–109.
2 Sacvan Bercovitch, "The Problem of Ideology in American Literary History," *Critical Inquiry* 12 (Summer 1986): 633ff.

3 See my *Professing Literature.*

4 Allan Bloom, *The Closing of the American Mind: How Higher Education Has Failed Democracy and Impoverished the Souls of Today's Students* (New York, 1987), 344.

5 Ibid., 375.

6 Richard Rorty, "That Old Time Philosophy," *New Republic*, 4 April 1988, 32.

7 See my essay "What Should We Be Teaching?" 204–7.

Barbara Herrnstein Smith

Cult-Lit: Hirsch, Literacy, and the "National Culture"

It should be a matter of some concern, I think, that the current movement for educational reform duplicates so many of the perennial (indeed classic) themes of apocalyptic cultural criticism: most obviously, of course, the recurrent images of a civilization in decline (the young corrupted, the masses stupefied, barbarians at the gates of the *polis*), but also the nostalgic invocations of an allegedly once "whole" but now "fragmented" community (lost shared values, lost shared knowledge, lost shared attitudes, and so forth), where historical as well as contemporary diversities are, in one stroke, both forgotten and wishfully obliterated.

The force of this general concern will be apparent in my remarks, but I mean to focus specifically on E. D. Hirsch's book, *Cultural Literacy*, and I don't mean to mince words.[1] I believe that the immediate objective it proposes—that is, the acquisition, by every American child, of the alleged "common," "traditional," information, attitudes, and values shared by all literate Americans

or, as Hirsch also refers to it, "*the* national culture"—is meaningless as stated and if not meaningless then, given what it evidently
means to Hirsch, undesirable; that such an objective, if it were desirable, could not be achieved by the pedagogic methods it proposes;
and that, if it were actually adopted on a national scale (as is clearly
Hirsch's serious and now institutionalized intention[2]), the pursuit of
that objective by those methods—that is, the attempt to equip every
child in the country with a putatively finite, determinate, measurable
store of basic "American knowledge" in the form of standard definitions or "sets of associations" attached to disarticulated terms and
phrases—would not only *not* alleviate the conditions it is supposedly
designed to cure (among them, widespread illiteracy and a cycle of
economic deprivation, social marginalization, and political ineffec-
tuality), but would postpone even longer adequate analyses of, and
appropriate responses to, those and other problems of the nation's
schools.

I will amplify these points by examining several key passages in
Cultural Literacy, beginning with the one, early in the book, in which
Hirsch introduces the notion of a "national culture" and sets up his
argument for a uniform national school curriculum based on his now-
famous List.

========

The failure of our schools, Hirsch tells us, can be attributed to the
educational theories of Rousseau, Dewey, and "their present-day dis-
ciples." In contrast to these, he writes, his own "anthropological"
theory of education

> deems it neither wrong nor unnatural to teach young children
> adult information before they fully understand it. The anthropo-
> logical view stresses the universal fact that a human group must
> have effective communications to function effectively, that ef-
> fective communications require shared culture, and that shared
> culture requires transmission of specific information to children.[3]

Each link in this argument bears scrutiny, as does also the nature of
the logical/rhetorical syntax by which they are joined.

To begin with, the term "human group" is vague and, as Hirsch uses it here, slippery. The statement containing the phrase—that is, "a human group must have effective communications to function effectively"—makes sense when we think of a relatively small group of mutually interacting people, such as a family, a company of co-workers, or, given the quasi-anthropological auspices, a tribal community. A *nation*, however, and particularly what Hirsch refers to repeatedly as "a modern industrial nation," is not a "human group" in that sense; and, although his subsequent allusions to "our national community" manage to evoke, under the sign of scientific precision, a questionable (and, as will be seen, otherwise disturbing) nationalist communitarianism, the phrase is clearly question-begging here and the concept has no anthropological or other scientific credentials whatsoever.

The existence of an American "national culture" is by no means self-evident. Every citizen of this nation belongs to numerous communities (regional, ethnic, religious, occupational, etc.) and shares different sets of beliefs, interests, assumptions, attitudes, and practices—and, in that sense, cultures—with the other members of each of those communities. There is, however, no single, comprehensive macroculture in which all or even most of the citizens of this nation actually participate, no numerically preponderant majority culture in relation to which any or all of the others are "minority" cultures, and no culture that, in Hirsch's term, "transcends" any or all other cultures.[4] Nor do these multiplicities describe a condition of cultural "fragmentation" except by implicit contrast to some presumed prior condition of cultural unity and uniformity—a condition that could obtain only among the members of a relatively isolated, demographically homogeneous and stable community, and has never obtained in this nation at any time in its history.

The invocation of *transcendence* noted above is justified in the book by an illegitimate analogy between language and culture: indeed, doubly illegitimate, for not only are cultures not like languages in the way Hirsch implies (that is, sets of discrete items of "information" analogous to "vocabulary" lists), but languages themselves are not the way he describes them and requires them to be for the analogies in question. Just as every national language, Hirsch writes, "*transcends* any particular dialect, region, or social class," so also does the "national culture."[5] There is, however, no "national language," either in the United States or anywhere else, that all or most of the inhabitants of a nation speak *over and above* various regional and other (ethnic, class, etc.) dialects. There are only *particular* regional and other dialects, some—or one—of which may be privileged over and above all others in the state educational system and/or by various cultural agencies. An analogy from language to culture, then, would support a view of the latter quite different from that urged by Hirsch. Indeed, as his critics observe, what he refers to as "*the* national culture," and exemplifies by his List, is nothing but a *particular* (egregiously classbound and otherwise parochial) set of items of "knowledge" that Hirsch himself privileges and that he *wants* the state educational system to make "standard." (His recurrent reply to this observation is to dismiss it as "ideological," in presumed contrast to his own beliefs and proposals.)

Hirsch puts the culture/language analogy to other, remarkable uses. "[F]ixing the vocabulary of a national culture," he writes, "is analogous to fixing a standard grammar, spelling, and pronunciation"; and, he claims, Americans "need to learn not just the associations of such words as *to run* but also the associations of such terms as *Teddy Roosevelt, DNA*, and *Hamlet*."[6] Indeed, he assures us, if children can all learn the associations of common words such as *to run*, there is no reason why they cannot all learn the associations of *Teddy Roosevelt, DNA*, and *Hamlet*. To speak of the "vocabulary" of a culture, however, is to presuppose the altogether Hirsch-generated culture/language analogy and thus, as usual, to beg the question. (It is because Hirsch characteristically presupposes the key points of his arguments —either as self-evident or as already proved by his mere statement of them—that question-begging formulations are so recurrent in *Cultural Literacy*.) Moreover, the dubiousness—and, in fact, absurdity —of the analogy becomes increasingly apparent from the very use he makes of it. Can we really speak of "*the* associations" of *Teddy Roosevelt, DNA*, and *Hamlet* or, to choose some other items from Hirsch's List, of *Woodie Guthrie* or *Harlem*? Are there "standard associations" and, as he also claims, "traditional values" already in existence for such items, and are they really shared by all literate Americans? Or, if they are not already in existence (Hirsch is equivocal on the point), could associations and values for such items be "fixed" or "standardized" so that they really would be *independent*, as he implies, of the specific personal histories of whoever was doing the sharing and associating and valuing? And, if we really managed to teach children from Houston, Boston, Alaska, and Nebraska to memorize and recite standard associations and values for *Teddy Roosevelt, Woodie Guthrie, Hamlet, Harlem, DNA*, and five thousand other terms, do we really suppose that the "human group" constituted by the citizens of this country would have acquired a "shared culture," and would only then "have effective communications," and would only thereby and thereupon "function effectively"? What *are* we talking about?

Hirsch's claim that "effective communications require shared culture" is, in fact, false. For, given any sense of the term "culture" relevant to the passage under discussion—that is, either (a) as anthropologists would define it, the system of beliefs, skills, routine practices, and communal institutions shared by the members of some society as such, or (b) as Hirsch implies, familiarity with a list of academic set-phrases and vintage items of middle-class cultural lore —then it is a "universal fact" that people can communicate *without* a "shared culture" and that they do it all the time. Japanese suppliers, for example (a group whose presence hovers over the pages of *Cultural Literacy*), communicate with European and African buyers without sharing the latter's cultures in the anthropological sense; and, just to speak of other Americans, I communicate quite effectively with my eighty-five-year-old ex-mother-in-law from Altoona, Pennsylvania, my twenty-five-year-old hairdresser from Hillsborough, North Carolina, my five-year-old grandson from Brooklyn, New York, and my *cat*, without sharing much, if anything, of what Hirsch calls "the shared national culture" with any of them. The reason I can do so is that all the activities that Hirsch classifies as "communication" and sees as *duplicative transmissions* that presuppose *sameness*—"common" knowledge, "shared" culture, "standardized" associations—are, in fact, always *ad hoc*, context-specific, pragmatically adjusted negotiations of (and through) *difference*. We never have sameness; we cannot produce sameness; we do not need sameness.[7]

———

From the conjunction of the two questionable statements considered above, Hirsch would have us conclude that "[o]nly by accumulating shared symbols, and the shared information that the symbols represent, can we learn to communicate effectively with one another in our national community"—from their conjunction, that is, by way of a crucial link in the argument: namely, the observation that "[l]iteracy, an essential aim of education in the modern world, is no autonomous, empty skill but *depends upon literate culture*."[8] The link is crucial because it joins the two terms, *literacy* and *culture*, the recurrent, varied, and thoroughly ambiguous operations of each of which underwrite the remarkable notion of "cultural literacy" and, with it, the rhetorical force of Hirsch's entire program for educational reform.

Literacy, Hirsch tells us, is no empty, autonomous skill. To be sure. But does it follow that it depends on "literate culture"? Indeed, what does this latter, rather barbaric phrase mean? It seems to be equivalent to the condition of "cultural literacy," or what he characterizes, for the citizens of this nation, as that which "all literate [but *not illiterate*] Americans know"—as represented by his List.[9] But it is not clear, then, whether "literate culture" is the information possessed by people who *are able to read adequately* or, alternatively—and, of course, quite differently—the knowledge had by people who are "literate" in the sense of *well-educated* and thus also, as we say and as Hirsch's own uses of the term certainly suggest, "cultured."

In the first case, the statement in question (that literacy depends on literate culture) is, as formulated, vacuous, self-contradictory, or a Catch-22 clause: that is, it is the same as saying that, in order to read, you must know what is known (only) by people who are able to read. In the second case, it is empirically wrong, and—in relation to the ambitious claims made for it—importantly wrong. For one's ability to read adequately (including one's ability to understand what one reads) certainly does not depend on one's having already read many worthy books, or having a B.A. degree, or being familiar with high culture. And, more significantly for the specific pedagogic reforms Hirsch proposes, it certainly does not depend on one's ability to identify or recite standard definitions for all (or even a large number) of the items on Hirsch's List—or, which may or may not be the same thing, having one's head furnished with the particular assortment of bric-a-brac that furnishes the heads of people like the Kenan Professor of English at the University of Virginia and his various friends, relatives, and associates.

The verbal slippage noted above—that is, between "literate" in the sense of being able to read adequately and "literate" in the sense of being well-read, well-educated, and, in that sense, "cultured"—is crucial to the shimmering ambiguity of the term and concept "cultural literacy" and, one suspects, responsible for a good bit of the popularity of the book (which seems to offer easy access to the socially desirable states thus named). It also permits Hirsch to deal handily with a number of significant objections:

> There are many things to be said against making a list, and in the past two years I have heard them. Ideological objections to codifying and imposing the culture of the power structure have been among them. These are objections to the whole concept of spreading cultural literacy and are consequently objections to spreading literacy itself, not to making lists.[10]

Period. End of reply. Hirsch's answer to these objections consists, in other words, of labeling them (as usual) "ideological," putting the rabble-rousing words "power structure" in the mouths of those who raise them, and deftly identifying the questioning of his List and its use in the schools with not wanting people to be literate. The deftness of this identification depends, of course, on the verbal slippage just noted.[11]

We may turn, however, to the more general operation of the idea of "literacy" in Hirsch's book. As everyone who has dealt with the question knows, the term names something notoriously difficult to determine or measure, even taken in its common, pedagogic sense of adequate reading competence.[12] For not only are there many different levels of reading competence, but also many different varieties, and "adequacy" itself is, of course, a variable concept, changing its specific value in relation to different criteria, including specific purposes. It is also well known that the ease with which someone reads a text plus the extent to which she or he understands it—a legal contract, a newspaper editorial, a historical novel, printed directions for installing and operating an appliance, etc.—will always depend on a number of variable conditions, including the extent of (a) the reader's interest in that *particular* text, (b) his or her prior experience with its *particular* subject matter and domain, and (c) his or her skill in handling its *particular* verbal idiom. Contrary, however, to Hirsch's unshakable belief and central contention, none of these conditions can be equated with or reduced to the reader's mastery of *general* "background information," nor could the interests, experiences, and skills in question be derived from someone's knowledge of some list of things—any list, no matter who compiled it or how long it was.

As it happens, Hirsch cites a number of studies bearing on these points, but he interprets them bizarrely. Since appeals to the laboratory lend authority to many of his claims, it will be useful, for this and other reasons, to look at one such characteristic appeal. Citing a particular study of the conditions that enhance reading facility, Hirsch maintains that its results demonstrate the "*national* character of the knowledge needed in reading and writing." [13] The experiment apparently consisted of a comparison of the rates of speed with which people from India and the United States could read texts that described either "an Indian wedding" or "an American wedding." [14] As Hirsch reports it, what the data indicated (hardly surprisingly) was that the Indians read the descriptions of the Indian wedding faster, and the Americans read the description of the American wedding faster. But, of course, the same contrasts would have been obtained if the study had compared the ease with which auto mechanics and pastry chefs could read texts that described either how to take apart a carburetor or how to bake a strudel, since what mattered was not the different nationalities of the readers as such but, rather, the different extents of their prior familiarity with the particular practices described in those texts—a difference that would, with other texts, fall along occupational lines, age lines, class lines, or regional lines rather than, as was the case here, along national lines. In other words, whatever else the study demonstrated, it did not support Hirsch's views either of the general conditions required for reading facility or of the specifically "national character" of the knowledge presupposed by literacy. [15]

The idea that "background information" is in some sense *"national"* is attended by a set of claims that are crucial to Hirsch's general argument, dubious in every detail, and worth examining very closely:

> Although nationalism may be regrettable in some of its world-wide political effects, a mastery of national culture is essential to a mastery of the standard language in every modern nation. This point is important because educators often stress the importance of a multicultural education. Such study is indeed valuable in itself; it inculcates tolerance and provides a perspective on *our own* traditions and values. But however laudable it is it should not be the primary focus of national education. It should not be allowed to supplant or interfere with *our* schools' responsibility to insure *our* children's mastery of American literate culture.[16]

It is not clear what Hirsch understands and implies here by "multi-cultural education," and the vagueness is not without consequences. For many educators in this country, it would mean schooling that recognizes either the internal multiplicity of American culture and/or the significance for Americans of the cultures of other groups and nations. The indeterminate reference here permits Hirsch to ignore the former as such and, at the same time, to conflate it with the latter: in other words, he can imply (and may, of course, himself believe) that (certain) internal American cultures are *foreign* or, in any case, not "our own." The question is, which traditions and values *are* "our own," or, to put it the other way around, which traditions and values, shared by members of various communities in America and/or elsewhere in the world, are *not* "our own," and who exactly are "we"? Hirsch's answer to each part of this question, though never explicit, is a subtextual drumbeat throughout the passage and the book.

Because the reference of "multicultural education" is vague, we also do not know what specific curricular practices Hirsch's imperatives are meant to discourage. The study of African-American fiction and the history of jazz by Philadelphia schoolchildren, for example? The study of Chinese and Mayan art in some California high school where Asian-American and Hispanic-American students are a majority? The study of French literature, architecture, and cooking in an elite New England prep school? Never mind the details; we are given to understand that, whatever we suspect it is (probably not a course in French civilization at the Concord Academy for Girls), we don't want too much of it. The passage concludes as follows:

> To teach the ways of *one's own* community has always been and still remains the essence of the education of *our* children, who enter neither a narrow tribal culture nor a transcendent world culture but a national literate culture. For profound historical reasons, this is the way of the modern world. It will not change soon, and it will certainly not be changed by educational policy alone.[17]

What this deeply allusive and determinedly grim statement is meant to suggest, I take it, is that, however much pluralistic- or international-minded educators might wish to ignore the stark realities of life, modern (American) children have no use for local, ethnic cultures (at least not for *certain* of them—dare we guess which?), and, furthermore, should not be encouraged to identify, as their own community, any social unit either smaller, larger, or other than the *nation*. What is indicated here as ironclad fact, however ("This is the way of the modern world"), is, of course, thoroughly ideological and, for "profound historical reasons" plus many other—sociological, geopolitical, etc.—reasons, profoundly questionable.

American children "need to know" a great many things, and no doubt many more than the schools are now teaching most of them. It would be all to the good—in many different ways and for various reasons (including, but not only, their chances of prospering economically)—for them to know things about the history, government, demography, and geography of their own nation, their own state, and their own local region, *and* various other regions of the world that quite properly engage their attention. It would also be all to the good for them to know things about the ecologically, economically, and politically global, international world that they "enter" just as surely as they enter the United States of America when they are born somewhere within its borders. And, of course, it would be good for children everywhere to know things such as mathematics, biology, ecology, and computers that are not about—and the knowledge of which is not confined to or especially distinctive of—any particular society or culture, American or otherwise; for, contrary to Hirsch's odd notions regarding its "national character," most knowledge in "the modern world" (background, foreground, and middle ground) does not have any citizenship papers attached to it at all.

Given that there is more that American children "need to know" than they can be taught during their school years, the schools must, of course, establish educational priorities. Given also, however, that the social backgrounds and individual competencies of American schoolchildren vary in numerous ways related to the unique social/regional/demographic history of this very large, very populous, and exceptionally diverse nation, the *specific* priorities of their education (and sequence of their studies) are most responsively and effectively determined on a local—region by region, school by school, classroom by classroom—level, not a national level. This is not to say that those priorities are being determined now as well as they should be. But there is no reason to think that attempting to determine them uniformly at a national level would be more responsive and effective, and, moreover, no reason, aside from Hirsch's personal illusion of the essentialness, basicness, and proper standardness of some particular bag of things that he (along with what he is pleased to call "all literate Americans") happens to know, why the alphabetically listed contents of that bag should be given absolute priority in this regard.

====

What literate Americans know. What every American needs to know. So Hirsch claims for his List, and so Americans in the hundreds of thousands may now be inclined to believe. The force of the claim is equivocal, however, and hedged throughout the book. Hirsch states, for example, that the appendix to *Cultural Literacy* is not meant to be "prescriptive" but is only "a *descriptive* list of the information actually possessed by literate Americans," forgetting the book's subtitle and his recurrent imperatives concerning the centrality of the List to the educational reforms he is proposing.[18] The continuous eliding of the prescriptive/descriptive distinction is significant because it permits Hirsch to evade the responsibilities of each kind of claim by moving to the other when criticisms are pressed. Thus, if the List's claims to descriptive adequacy and accuracy are questioned (is it really what literate Americans—*all* of them?—"actually" know?), Hirsch can claim to be offering only provisional recommendations and "guideposts"; conversely, when objections are raised to the manifestly patrician, self-privileging norms promoted by the List, Hirsch can claim that it has nothing to do with what *he* knows or thinks should be known, but simply describes the way things are among "literate Americans."

The method by which the List was generated is, in any case, exceedingly mysterious. According to Hirsch, it is not "a complete catalogue of American knowledge," but "is intended to illustrate the character and range of the knowledge literate Americans tend to share" and to "establish guideposts that can be of practical use to teachers, students, and all others who need to know our literate culture" (which is, of course, according to Hirsch, "every American").[19] But, one might ask (granting the double absurdity of a specifically "*American* knowledge" and a possible catalog of *any* actual human knowledge), what sorts of persons *are* the "literate Americans" whose knowledge is illustrated or represented by the List? How, for example, could one distinguish them from Americans who merely know how to read? And how does Hirsch himself know what "the literate reader" knows?

The answers to these questions cannot be determined from any explicit statements of procedure in the book. Indeed, the accounts of the List given by way of introduction and explanation could hardly be briefer or vaguer. Hirsch notes that "different literate Americans have slightly [*sic*] different conceptions of our shared knowledge," but assures his readers that "more than one hundred consultants reported agreement on over 90 percent of the items listed."[20] Wonderful: more than one hundred, over 90 percent. But agreement on *what*? Was each "consultant" asked to compile an individual list and then all the lists compared for overlap? Or, quite differently, were the consultants asked, for each item on an already compiled list, to say whether they were themselves familiar with it? Or, again, and again quite differently, were the consultants asked, for each item, whether they agreed that every "literate American" (however defined for them—if at all) *knew* it—or, and also quite differently, whether they thought every literate American *should* know it?[21] Nor does Hirsch indicate how the consultants themselves were chosen. At random from the Charlottesville telephone directory? From among his classiest friends, best students, and most congenial colleagues at the University of Virginia? Were they, by any chance, selected to be representative of various regions of the nation, and a range of ages, occupations, and degrees of formal education? Were they chosen, in fact, by any consistent and appropriate sampling principle?

The questions raised here are important because, depending on the specific procedures and selection criteria used, very different lists would have been produced. Moreover, without consistent and appropriate procedures and criteria, the claims of representativeness (not to mention implications of unbiased, statistical authority) made for Hirsch's List—copies of which are now being delivered by the truckful to teachers and children across the nation[22]—might seem, relative to the standards of responsible social science research, dubious. But never mind all that: like the old Ivory Soap ads, *99 and 44/100 percent pure—it floats*!

=====

Toward the end of the book, Hirsch acknowledges the objection from "some educators" that there might be some "difficulties" putting the idea of cultural literacy into practice since information is not remembered "unless it is embedded in interesting material" and, as he phrases the objection, knowledge of that sort is acquired only through "years of communication with other literate people." His reply is that "the predicted difficulties . . . simply do not apply to young children" because the latter are "fascinated by straightforward information and absorb it without strain": young children, Hirsch remarks, really *like* "to pick up adult information long before they can make sense of it" and, besides, "even untraditional schools have not found a way to avoid rote learning," as in the alphabet and multiplication tables.[23]

But Hirsch's reply evades the point of such objections and misses their decisive implications for the value of his educational program. If "cultural literacy," as he defines it, cannot be formally taught, then it makes no difference how early you start teaching it; if it cannot be acquired by memorizing lists and dictionaries, then it makes no difference that children memorize alphabets and multiplication tables. Moreover, if children learn List-items such as *coup d'état, The Charge of the Light Brigade,* and *consumer price index* only as "adult information" that they cannot "make sense of," and their lives, then and subsequently, give them no other way to use that information or otherwise make sense of it, then it will not operate as knowledge at all. It will not, that is, function for those children in the way one presumably wants it to function (in relation to reading or otherwise), namely as a part of their intellectual resources—to say nothing of their creative or critical thinking, the first of which (and, indeed, creativity of any kind) Hirsch never mentions in the book, and the second of which elicits only his patient condescension as among the sadly misguided goals of progressive education.

Indeed, the acquisition of information of that sort in those ways (that is, children's memorization and recitation-on-cue of discrete pieces of information that they did not understand and never had any need or extra-academic occasion to use) would be no different in kind and effect from that bare "word recognition" and mere "knowledge of phonics" that Hirsch always contrasts to genuine literacy and excoriates as only a facsimile of competence. It appears, then, that this "educational reform" would not, as it promises, eliminate illiteracy and make all merely technically literate Americans truly, functionally literate, but would only create a new classification of functional illiteracy—"functional *cultural* illiteracy"—on which we can blame all our national problems and by which we can explain why the jobless can't get jobs, the powerless don't vote, and the poor don't have enough money.

═══

It is no wonder that Hirsch's book is acclaimed by numerous government officials and by the neoconservative wing of the nation's intellectual/educational establishment. For *Cultural Literacy* (book, list, term, and concept) does a very good job of obscuring the nation's very real educational problems and assuring the American public, many of whom are naturally happy to hear it, that those problems (along with other social and economic ills, both real and imaginary, from poverty and unemployment to "cultural fragmentation" and the "competitive edge" of the Japanese) are caused primarily by befuddled education professors and school administrators following what scientists have shown to be the incorrect principles of progressive education—and, consequently, can be solved by school reforms that require no funding, entail no social or political changes, create no uncomfortable feelings for anyone except teachers and school administrators, and do not touch the structure of a single American institution, including its school system.

Cultural Literacy promises practically everything, costs practically nothing, and is produced, packaged, and promoted in a form quite familiar to Americans, whose shared national culture consists as much of media hype and 4th of July speeches as it does of anything on Hirsch's List from *auf wiedersehen* to *vestal virgins*. "[O]nly a few hundred pages of information," says Hirsch, "stand between" literacy and illiteracy, "between dependence and autonomy"—only a few hundred pages between us and the fulfillment of our dreams.[24] And not only our individual dreams but the American Dream. For, as he tells us in the concluding words of the book, the stakes here are high:

> breaking the cycle of illiteracy for deprived children; raising the living standard of families who have been illiterate; making our country more competitive in international markets; achieving greater social justice; enabling all citizens to participate in the political process; bringing us that much closer to the Ciceronian ideal of universal public discourse—in short, achieving the fundamental goals of the Founders at the birth of the republic.[25]

Wild applause; fireworks; music—*America the Beautiful*; all together, now: *Calvin Coolidge, Gunga Din, Peter Pan, spontaneous combustion*. Hurrah for America and the national culture! Hurrah!

=======

The project of cult-lit will, I am certain, fail. It will fail because, even if children all over the country began to study cultural literacy lists, it would make little if any dent in the conditions that actually produce and perpetuate illiteracy, poverty, social inequities, and political ineffectiveness (not to mention the prosperity of the Japanese in industry and business, and the communication gap between Puerto Rican teenagers and Bridgeport bank executives or between middle-class grandparents and their postmodern grandchildren).[26] As I have been suggesting, however, the very pursuit of Hirsch's project would itself have substantial consequences and, it seems, is already having them, not the least of which is the continued deferral of responsible analysis of the nation's enormous—but quite complex and *various*—educational problems (in some places, deteriorated facilities and insufficient, obsolete materials; in other places, large numbers of children from poor, illiterate, non-English speaking, and otherwise educationally disadvantaged families; in most places, underpaid, undervalued, overburdened teachers; and, throughout the system, but for different reasons and to different extents, unresponsive and ineffective teaching), and the deferral also of the identification and mobilization of the substantial and *varied* resources that would be needed to begin to address those problems adequately.[27]

It is for this reason that I think members of the educational community should not dismiss Hirsch's book as silly, well-meaning, and harmless but, rather, should examine it closely, devote some energy to the exposure of its oversimplifications and incoherences, and remain alert to its echo and endorsement by state officials and agencies. For, we must remember, the fact that the arguments for a proposal are vague and muddled, that its recommendations are patently absurd, and that the possibility of its success is rejected by all of the most eminent people in the field does not mean that it won't become national policy. After all, just think of Star Wars.[28]

Notes

1   E. D. Hirsch, Jr., *Cultural Literacy: What Every American Needs to Know* (Boston, 1987). The title of this article (originally the name I gave to my computer file on the topic) refers to the ever-expanding complex consisting of the term "cultural literacy," the concept of it as developed in Hirsch's book, the book's appended List, the subsequently published dictionary (E. D. Hirsch, Jr., Joseph F. Kett, and James Trefil, *The Dictionary of Cultural Literacy* [Boston, 1988]), the federation of schools apparently committed to instituting List-based curricula (see n. 22), and the foundation apparently created to promote all of them (see n. 2).

2 For a description of the Cultural Literacy Foundation, see Scott Heller, "Author Sets Up Foundation to Create 'Cultural Literacy' Tests," *Chronicle of Higher Education*, 5 August 1987.

3 Hirsch, *Cultural Literacy*, xvi–xvii.

4 Ibid., 82.

5 Ibid.; emphasis mine.

6 Ibid., 84.

7 A thorough critique of Hirsch's conception of communication is beyond the scope of this article. I discuss the widely discredited telegraphic model it presupposes in *Contingencies of Value: Alternative Perspectives for Critical Theory* (Cambridge, Mass., 1988), 94–110.

8 Hirsch, *Cultural Literacy*, xvi; emphasis mine.

9 Explaining how the List was generated, Hirsch notes that various proposed items were rejected because they were known to illiterates as well as literates (*Cultural Literacy*, 146).

10 Ibid., 142.

11 In a recent piece, Hirsch writes:

> Those who evade the inherent conservatism of literacy in the name of anti-elitism are, in effect, elitists of an extreme sort. Traditionally educated and economically secure, these self-appointed protectors of minority cultures have advised schools to pursue a course that sentences minorities to illiteracy and poverty. ("A Postscript by E. D. Hirsch, Jr.," *Change* [July/August 1988]: 25)

This is as disturbing for the wildness of its aim as for the irresponsibility of the charge itself: aside from Wayne C. Booth, to whose article in the same issue ("Cultural Literacy and Liberal Learning: An Open Letter to E. D. Hirsch, Jr.") Hirsch is replying (or, rather, *not* replying), he names no specific "self-appointed protectors." See also E. D. Hirsch, Jr., "From Model to Policy," *New Literary History* 20 (Winter 1989): 451–56, for his patronizing rejoinder to the rigorously detailed critique of his accounts of cognitive processing by his former student, Gregory G. Colomb, in whom Hirsch also detects contaminating "ideological" motives.

12 For a recent survey and assessment of research on literacy in cognitive psychology and related fields, see George A. Miller, "The Challenge of Universal Literacy," *Science*, 9 September 1988, 1293–99. Although Miller cites a number of the studies invoked in *Cultural Literacy*, his analyses of their pedagogic and other implications lead to conclusions quite different from Hirsch's.

13 Hirsch, *Cultural Literacy*, 17; emphasis mine.

14 Ibid., 18. See M. S. Steffensen, C. Joag-Des, and R. C. Anderson, "A Cross-Cultural Perspective on Reading Comprehension," *Reading Research Quarterly* 15 (1979): 10–29 (cited by Hirsch, *Cultural Literacy*, 218 n. 17).

15 Numerous instances of Hirsch's questionable understanding and application of sociological, psychological, and anthropological studies have been noted by other

commentators. See Robert Scholes, "Three Views of Education: Nostalgia, History, and Voodoo," *College English* 50 (March 1988): 323–32; Andrew Sledd and James Sledd, "Hirsch's Use of His Sources in *Cultural Literacy*: A Critique," *Profession 88* (1988): 33–39; and Gregory G. Colomb, "Cultural Literacy and the Theory of Meaning: Or, What Educational Theorists Need to Know about How We Read," *New Literary History* 20 (Winter 1989): 411–50. For Hirsch's dismissive replies, see E. D. Hirsch, Jr., "Comments on Profession 88," *Profession 88* (1988): 77–80. In his more recent public statements, Hirsch cites the validation of his convictions by the "common sense" of "ordinary people" whose heads are not cluttered by "theories" and the objections of "experts" (presumably people in such fields as cognitive psychology, social psychology, and sociolinguistics), whom he tends increasingly to patronize, ridicule, and dismiss except when he is claiming that they (or, as suits his needs, their Hirsch-interpreted data) confirm his views. See E. D. Hirsch, Jr., "The Primal Scene of Education," *New York Review of Books*, 2 March 1989, 29–35, for the general point, and "Correspondence," *MLA Newsletter*, Spring 1989, 26–28, for his strained reply to Robert Scholes in their ongoing dispute over Hirsch's citation, in *Cultural Literacy*, of the work of British sociologist Basil Bernstein. (For a follow-up reply by Scholes, see "Correspondence," *MLA Newsletter*, Summer 1989, 21–22.)

16 Hirsch, *Cultural Literacy*, 18; emphasis mine.

17 Ibid.; emphasis mine. The slippery pronouns here simultaneously mask and flash the social and educational import of this assertion. For, given what Hirsch means here by "*one's* own community," namely (as he says immediately thereafter) the community of "literate Americans" (as defined, of course, by Hirsch), it would be, for many Americans, not *their* "own" community but *someone else's* "own," the "ways" of which *their* children would be taught by the schools—that being, according to Hirsch, the "essence" of the education of "*our* children."

18 Hirsch, *Cultural Literacy*, xiv.

19 Ibid., 146.

20 Ibid.

21 The prescriptiveness of the science-related entries is acknowledged by one of the List's coauthors, James Trefil. Trefil, who is a professor of physics at the University of Virginia, notes that "the kind of criteria used to compile our lists for the humanities and social sciences—for example, Would a literate person be familiar with this term?—simply can't be used for the natural sciences" because of the size of "the gap between *the essential basic knowledge* of science and what the general reader can be expected to know" (Hirsch, *Cultural Literacy*, 148; emphasis mine).

22 See "Primal Scene," where Hirsch describes the activities of the Cultural Literacy Federation and its "network" of participant schools.

23 Hirsch, *Cultural Literacy*, 130–31.

24 Ibid., 143.

25 Ibid., 145.

26 I allude here to the ever-expanding claims Hirsch makes for his educational pro-

gram (for example, in his preface to the recent paperback edition of *Cultural Literacy* [New York, 1988]).

27 Other analyses and proposals for reform—not as simple or cheap as Hirsch's, but empirically richer, analytically more subtle and sophisticated, and, with respect to the problems and objectives involved here, pragmatically more promising— include Shirley Brice Heath, *Ways with Words: Language, Life, and Work in Communities and Classrooms* (Cambridge, 1983), and James P. Comer, "Educating Poor Minority Children," *Scientific American,* November 1988, 42–48. As Comer observes in his conclusion, "All the money and effort expended for educational reform will have only limited benefits—particularly for poor minority children— as long as the underlying developmental and social issues remain unaddressed" (48). The long-term project that he and his colleagues have developed at Yale University's Child Care Center for two inner-city schools in New Haven attempts to address those issues and shows impressive results.

Hirsch cites the work of the Yale group in "Primal Scene," but in a highly equivocal way, concluding with the sober observation that "simply offering children systematic knowledge" will not improve their performance "when they are emotionally unprepared to believe that they can learn or use academic knowledge at all" (34). Whether the "simple" offer of "systematic knowledge" (that is, a List-based curriculum) would work for *any* children is, of course, the question begged here, while the otherwise damaging conclusion deftly skirted is that what *would* work for "emotionally unprepared" children is *not* a uniform List-centered curriculum at all but, *instead,* an intensive, locally specific, school-home program.

Hirsch insulates his reforms from comparison and competition by describing alternatives misleadingly. Thus, in the same article, he states that "educational specialists" attribute the "boredom, discomfort, and hostility" of poor, minority children to "social forces beyond anyone's control," and implies that other programs directed at alleviating such effects are pointless because, "unfortunately," they seek only to supply "higher-order thinking skills" ("Primal Scene," 31). It is simply not true, however, that all education specialists believe that the relevant "social forces" (such as racial discrimination, poverty, inadequate housing, and drug addiction) are "beyond anyone's control," and it is clear from the work of the Yale group, as cited by Hirsch himself, that not all alternative programs are thus restricted in educational focus. Nor, in fact, is it at all self-evident that the particular skills and strategies that such programs seek *among other things* to develop —and which Hirsch simply *contrasts* to the "impart[ing of] shared background knowledge"—are irrelevant to academic performance. (See Miller, "Challenge of Universal Literacy," 1296–97, for the opposite conclusion drawn from recent research.)

28 The comments that follow were elicited by exchanges that took place during the discussion of this and other papers at the Liberal Arts Education conference.

Cultural Literacy is, I think, a conceptual shambles, but it is also a skillful piece of verbal showmanship, promoting a deeply conservative view of American society and culture through a rousing populist rhetoric. That rhetoric, and not this nation's founding or institutions, was the object of my 4th of July satire. I thought the target would be obvious, but the atmosphere surrounding the current educational debate is evidently such that the adequacy of a speaker's *patriotism* can become an issue in it—as it did, with egregious irrelevance, in the discussion of my paper at the conference.

Hirsch was praised at the conference for his readiness to address his readers directly and, in effect, at their own level. Accessibility of idiom is desirable, of course, from any speaker addressing any public audience—and, for polemical effectiveness, necessary. To claim, however, that Hirsch speaks to his readers "simply as one citizen to another" is to obscure the force of his institutional authority and the relevance of numerous other disparities of resources (professional experience, material facilities, government sponsorship, a national platform) that not only distinguish him from most members of his public audiences but that give him significant advantages over them—advantages which he does not appear to forbear from exploiting—in this altogether asymmetrical "conversation."

In view of the common disdain among academic intellectuals for the world of primary and secondary school education, the fact that Hirsch ventures into the schools, talks to teachers and school administrators, and spends a good deal of time and effort promoting his ideas of educational reform may be put to his credit. It would seem obvious, however, that none of this—or what was spoken of at the conference as his "getting his hands dirty"—vouches for the relevance or adequacy of the analyses in *Cultural Literacy* or for the value of the reforms themselves. Nor should any of it be thought to shield Hirsch's claims and arguments from criticism, including criticism from those who have not—at least not in quite those ways—gotten their hands dirty.

Henry Louis Gates, Jr.

The Master's Pieces: On Canon Formation and the African-American Tradition

William Bennett and Allan Bloom, the dynamic duo of the new cultural right, have become the easy targets of the cultural left—which I am defining here loosely and generously, as that uneasy, shifting set of alliances formed by feminist critics, critics of so-called "minority" discourse, and Marxist and post-structuralist critics generally, the Rainbow Coalition of contemporary critical theory. These two men symbolize for us the nostalgic return to what I think of as the "antebellum aesthetic position," when men were men, and men were white, when scholar-critics were white men, and when women and persons of color were voiceless, faceless servants and laborers, pouring tea and filling brandy snifters in the boardrooms of old boys' clubs. Inevitably, these two men have come to play the roles for us that George Wallace and Orville Faubus played for the civil rights movement, or that Nixon and Kissinger played for us during Vietnam—the "feel good" targets, who, despite our internal differences and contradictions, we all love to hate.

And how tempting it is to juxtapose their "civilizing mission" to the racial violence that has swept through our campuses since 1986—at traditionally liberal northern institutions such as the University of Massachusetts at Amherst, Mount Holyoke College, Smith College, the University of Chicago, Columbia, and at southern institutions such as the University of Alabama, the University of Texas, and at the Citadel. Add to this the fact that affirmative action programs on campus have meanwhile become window-dressing operations, necessary "evils" maintained to preserve the fiction of racial fairness and openness, but deprived of the power to enforce their stated principles. When unemployment among black youth is 40 percent, when 44 percent of black Americans can't read the front page of a newspaper, when less than 2 percent of the faculty on campuses is black, well, you look for targets close at hand.

And yet there's a real danger of localizing our grievances, of the easy personification, assigning a celebrated face to the forces of reaction and so giving too much credit to a few men who are really symptomatic of a larger political current. Maybe our eagerness to do so reflects a certain vanity that academic cultural critics are prone to. We make dire predictions, and when they come true, we think we've changed the world.

It's a tendency that puts me in mind of my father's favorite story about Father Divine, that historic con-man of the cloth; the guy made Al Sharpton look like someone out of *Paper Moon*. In the 1930s he was put on trial for using the mails to defraud, I think, and was convicted. At sentencing, Father Divine stood up and told the judge: I'm warning you, you send me to jail, something terrible is going to happen to you. Father Divine, of course, was sent to prison, and a week later, by sheer coincidence, the judge had a heart attack and died. When the warden and the guards found out about it in the middle of the night, they raced to Father Divine's cell and woke him up. Father Divine, they said, your judge just dropped dead of a heart attack. Without missing a beat, Father Divine lifted his head and told them: "I *hated* to do it."

As writers, teachers, or intellectuals, most of us would like to claim greater efficacy for our labors than we're entitled to. These days, literary criticism likes to think of itself as "war by other means."

But it should start to wonder: Have its victories come too easily? The recent turn toward politics and history in literary studies has turned the analysis of texts into a marionette theater of the political, to which we bring all the passions of our real-world commitments. And that's why it is sometimes necessary to remind ourselves of the distance from the classroom to the streets. Academic critics write essays, "readings" of literature, where the bad guys (for example, racism or patriarchy) lose, where the forces of oppression are subverted by the boundless powers of irony and allegory that no prison can contain, and we glow with hard-won triumph. We pay homage to the marginalized and demonized, and it feels almost like we've righted a real-world injustice. I always think about the folktale about the fellow who killed seven with one blow.

Ours was the generation that took over buildings in the late sixties and demanded the creation of black and women's studies programs, and now, like the return of the repressed, has come back to challenge the traditional curriculum. And some of us are even attempting to redefine the canon by editing anthologies. Yet it sometimes seems that blacks are doing better in the college curriculum than they are in the streets.

This is not a defeatist moan. Just an acknowledgment that the relation between our critical postures and the social struggles they reflect upon is far from transparent. That doesn't mean there's no relation, of course, only that it's a highly mediated one. In any event, I do think we should be clear about when we've swatted a fly and when we've toppled a giant.

In the swaddling clothes of our academic complacencies, few of us are prepared when we bump against something hard, and sooner or later, we do. One of the first talks I ever gave was to a packed audience at the Howard University Honors Seminar, and it was one of those mistakes you don't do twice. Fresh out of graduate school, immersed in the arcane technicalities of contemporary literary theory, I was going to deliver a crunchy structuralist analysis of a slave narrative by Frederick Douglass, tracing the intricate play of its "binary oppositions." Everything was neatly schematized, formalized, analyzed; this was my Sunday-best structuralism, crisp white shirt and shiny black shoes. And it wasn't playing. If you've seen an audience glaze over, this was double-glazing. Bravely, I finished my talk and, of course, asked for questions. Long silence. Finally, a young man in the very back of the room stands up and says, "Yeah, brother, all we want to know is, was Booker T. a Tom or not?"

The funny thing is, this happens to be an interesting question, a lot more interesting than my talk was. And while I didn't exactly appreciate it at the time, the exchange did draw my attention, a little rudely perhaps, to the yawning chasm between our critical discourse and the traditions they discourse on. You know—Is there a canon in this class? People often like to represent the high canonical texts as the reading matter of the power elite. I mean, you have to try to imagine James Baker curling up with the *Four Quartets*, Dan Quayle leafing through the *Princess Cassimassima*. I suppose this is the vision, anyway. What is wrong with this picture? Now, Louis L'Amour or Ian Fleming, possibly. But that carries us a ways from the high canonical.

It's funny, when I think back to that Howard talk, I think back to why I went into literature in the first place. I suppose the literary canon is, in no very grand sense, the commonplace book of our shared culture, in which we have written down the texts and titles that we want to remember, that had some special meaning for us. How else did those of us who teach literature fall in love with our subject than through our own commonplace books, in which we inscribed, secretly and privately, as we might do in a diary, those passages of books that named for us what we had for so long deeply felt, but could not say? I kept mine from the age of twelve, turning to it to repeat those marvelous passages that named myself in some private way. From H. H. Munro and O. Henry—I mean, some of the popular literature we had on the shelves at home—to Dickens and Austen, to Hugo and de Maupassant, I found resonant passages that I used to inscribe in my book. Finding James Baldwin and writing him down at an Episcopal church camp during the Watts riots in 1965 (I was fifteen) probably determined the direction of my intellectual life more than did any other single factor. I wrote and rewrote verbatim his elegantly framed paragraphs, full of sentences that were at once somehow Henry Jamesian and King Jamesian, yet clothed in the cadences and figures of the spirituals. I try to remind my graduate students that each of us turned to literature through literal or figurative commonplace books, a fact that we tend to forget once we adopt the alienating strategies of formal analysis. The passages in my commonplace book formed my own canon, just as I imagine each of yours did for you. And a canon, as it has functioned in every literary tradition, has served as the commonplace book of our shared culture.

But the question I want to turn to now is this: How does the debate over canon formation affect the development of African-American literature as a subject of instruction in the American academy?

Curiously enough, the first use of the word "canon" in relation to the African-American literary tradition occurs in 1846, in a speech delivered by Theodore Parker. Parker was a theologian, a Unitarian clergyman, and a publicist for ideas, whom Perry Miller described eloquently as "the man who next only to Emerson . . . was to give shape and meaning to the Transcendental movement in America." In a speech on "The Mercantile Classes" delivered in 1846, Parker laments the sad state of "American" letters:

> Literature, science, and art are mainly in [poor men's] hands, yet are controlled by the prevalent spirit of the nation. . . . In England, the national literature favors the church, the crown, the nobility, the prevailing class. Another literature is rising, but is not yet national, *still less canonized*. We have no American literature which is permanent. Our scholarly books are only an imitation of a foreign type; they do not reflect our morals, manners, politics, or religion, not even our rivers, mountains, sky. They have not the smell of our ground in their breath.

Parker, to say the least, was not especially pleased with American letters and their identity with the English tradition. Did Parker find any evidence of a truly American literature?

> The American literature is found only in newspapers and speeches, perhaps in some novel, hot, passionate, but poor and extemporaneous. That is our national literature. Does that favor man—represent man? Certainly not. All is the reflection of this

most powerful class. The truths that are told are for them, and
the lies. Therein the prevailing sentiment is getting into the form
of thoughts.

Parker's analysis, we see plainly, turns upon an implicit reflection
theory of base and superstructure. It is the occasional literature,
"poor and extemporaneous," wherein "American" literature dwells,
but a literature, like English literature, which reflects the interests
and ideologies of the upper classes.

Three years later, in his major oration on "The American Scholar,"
Parker had at last found an entirely original genre of American literature:

> Yet, there is one portion of our permanent literature, if literature
> it may be called, which is wholly indigenous and original. . . .
> [W]e have one series of literary productions that could be writ-
> ten by none but Americans, and only here; I mean the Lives of
> Fugitive Slaves. But as these are not the work of the men of su-
> perior culture they hardly help to pay the scholar's debt. Yet all
> the original romance of Americans is in them, not in the white
> man's novel.

Parker was right about the originality, the peculiarly *American*
quality, of the slave narratives. But he was wrong about their inherent inability to "pay the scholar's debt"; scholars had only to learn
to *read* the narratives for their debt to be paid in full, indeed many
times over. Parker was put off by the language of the slaves' narratives. He would have done well to heed the admonition that Emerson had made in his 1844 speech, "Emancipation in the British West
Indies": "Language," Emerson wrote, "must be raked, the secrets of
slaughter-houses and infamous holes that cannot front the day, must
be ransacked, to tell what negro slavery has been." The narratives,
for Parker, were not instances of greater literature, but they were
prime site of America's "original romance." As Charles Sumner said
in 1852, the fugitive slaves and their narratives "are among the heroes
of our age. Romance has no storms of more thrilling interest than
theirs. Classical antiquity has preserved no examples of adventurous
trial more worthy of renown." Parker's and Samuel's divergent views

reveal that the popularity of the narratives in antebellum America most certainly did not reflect any sort of common critical agreement about their nature and status as art. Still, the implications of these observations upon black canon formation would not be lost upon those who would soon seek to free the black slave, or to elevate the ex-slave, through the agency of literary production.

Johann Herder's ideas of the "living spirit of a language" were brought to bear with a vengeance upon eighteenth- and nineteenth-century considerations of the place in nature of the black. Indeed the relationship between the social and political subjectivity of the Negro and the production of art was discussed by a host of commentators, including Hume, Hegel, and Kant, since Morgan Godwyn wondered aloud about it in 1684. But it was probably Emerson's comments that generated our earliest efforts at canon formation. As Emerson said, again in his speech on "Emancipation in the West Indies,"

> If [racial groups] are rude and foolish, down they must go. When at last in a race a new principle appears, an idea—*that* conserves it; ideas only save races. If the black man is feeble and not important to the existing races, not on a parity with the best race, the black man must serve, and be exterminated. But if the black man carries in his bosom an indispensable element of a new and coming civilization; for the sake of that element, no wrong nor strength nor circumstance can hurt him; he will survive and play his part. . . . [N]ow let [the blacks] emerge, clothed and in their own form.

The forms in which they would be clothed would be registered in anthologies that established the canon of black American literature.

The first attempt to define a black canon that I have found is that by Armand Lanusse, who edited *Les Cenelles*, an anthology of black French verse published at New Orleans in 1845—the first black anthology, I believe, ever published. Lanusse's introduction is a defense of poetry as an enterprise for black people, in their larger efforts to defend the race against "the spiteful and calumnious arrows shot at us," at a target defined as the collective black intellect. Despite this stated political intention, these poems imitate the styles and themes of the French Romantics, and never engage directly the social and political experiences of black Creoles in New Orleans in the 1840s. *Les Cenelles* argues for a political effect—that is, the end of racism—by publishing apolitical poems, poems which share as silent second texts the poetry written by Frenchmen three thousand miles away. We are just like the French—so, treat us like Frenchmen, not like blacks. An apolitical art being put to uses most political.

Four years later, in 1849, William G. Allen published an anthology in which he canonized Phillis Wheatley and George Moses Horton. Like Lanusse, Allen sought to refute intellectual racism by the act of canon formation. "The African's called inferior," he writes. "But what race has ever displayed intellect more exaltedly, or character more sublime?" Pointing to the achievements of Pushkin, Placido, and Augustine, as the great African tradition to which African-Americans are heir, Allen claims Wheatley and Horton as the exemplars of this tradition, Horton being "decidedly the superior genius," no doubt because of his explicitly racial themes, a judgment quite unlike that which propelled Armand Lanusse into canon formation. As Allen puts it, with the publication of their anthology:

> Who will now say that the African is incapable of attaining to intellectual or moral greatness? What he now is, degrading circumstances have made him. What he is capable of becoming, the past clearly evinces. The African is strong, tough and hardy. Hundreds of years of oppression have not subdued his spirit, and though Church and State have combined to enslave and degrade him, in spite of them all, he is increasing in strength and power, and in the respect of the entire world.

Here, then, we see the poles of black canon formation, established firmly by 1849: Is "black" poetry racial in theme, or is black poetry any sort of poetry written by black people? This quandary has been at play in the tradition ever since.

I do not have time to trace in detail the history of this tension over definitions of the African-American canon, and the direct relation between the production of black poetry and the end of white racism. Suffice it to point to such seminal attempts at canon formation in the 1920s as James Weldon Johnson's *The Book of American Negro Poetry*

(1922), Alain Locke's *The New Negro* (1925), and V. F. Calverton's *An Anthology of American Negro Literature* (1929), each of which defined as its goal the demonstration of the existence of the black tradition as a political defense of the racial self against racism. As Johnson put it so clearly:

> A people may be great through many means, but there is only one measure by which its greatness is recognized and acknowledged. The final measure of the greatness of all peoples is the amount and standard of the literature and art that they have produced. The world does not know that a people is great until that people produces great literature and art. No people that has produced great literature and art has ever been looked upon by the world as distinctly inferior.
>
> The status of the Negro in the United States is more a question of national mental attitude toward the race than of actual conditions. And nothing will do more to change that mental attitude and raise his status than a demonstration of intellectual parity by the Negro through the production of literature and art.

Johnson, here, was echoing racialist arguments that had been used against blacks since the eighteenth century, especially those by Hume, Kant, Jefferson, and Hegel, which equated our access to natural rights with our production of literary classics. The Harlem Renaissance, in fact, can be thought of as a sustained attempt to combat racism through the very *production* of black art and literature.

Johnson's and Calverton's anthologies "frame" the Renaissance period, making a comparison between their ideological concerns useful. Calverton's anthology made two significant departures from Johnson's model, both of which are worth considering, if only briefly. Calverton's was the first attempt at black canon formation to provide for the influence and presence of black vernacular literature in a major way. "Spirituals," "Blues," and "Labor Songs" each comprises a genre of black literature for him. We all understand the importance of this gesture and the influence it had upon Sterling Brown, Arthur Davis, and Ulysses Lee, the editors of *The Negro Caravan* (1941). Calverton, whose real name was George Goetz, announces in his introductory essay, "The Growth of Negro Literature," that his selection principles have been determined by his sense of the history of black literary *forms*, leading him to make selections because of their formal "representative value," as he puts it. These forms, he continues, are *Negro* forms, virtually self-contained in a hermetic black tradition, especially in the vernacular tradition, where artistic American originality was to be found:

> . . . [I]t is no exaggeration whatsoever to contend that [the Negro's contributions to American art and literature] are more striking and singular in substance and structure than any contributions that have been made by the white man to American culture. In fact, they constitute America's chief claim to originality in its cultural history. . . . The white man in America has continued, and in an inferior manner, a culture of European origin. He has not developed a culture that is definitely and unequivocally American. In respect of originality, then, the Negro is more important in the growth of American culture than the white man. . . . While the white man has gone to Europe for his models, and is seeking still a European approval of his artistic endeavors, the Negro in his art forms has never sought the acclaim of any culture other than his own. This is particularly true of those forms of Negro art that come directly from the people.

And note that Calverton couched his argument in just that rhetoric of nationalism, of American exceptionalism, that had long been used to exclude, or anyway occlude, the contribution of the Negro. In an audacious reversal, it turns out that *only* the Negro is really American, the white man being a pale imitation of his European forebears.

If Calverton's stress upon the black vernacular heavily influenced the shaping of *The Negro Caravan*—certainly one of the most important anthologies in the tradition—his sense of the black canon as a formal self-contained entity most certainly did not. As the editors put it in the introduction to the volume:

> [We] . . . do not believe that the expression "Negro literature" is an accurate one, and . . . have avoided using it. "Negro literature" has no application if it means structural peculiarity, or a Negro school of writing. The Negro writes in the forms evolved

in English and American literature. . . . The editors consider
Negro writers to be American writers, and literature by American Negroes to be a segment of American literature. . . .

The chief cause for objection to the term is that "Negro literature" is too easily placed by certain critics, white and Negro, in
an alcove apart. The next step is a double standard of judgment,
which is dangerous for the future of Negro writers. "A Negro
novel," thought of as a separate form, is too often condoned as
"good enough for a Negro." That Negroes in America have had
a hard time, and that inside stories of Negro life often present
unusual and attractive reading matter are incontrovertible facts;
but when they enter literary criticism these facts do damage to
both the critics and the artists.

Yet immediately following this stern admonition, we're told the
editors haven't been too concerned to maintain "an even level of literary excellence," because the tradition is defined by both form and
content:

Literature by Negro authors about Negro experience . . . must
be considered as significant, not only because of a body of established masterpieces, but also because of the illumination it sheds
upon a social reality.

And later, in the introduction to the section entitled "The Novel," the
editors elaborate upon this idea by complaining about the relation
of revision between *Iola Leroy* (1892) and *Clotel* (1853), a relation
of the sort central to Calverton's canon, but here defined most dis-
approvingly: "There are repetitions of situations from Brown's *Clotel*,
something of a forecast of a sort of literary inbreeding which causes
Negro writers to be influenced by other Negroes more than should
ordinarily be expected." The black canon, for these editors, was that
literature which most eloquently refuted white racist stereotypes and
which embodied the shared "theme of struggle that is present in so
much Negro expression." Theirs, in other words, was a canon that
was unified thematically by self-defense against racist literary conventions, and by the expression of what the editors called "strokes
of freedom." The formal bond that Calverton had claimed was of no

academic or political use for these editors, precisely because they wished to project an integrated canon of American literature. As the editors put it,

> [i]n spite of such unifying bonds as a common rejection of the popular stereotypes and a common "racial" cause, writings by Negroes do not seem to the editors to fall into a unique cultural pattern. Negro writers have adopted the literary traditions that seemed useful for their purposes. . . . While Frederick Douglass brought more personal knowledge and bitterness into his antislavery agitation than William Lloyd Garrison and Theodore Parker, he is much closer to them in spirit and in form than to Phillis Wheatley, his predecessor, and Booker T. Washington, his successor. . . . The bonds of literary tradition seem to be stronger than race.

Form, then, or the community of structure and sensibility, was called upon to reveal the sheer arbitrariness of American "racial" classifications, and their irrelevance to American canon formation. Above all else, these editors sought to expose the essentialism at the center of racialized subdivisions of the American literary tradition. If we recall that this anthology appears just thirteen years before *Brown v. Board*, we should not be surprised by the "integrationist" thrust of the poetics espoused here. Ideological desire and artistic premise were one. African-American literature, then, is a misnomer; "American literature" written by Negroes more aptly designates this body of writing. So much for a definition of the African-American tradition based on formal relationships of revision, text to text.

At the opposite extreme in black canon formation is the canon defined by Amiri Baraka and Larry Neal in *Black Fire*, published in 1968, an anthology so very familiar to us all. This canon, the blackest canon of all, was defined by both formal innovations and by themes: formally, individual selections tended to aspire to the vernacular or to black music, or to performance; theoretically, each selection reinforces the urge toward black liberation, toward "freedom now" with an up-against-the-wall subtext. The hero, the valorized presence in this volume, is the black vernacular: no longer summoned or invoked through familiar and comfortable rubrics such as "The Spirituals" and "The Blues," but *embodied, assumed, presupposed* in a marvelous act of formal bonding often obscured by the stridency of the political message the anthology meant to announce. Absent completely was a desire to "prove" our common humanity with white people, by demonstrating our power of intellect. One mode of essentialism— African essentialism—was used to critique the essentialism implicit in notions of a common or universal American heritage. No, in *Black Fire*, art and act were one.

=======

I have been thinking about these strains in black canon formation because a group of us will be editing still another anthology, which will constitute still another attempt at canon formation: I am pleased to confirm that W. W. Norton will be publishing the *Norton Anthology of African-American Literature*. As some of you know, the editing of this anthology has been a great dream of mine for a long time. After a year of readers' reports, market surveys, and draft proposals, Norton has enthusiastically embarked upon the publishing of our anthology.

I think that I am most excited about the fact that we will have at our disposal the means to edit an anthology which will define a canon of African-American literature for instructors and students at any institution which desires to teach a course in African-American literature. Once our anthology is published, no one will ever again be able to use the unavailability of black texts as an excuse not to teach our literature. A well-marketed anthology—particularly a Norton Anthology—functions in the academy to *create* a tradition, as well as to define and preserve it. A Norton Anthology opens up a literary tradition as simply as opening the cover of a carefully edited and ample book.

I am not unaware of the politics and ironies of canon formation. The canon that we define will be "our" canon, one possible set of selections among several possible sets of selections. In part to be as eclectic and as democratically "representative" as possible, most other editors of black anthologies have tried to include as many authors and selections (especially excerpts) as possible, in order to preserve and "resurrect" the tradition. I call this the Sears and Roebuck approach, the "dream book" of black literature.

We have all benefited from this approach to collection. Indeed, many of our authors have managed to survive only because an enterprising editor was determined to marshal as much evidence as she or he could to show that the black literary tradition existed. While we must be deeply appreciative of that approach and its results, our task will be a different one.

Our task will be to bring together the "essential" texts of the canon, the "crucially central" authors, those whom we feel to be indispensable to an understanding of the shape, and shaping, of the tradition. A canon is often represented as the "essence" of the tradition, indeed, as the marrow of tradition: the connection between the texts of the canon is meant to reveal the tradition's inherent, or veiled, logic, its internal rationale.

None of us is naive enough to believe that "the canonical" is self-evident, absolute, or neutral. It is a commonplace of contemporary criticism to say that scholars make canons. But, just as often, writers make canons, too, both by critical revaluation and by reclamation through revision. Keenly aware of this—and, quite frankly, aware of my own biases—I have attempted to bring together as period editors a group of scholar-critics (five black women, five black men, one white man), each of whom combines great expertise in her or his period with her or his own approach to the teaching and analyzing of African-American literature. I have attempted, in other words, to bring together scholars whose notions of the black canon might not necessarily agree with my own, or with each others'. I have tried to bring together a diverse array of ideological, methodological, and theoretical perspectives, so that we together might produce an anthology that most fully represents the various definitions of what it means to speak of the African-American literary tradition, and what it means to *teach* that tradition. And while we are at the earliest stages of organization, I can say that my own biases toward canon formation are to stress the formal relationships that obtain among texts in the black tradition—relations of revision, echo, call and response, antiphony, what have you—and to stress the vernacular roots of the tradition. For the vernacular, or oral literature, in my tradition, has a canon of its own.

Accordingly, let me add that our anthology will include a major innovation in anthology production. Because of the strong oral and vernacular base of so much of our literature, we shall sell a cassette tape along with our anthology—precisely *because* the vernacular has a canon of its own, one which has always in its turn informed the written works of the tradition. I am ecstatic about this aspect of our project. This means that each period will include both the printed and spoken text of oral and musical selections of black vernacular culture: sermons, blues, spirituals, R & B, poets reading their own "dialect" poems, speeches—whatever. Imagine having Bessie Smith and Billie Holliday singing the blues, Langston Hughes reading "I Have Known Rivers," Sterling Brown reading "Ma Rainey," James Weldon Johnson, "The Creation," C. L. Franklin, "The Sermon of the Dry Bones," Martin Luther King speaking "I Have a Dream," Sonia Sanchez, "Talking in Tongues"—the list of possibilities is endless, and exhilarating. We will change fundamentally not only the way that our literature is taught, but the way in which any literary tradition is even conceived. So much of our literature seems dead on the page when compared to its performances. We will incorporate performance and the black and human voice into our anthology.

But my pursuit of this project has required me to negotiate a position between, on the one hand, William Bennett, who claims that black people can have no canon, no masterpieces, and, on the other hand, those on the critical left who wonder why we want to establish the existence of a canon, any canon, in the first place. On the right hand, we face the outraged reactions of those custodians of Western culture who protest that the canon, that transparent decanter of Western values, may become—breathe the word—*politicized*. But the only way to answer the charge of "politics" is with an emphatic *tu quoque*. That people can maintain a straight face while they protest the irruption of politics into something that has always been political from the beginning—well, it says something about how remarkably successful official literary histories have been in presenting themselves as natural and neutral objects, untainted by worldly interests.

I agree with those conservatives who have raised the alarm about our students' ignorance of history. But part of the history we need to teach has to be the history of the idea of the "canon," which involves (though it's hardly exhausted by) the history of literary pedagogy and of the institution of the school. Once we understand how they arose, we no longer see literary canons as *objets trouvés* washed up on the beach of history. And we can begin to appreciate their ever-changing configuration in relation to a distinctive institutional history.

Universal education in this country was justified by the argument that schooling made good citizens, good American citizens: and when American literature started to be taught in our schools, part of the aim was to show what it was to be an American. As Richard Brodhead, a leading scholar of American literature, has observed, "no past lives without cultural mediation. The past, however worthy, does not survive by its own intrinsic power." One function of "literary history" is, then, to disguise that mediation, to conceal all connections between institutionalized interests and the literature we remember. Pay no attention to the man behind the curtain, booms the Great Oz of literary history.

Cynthia Ozick once chastised feminists by warning that *strategies become institutions*. But isn't that really another way of warning that their strategies, heaven forfend, may *succeed*? Here we approach the scruples of those on the cultural left, who worry about, well, the price of success. "Who's co-opting whom?" might be their slogan. To them, the very idea of the canon is hierarchical, patriarchal, and otherwise politically suspect. They'd like us to disavow it altogether.

But history and its institutions are not just something we study, they're also something we live, and live through. And how effective and how durable our interventions in contemporary cultural politics will be depends upon our ability to mobilize the institutions that buttress and reproduce that culture. The choice isn't between institutions and no institutions. The choice is always: What kind of institutions shall there be? Fearing that our strategies will become institutions, we could seclude ourselves from the real world and keep our hands clean, free from the taint of history. But that is to pay obeisance to the status quo, to the entrenched arsenal of sexual and racial authority, to say that they shouldn't change, become something other, and, let's hope, better than they are now.

Indeed, this is one case where we've got to borrow a leaf from the right, which is exemplarily aware of the role of education in the reproduction of values. We must engage in this sort of canon deformation precisely because Mr. Bennett is correct: the teaching of literature *is* the teaching of values, not inherently, no, but contingently, yes; it is—it has become—the teaching of an aesthetic and political order, in which no women and people of color were ever able to discover the reflection or representation of their images, or hear the resonances of their cultural voices. The return of "the" canon, the high canon of Western masterpieces, represents the return of an order in which my people were the subjugated, the voiceless, the invisible, the unrepresented and the unrepresentable. Who would return us to that medieval never-never land?

The classic critique of our attempts to reconstitute our own subjectivity, as women, as blacks, etc., is that of Jacques Derrida. "This is the risk. The effect of Law is to build a structure of the subject, and as soon as you say, 'well, the woman is a subject and this subject deserves equal right,' and so on—then you are caught in the logic of phallocentricism and you have rebuilt the empire of Law." To expressions such as this, made by a critic whose stands on sexism and racism have been exemplary, we must respond that the Western male subject has long been constituted historically for himself and in himself. And, while we readily accept, acknowledge, and partake of the critique of *this* subject as transcendent, to deny us the process of exploring and reclaiming our subjectivity before we critique it is the critical version of the grandfather clause, the double privileging of categories that happen to be *preconstituted*. Such a position leaves us nowhere, invisible and voiceless in the republic of Western letters. Consider the irony: precisely when we (and other third world peoples) obtain the complex wherewithal to define our black subjectivity in the republic of Western letters, our theoretical colleagues declare that there ain't no such thing as a subject, so why should we be bothered with that? In this way, those of us in feminist criticism or African-American criticism who are engaged in the necessary work of canon deformation and reformation, confront the skepticism even of those who are allies on other fronts, over this matter of the death of the subject and our own discursive subjectivity.

So far I've been talking about social identity and political agency as if they were logically connected. I think they are. And that has a lot to do with what I think the task of the African-American critic today must be.

Simone de Beauvoir wrote that one is not born a woman; no, and one is not born a Negro; but then, as Donna Haraway has pointed out, one isn't even born an organism. Lord knows that black art has been attacked for well over a century as being "not universal," though no one ever says quite what this might mean. If this means an attack against *self-identification*, then I must confess that I am opposed to "universality." This line of argument is an echo from the political right. As Allan Bloom writes:

> . . . [T]he substantial human contact, indifferent to race, soul to soul, that prevails in all other aspects of student life simply does not usually exist between the two races. There are exceptions, perfectly integrated black students, but they are rare and in a difficult position. I do not believe this somber situation is the fault of the white students who are rather straightforward in such matters and frequently embarrassingly eager to prove their liberal credentials in the one area where Americans are especially sensitive to a history of past injustice. . . . Thus, just at the moment when everyone else has become "a person," blacks have become blacks. . . . "They stick together" was a phrase once used by the prejudiced, by this or that distinctive group, but it has become true by and large of the black students.

Self-identification proves a condition for agency, for social change. And to benefit from such collective agency, we need to construct ourselves, just as the nation was constructed, just as the class was, just as *all* the furniture in the social universe was. It's utopian to think we can now disavow our social identities; there's not another one to take its place. You can't opt out of a Form of Life. We can't become one of those bodiless vapor trails of sentience portrayed on that *Star Trek* episode, though often it seems like the universalists want us to be just that. You can't opt out of history. History may be a nightmare, as Joyce suggested, but it's time to stop pinching ourselves.

But there's a treacherous non sequitur here, from "socially constructed" to essentially unreal. I suppose there's a lurking positivism in the sentiment, in which social facts are unreal compared to putatively biological ones. We go from "constructed" to "unstable," which is one non sequitur; or to "changeable by will," which is a bigger problem still, since the "will" is yet another construction.

And theory is conducive to these slippages, however illegitimate, because of the real ascendancy of the paradigm of dismantlement. Reversals don't work, we're told; dismantle the scheme of difference altogether. And I don't deny the importance, on the level of theory, of the project; it's important to remember that "race" is *only* a socio-political category, nothing more. At the same time—in terms of its practical performative force—that doesn't help me when I'm trying to get a taxi on the corner of 125th and Lenox Avenue. ("Please sir, it's only a metaphor.")

Maybe the most important thing here is the tension between the imperatives of agency and the rhetoric of dismantlement. An example: Foucault says, and let's take him at his word, that the "homosexual" as life form was invented sometime in the mid-nineteenth century. Now, if there's no such thing as a homosexual, then homophobia, at least as directed toward people rather than acts, loses its rationale. But you can't respond to the discrimination against gay people by saying, "I'm sorry, I don't exist; you've got the wrong guy." The simple historical fact is, Stonewall was necessary, concerted action was necessary to take action against the very structures that, as it were, called the homosexual into being, that subjected certain people to this imaginary identity. To reverse Audre Lorde, *only* the master's tools will ever dismantle the master's house.

Let me be specific. Those of us working in my own tradition confront the hegemony of the Western tradition, generally, and of the larger American tradition, specifically, as we set about theorizing about our tradition, and engaging in attempts at canon formation. Long after white American literature has been anthologized and canonized, and recanonized, our attempts to define a black American canon—foregrounded on its own against a white backdrop—are often decried as racist, separatist, nationalist, or "essentialist"—my favorite term of all. Attempts to derive theories about our literary tradition from the black tradition—a tradition, I might add, that must include black vernacular forms as well as written literary forms—are often greeted by our colleagues in traditional literature departments as misguided attempts to secede from a union which only recently, and with considerable kicking and screaming, has been forged. What is *wrong* with you people, our friends ask us in genuine passion and concern; after all, aren't we all just citizens of literature here?

Well, yes and no. It is clear that every black American text must confess to a complex ancestry, one high and low (literary and vernacular), but also one white and black. There can be no doubt that white texts inform and influence black texts (and vice versa), so that a thoroughly integrated canon of American literature is not only politically sound, it is *intellectually* sound as well. But the attempts of scholars such as Arnold Rampersad, Houston Baker, M. H. Washington, Nellie McKay, and others to define a black American canon, and to pursue literary interpretation from within this canon, are not meant to refute the soundness of these gestures of integration. Rather, it is a question of perspective, a question of emphasis. Just as we can and must cite a black text within the larger American tradition, we can and must cite it within its own tradition, a tradition not defined by a pseudoscience of racial biology, or a mystically shared essence called blackness, but by the repetition and revision of shared themes, topoi, and tropes, a process that binds the signal texts of the black tradition into a canon just as surely as separate links bind together into a chain. It is no more, or less, essentialist to make this claim than it is to claim the existence of French, English, German, Russian, or American literature—as long as we proceed inductively, from the texts to the theory. For nationalism has always been the dwarf in the critical, canonical chess machine. For anyone to deny us the right to engage in attempts to constitute ourselves as discursive subjects is for them to engage in the double privileging of categories that happen to be preconstituted.

In our attempts at canon formation we are demanding a return to history in a manner scarcely conceived of by the new historicists. Nor can we opt out of our own private histories, which Houston Baker called the African-American autobiographical moment, and which I call the auto-critography. Let me end, as I began, with an anecdote, one that I had forgotten for so long until just the other day.

Earlier this year at Cornell, I was listening to Hortense Spillers, the great black feminist critic, read her important essay, "Mama's Baby,

Papa's Maybe." Her delivery, as usual, was flawless, compelling, inimitable. And although I had read this essay as a manuscript, I had never before felt—or heard—the following lines:

> The African-American male has been touched, therefore, by the *mother*, handled by her in ways that he cannot escape, and in ways that the white American male is allowed to temporize by a fatherly reprieve. This human and historic development— the text that has been inscribed on the benighted heart of the continent—takes us to the center of an inexorable difference in the depths of American women's community: the African-American woman, the mother, the daughter, becomes historically the powerful and shadowy evocation of a cultural synthesis long evaporated—the law of the Mother—only and precisely because legal enslavement removed the African-American male not so much from sight as from *mimetic* view as a partner in the prevailing social fiction of the Father's name, the Father's law.
>
> Therefore, the female, in this order of things, breaks in upon the imagination with a forcefulness that marks both a denial and an "illegitimacy." Because of this peculiar American denial, the black American male embodies the *only* American community of males which has had the specific occasion to learn *who* the female is within itself, the infant child who bears the life against the could-be fateful gamble, against the odds of pulverization and murder, including her own. It is the heritage of the *mother* that the African-American male must regain as an aspect of his own personhood—the power of "yes" to the "female" within.

How curious a figure—men, black men, gaining their voices through the black mother. Precisely when some committed feminists or some committed black nationalists would essentialize all "others" out of their critical endeavor, Hortense Spillers rejects that glib and easy solution, calling for a revoicing of the master's discourse in the cadences and timbres of the Black Mother's voice.

As I sat there before her, I recalled, to my own astonishment, my own first public performance, when I was a child of four years. My mom attended a small black Methodist Church in Piedmont, West Virginia, just as her mom had done for the past fifty years. I was a fat little kid, a condition that my mom defended as "plump." I remember that I had just been given a brand new grey suit for the occasion, and a black stringy brim Dobbs hat, so it must have been Easter, because my brother and I always got new hats for Easter, just like my dad and mom did.

At any rate, the day came to deliver my Piece. What is a Piece? A Piece is what people in our church called a religious recitation. I don't know what the folk etymology might be, but I think it reflects the belief that each of the fragments of our praise songs, taken together, amounts to a Master Text. And each of us, during a religious program, was called upon to say our Piece. Mine, if you can believe it, was "Jesus was a boy like me, and like Him I want to be." That was it—I was only four. So, after weeks of practice in elocution, hair pressed and greased down, shirt starched and pants pressed, I was ready to give my Piece.

I remember skipping along to the church with all of the other kids, driving everyone crazy, saying over and over, "Jesus was a boy like me, and like Him I want to be." "Will you shut up!" my friends demanded. Just jealous, I thought. They probably don't even know their Pieces.

Finally, we made it to the church, and it was packed—bulging and glistening with black people, eager to hear Pieces, despite the fact that they had heard all of the Pieces already, year after year, bits and fragments of a repeated Master Text.

Because I was the youngest child on the program, I was the first to go. Miss Sarah Russell (whom we called Sister Holy Ghost—behind her back, of course) started the program with a prayer, then asked if little Skippy Gates would step forward. I did so.

And then the worst happened: I completely forgot the words of my Piece. Standing there, pressed and starched, just as clean as I could be, in front of just about everybody in our part of town, I could not for the life of me remember one word of that Piece.

After standing there I don't know how long, struck dumb and captivated by all of those staring eyes, I heard a voice from near the back of the church proclaim, "Jesus was a boy like me, and like Him I want to be."

And my mother, having arisen to find my voice, smoothed her dress and sat down again. The congregation's applause lasted as long as its laughter as I crawled back to my seat.

For me, I realized as Hortense Spillers spoke, much of my scholarly and critical work has been an attempt to learn how to speak in the strong, compelling cadences of my mother's voice. To reform core curricula, to account for the comparable eloquence of the African, the Asian, and the Middle Eastern traditions, is to begin to prepare our students for their roles as citizens of a world culture, educated through a truly human notion of "the humanities," rather than—as Bennett and Bloom would have it—as guardians at the last frontier outpost of white male Western culture, the Keepers of the Master's Pieces. And for us as scholar-critics, learning to speak in the voice of the black female is perhaps the ultimate challenge of producing a discourse of the critical Other.[1]

Notes

1   This essay was published in the 26 February 1989 *New York Times Book Review* (in slightly different form) and appears in *Conversations: Contemporary Critical Theory and the Teaching of Literature*, ed. Charles Moran and Elizabeth F. Penfield (Urbana: National Council of Teachers of English, 1990).

Henry A. Giroux

Liberal Arts Education and the Struggle for Public Life: Dreaming about Democracy

I will begin with what has become a commonplace but no less significant assertion: that the most important questions facing both the liberal arts and higher education in general are moral and political.[1] More specifically, the various questions that have been raised recently about either defending, reconstructing, or eliminating a particular canon in higher education can only be understood within a broader range of political and theoretical considerations that bear directly on the issue of whether a liberal arts education in this country should be considered a privilege for the few or a right for the vast majority of citizens. This is not merely a matter of deciding who is eligible or can financially afford a liberal arts education; it is part of a wider discourse that has increasingly challenged the American public in the last decade to rethink the role of higher education and its relationship to democratic public life. Moreover, this debate raises anew important questions regarding the social and political implications of viewing curriculum as a historically specific narrative and pedagogy as a form of cultural politics that either enables or silences the differentiated human capacities which allow students to speak from their own experiences, locate themselves in history, and act so as to create social forms that expand the possibility of democratic public life.[2] I believe that the current debate on higher education opens up new possibilities for rethinking the role that university educators might play as critically engaged public intellectuals. But before I discuss these issues in detail, I want to stress the importance of recognizing that the university is not simply a place that provides students with the knowledge and skills they will need to secure decent employment and the benefits of social mobility; neither is it a place whose purpose is merely to cultivate the life of the mind or reproduce the cultural equivalent of "masterpiece theater." I firmly believe that the institutions of higher education, regardless of their academic status, represent places that affirm and legitimate existing views of the world, produce new ones, and authorize and shape particular social relations; put simply, they are places of moral and social regulation "where a sense of identity, place, and worth is informed and contested through practices which organize knowledge and meaning."[3] The university is a place that produces a particular selection and ordering of narratives and subjectivities. It is a place that is deeply political and unarguably normative.

Unfortunately, questions concerning higher education in general, and liberal arts in particular, are often discussed as if they have no relation to existing arrangements of social, economic, and political power. Central to this essay is the argument that as a social and political as well as pedagogical site the university is a terrain of contestation and that one can neither understand the nature of the struggle itself nor the nature of the liberal arts unless one raises the question as to what the purpose of the university actually is or might be. Or, as Jacques Derrida has put it, "To ask whether the university has a reason for being is to wonder why there is a university, but the question 'why' verges on 'with a view to what?' "[4] It is this question of purpose and practice that illuminates what the limits and possibilities are that exist within the university at a given time in history. Putting aside Derrida's own political agenda, this is essentially a question of politics, power, and possibility. For as we know the liberal arts and various other programs and schools within the university presuppose and legitimate particular forms of history, community, and authority. The question is, of course, what and whose history, community, knowledge, and voice prevails? Unless this question is addressed, the issues of what to teach, how we should teach, how we should engage our students, and how we should function as intellectuals become removed from the wider principles that inform such issues and practices.

The sphere of higher education represents an important public culture that cultivates and produces particular stories of how to live ethically and politically; its institutions reproduce selected values, and they harbor in their social relations and teaching practices specific notions regarding what knowledge is of most worth, what it means to know something, and how one might construct representations of themselves, others, and the social environment. In many respects, the normative and political language taught in the university can be compared to what Ernst Bloch called the utopian impulse of daydreams:

> Dreams come in the day as well as the night. And both kinds of dreaming are motivated by the wishes they seek to fulfill. But daydreams differ from night dreams; for the daydreaming "I" persists throughout, consciously, privately, envisaging the circumstances and images of a desired, better life. The content of the daydream is not, like that of the night dream, a journey back into repressed experiences and their association. It is concerned with, as far as possible, an unrestricted journey forward, so that instead of reconstituting that which is no longer conscious, the images of that which is not yet can be fantasized into life and into the world.[5]

Bloch's analysis points to an important relation between daydreaming and the liberal arts that is often overlooked. As an introduction to, preparation for, and legitimation of social life, a liberal arts education always presupposes a vision of the future. In other words, like the process of daydreaming, the liberal arts is fundamentally involved in the production of images of that which is "not yet." As Roger Simon points out, "the utopian impulse of such programs is represented in the notion that without a perspective on the future, conceivable as a desired future, there can be no human venture."[6] In this respect, the language of education that students take with them from their university experience should embody a vision capable of providing them with a sense of history, civic courage, and democratic community. It is important to emphasize that visions are not only defined by the representations they legitimate and the practices they structure, but also by the arguments they embody for justifying why meaning, knowledge, and social action matter as part of the re-writing and remapping of the events that make up daily life as well as the dynamics of the larger world. The question becomes: To what vision of the future do the daydreams of our students speak? To whom do such visions matter and why? As a matter of pedagogical practice students need to take up these questions through a language of critique and possibility, a language that cultivates a capacity for reasoned criticism, for undoing the misuses of power and the relations of domination, and for exploring and extending the utopian dimensions of human potentiality. Needless to say, such a language is at odds with the language of cultural despair, conservative restoration, and aristocratic elitism trumpeted by the educational theorists of the new right.[7]

It serves us well to remember that dreams are neither ideologically neutral nor politically innocent. Dreams always belong to someone, and to the degree that they translate into curricula and pedagogical practices they not only denote a struggle over forms of political authority and orders of representation, they also weigh heavily in regulating the moral identities, collective voices, and the futures of others.[8] As institutionalized practices, dreams draw upon specific values, uphold particular relations of power, class, gender, ethnicity, and race, and often authorize official forms of knowledge. For this reason dreams always have a moral and political dimension: they are important not as a signal for a single-minded preoccupation with academic achievement or social status but as a context from which to organize the energies of a moral vision, to believe that one can make a difference both in combating domestic tyranny and assaults on human freedom and in creating a society that exhibits in its institutional and everyday relations moral courage, compassion, and cultural justice. This is, after all, what university life should be all about: the politics and ethics of dreaming, dreaming a better future and dreaming a new world.

=======

The current debate about education represents more than a commentary on the state of public and higher education in this country; it is a debate about the meaning of democracy, social criticism, and the status of utopian thought in constituting both our dreams and the stories that we devise in order to give meaning to our lives. This debate has taken a serious turn in the last decade and now as before its terms are being principally set by extremists and anti-utopians. Critics such as Allan Bloom, William Bennett, and E. D. Hirsch have presented an agenda and purpose for shaping public schooling and higher education that abstracts equity from excellence and cultural criticism from the discourse of social responsibility. Under the guise of attempting to revitalize the language of morality, these critics and politicians have, in reality, launched a dangerous attack on some of the most basic aspects of democratic public life and the social, moral, and political obligations of responsible, critical citizens. What has been valorized in this language is, in part, a view of schooling based on a celebration of cultural uniformity, a rigid view of authority, an uncritical support for remaking school curricula in the interest of labor-market imperatives, and a return to the old transmission model of teaching.

Within this new public philosophy there is a ruthlessly frank expression of doubt about the viability of democracy.[9] The loss of utopian vision that characterizes this position is nowhere more evident than in Allan Bloom's *The Closing of the American Mind* and E. D. Hirsch's *Cultural Literacy*.[10] For Bloom, the impulse to egalitarianism and the spirit of social criticism represent the chief culprits in the decay of higher learning. Bloom argues that the university must give up educating intellectuals, whose great crime is that they sometimes become adversaries of the dominant culture or speak to a wider culture about the quality of contemporary politics and public life. He would prefer that the university curriculum be organized around the "great books" and be selectively used to educate students from what he calls the top twenty elite schools to be philosopher-kings. Of course, what Bloom means by reform is nothing less than an effort to make explicit what women, blacks, and working-class students have always known: the precincts of higher learning are not for them, and the educational system is meant to reproduce a new mandarin class.

Hirsch, like Bloom, presents a frontal attack aimed at providing a programmatic language with which to defend schools as cultural sites; that is, as institutions responsible for reproducing the knowledge and values necessary to advance the historical virtues of Western culture. Hirsch presents his view of cultural restoration through a concept of literacy that focuses on the basic structures of language, and applies this version of cultural literacy to the broader consideration of the needs of the business community as well as to maintenance of American institutions. For Hirsch, the new service economy requires employees who can write a memo, read within a specific cultural context, and communicate through a national language composed of the key words of Western culture.

Central to Hirsch's concept of literacy is a view of culture removed from the dynamics of struggle and power. Culture is seen as the totality of language practices of a given nation and merely "presents" itself for all to participate in. Not unlike Bloom's position, Hirsch's view of culture expresses a single durable history and vision, one which is at odds with a critical notion of democracy and difference. Such a position maintains an ideological silence, a political amnesia of sorts, regarding either how domination works in the cultural sphere or how the dialectic of cultural struggle between different groups over competing orders of meaning, experience, and history emerges within unequal relations of power and struggle. By depoliticizing the issue of culture, Hirsch ends up with a view of literacy cleansed of its own complicity in producing social forms that create devalued others. This is more than a matter of cultural forgetting on Hirsch's part, it is also an attack on difference as possibility. Hirsch's discourse undermines the development of a curriculum committed to reclaiming higher education as an agency of social justice and critical democracy and to developing forms of pedagogy that affirm and engage the often-silenced voices of subordinate groups.

In the most general sense, Bloom and Hirsch represent the latest cultural offensive by the new elitists to rewrite the past and construct the present from the perspective of the privileged and the powerful.[11] They disdain the democratic implications of pluralism and argue for a form of cultural uniformity in which difference is consigned to the margins of history or to the museum of the disadvantaged. From this perspective, culture, along with the authority it sanctions, becomes merely an artifact, a warehouse of goods, posited either as a canon of knowledge or a canon of information that simply has to be transmitted as a means for promoting social order and control. In this view, pedagogy becomes an afterthought, a code word for the transmission and imposition of a predefined and unproblematic body of knowledge. For educators like Bloom and Hirsch, pedagogy is something one does in order to implement a preconstituted body of knowledge or information. The notion that pedagogy is itself part of the production of knowledge, a deliberate and critical attempt to influence the ways in which knowledge and identities are produced within and among particular sets of social relations, is far removed from the language and ideology of Hirsch and Bloom.

What is at stake here is not simply the issue of bad teaching but the broader refusal to take seriously the categories of meaning, experience, and voice that students use to make sense of themselves and the world around them. It is through this refusal to enable those who have been silenced to speak, to acknowledge the voices of the Other, and to legitimate and reclaim experience as a fundamental category in the production of knowledge that the character of the current dominant discourse on the canon reveals its totalitarian and undemocratic ideology.

Put in Bloch's terms, this new conservative public philosophy represents a form of daydreaming in which tradition is not on the side of democracy and difference; it is a form of the "not yet" expunged of the language of hope and strangled by a discourse in which history and culture are closed. It is a public philosophy in which teaching is reduced to a form of transmission, the canon is posited as a relationship outside of the restless flux of knowledge and power, and intellectuals are cheerfully urged to take up their roles as clerks of the empire.[12]

It is worth noting that Bloom, Hirsch, Bennett, and other neoconservatives have been able to perform a task that humanists and progressives have generally failed to do. They have placed the question of curriculum at the center of the debate about both education and democracy. But they have argued for a view of the liberal arts fashioned as part of an anti-utopian discourse that serves to disconnect the purpose of higher education from the task of reconstructing democratic public life. This is not to suggest that they have not invoked the notions of democracy and citizenship in their arguments. But in doing so they have reduced democracy to gaining access to the fruits of "Western civilization" and defined learning as the training of "good" citizens: that is, "willing subjects and agents of hegemonic authority."[13] By refusing to link democracy to forms of self and social empowerment, neoconservatives have been able to suppress the relationship between learning and critical citizenship.[14] This new cultural offensive presents a formidable challenge to humanists who have attempted to defend liberal arts education from the perspective of a highly specialized, self-referential discipline that holds up either a plurality of canons or a canon that serves as a model of scientific rigor and sophisticated methodological inquiry. In such cases, the purpose of the liberal arts is defined, though from different ideological perspectives, from within the perspective of creating a free, enterprising, educated, well-rounded individual. Though well-meaning, this discourse discounts the most important social relations that constitute what it means to be educated by ignoring the social and political function of particular knowledge/power/pedagogy relations and how they serve to construct students individually and collectively within the boundaries of a political order that they often take for granted.

The liberal arts cannot be defended either as a self-contained discourse legitimating the humanistic goal of broadly improving the so-called "life of the mind" or as a rigorous science that can lead students to indubitable truths. Similarly, it is insufficient to defend the liberal arts by rejecting technocratic education as a model of learning. All of these positions share the failure of abstracting the liberal arts from the intense problems and issues of public life. Moreover, the defense of the liberal arts as a gateway to indubitable truths, whether through the discourse of Western civilization or science, often collapses into a not too subtle defense of higher education as a training ground for a "dictatorship of enlightened social engineers."[15] This issue is not one of merely creating a more enlightened or scientific canon but of raising fundamental questions about how canons are used, what interests they legitimate, what relations they have to the dominant society, and how students are constituted within their prevailing discourses and social relations. How we read or define a "canonical" work may not be as important as challenging the overall function and social uses the notion of the canon has served. Within this type of discourse, the canon can be analyzed as part of a wider set of relations that connect the academic disciplines, teaching, and power to considerations defined through broader, intersecting political and cultural concerns such as race, class, gender, ethnicity, and nationalism. What is in question here is not merely a defense of a particular canon, but the issue of struggle and empowerment.[16] In other words, the liberal arts should be defended in the interest of creating critical rather than "good" citizens. The notion of the liberal arts has to be reconstituted around a knowledge-power relationship in which the question of curriculum is seen as a form of cultural and political production grounded in a radical conception of citizenship and public wisdom.

By linking the liberal arts to the imperatives of a critical democracy, the debate on the meaning and nature of higher education can be situated within a broader context of issues concerned with citizenship, politics, and the dignity of human life. In this view it becomes possible to provide a rationale and purpose for higher education which aims at developing critical citizens and reconstructing community life by extending the principles of social justice to all spheres of economic, political, and cultural life. This position is not far from the arguments posed by John Dewey, George S. Counts, C. Wright Mills, and more recently by Hannah Arendt and Alvin Gouldner. These theorists fashioned the elements of a public philosophy in which the liberal arts was seen as a major social site for revitalizing public life. John Dewey, for example, argued that a liberal education afforded people the opportunity to involve themselves in the deepest problems of society, to acquire the knowledge, skills, and ethical responsibility necessary for "reasoned participation in democratically organized publics." [17] C. Wright Mills urged intellectuals to define the liberal arts and their own roles through a commitment to the formation of an engaged citizenry. Mills envisioned the liberal arts as social site from which intellectuals could mobilize a moral and political vision committed to the reclamation and recovery of democratic public life. [18] In the most general sense, this means fashioning the purpose of higher education within a public philosophy committed to a radical conception of citizenship, civic courage, and public wisdom. In more specific terms this means challenging the image of higher education as an adjunct of the corporation. It means rejecting those ideologies and human capital theories which reduce the role of university intellectuals to the status of industrial technicians and academic clerks whose political project, or lack of one, is often betrayed by claims to objectivity, certainty, and professionalism. It means challenging the sterile instrumentalism, selfishness, and contempt for democratic community that has become the hallmark of the Reagan/Bush era. [19] It means recognizing and organizing against the structured injustices in society which prevent us from extending our solidarity to those others who strain under the weight of various forms of oppression and exploitation. It also means enhancing and ennobling the meaning and purpose of liberal arts education by giving it a truly central place in the social life of a nation where it can become a public forum for addressing preferentially the needs of the poor, the dispossessed, and the disenfranchised.

A public philosophy that offers the promise of reforming liberal arts education as part of a wider revitalization of public life raises important questions regarding what the notion of empowerment would mean for developing classroom pedagogical practices. That is, if liberal arts education is to be developed in relation to principles consistent with a democratic public philosophy, it is equally important to develop forms of critical pedagogy that embody these principles and practices, a pedagogy in which such practices are understood in relation *to* rather than *in* isolation from those economies of power and privilege at work in wider social and political formations.

———

For many educators, pedagogy is often theorized as what is left after curriculum content is determined. In this view, knowledge "speaks" for itself and teaching is a matter of providing an occasion for the text to reveal itself. Guided by a concern with producing knowledge that is academically correct and/or ideologically relevant, educational theorists have largely sidestepped the issue of how a teacher can work from sound ethical and theoretical principles and still end up pedagogically silencing students. Put another way, if educators fail to recognize that the legitimating claims they make in defense of the knowledge they teach is not enough to ensure that they *do not* commit forms of symbolic violence in their pedagogical relations with students, they will not adequately understand the ways in which students are both enabled and disabled in their own classrooms.

Central to the development of a critical pedagogy is the need to explore how pedagogy functions as a cultural practice to *produce* rather than merely *transmit* knowledge within the asymmetrical relations of power that structure teacher-student relations. There have been few attempts to analyze how relations of pedagogy and relations of power are inextricably tied not only to what people know but also to how they come to know in a particular way within the constraints of specific cultural and social forms.[20] Rendered insignificant as a form of cultural production, pedagogy is often marginalized and devalued as a means of recognizing that what we teach and how we do it are deeply implicated not only in producing various forms of domination but also in constructing active practices of resistance and struggle. Lost here is an attempt to articulate pedagogy as a form of cultural production that addresses how knowledge is produced, mediated, refused, and represented within relations of power both in and outside of the university.

Critical pedagogy as a form of cultural politics is not merely the discourse of skills and techniques teachers use in order to meet predefined, given objectives. The teaching of skills is insufficient for referencing both what teachers actually do in terms of underlying principles and values and for providing the language necessary to analyze how classroom practice relates to future visions of community life. As part of a broader set of theoretical and political considerations, critical pedagogy refers to a deliberate attempt to influence how and what knowledge and subjectivities are produced within particular sets of social relations. It draws attention to the ways in which knowledge, power, desire, and experience are produced under specific conditions of learning. It does not reduce classroom practice to the question of what works; it stresses the realities of what happens in classrooms by raising questions regarding "what knowledge is of most worth, in what direction should we desire, and what it means to know something."[21] But the discourse of pedagogy does something more. Pedagogy is simultaneously about the knowledge and practices that teachers and students might engage in together and the cultural politics such practices support. It is in this sense that to propose a pedagogy is at the same time to construct a political vision. The notion of pedagogy being argued for in this case is not organized in relation to a choice between elite or popular culture, but as part of a political project which takes issues of liberation and empowerment as its starting point. It is a pedagogy that rejects the notion of culture as an artifact immobilized in the image of a storehouse. Instead, the pedagogical principles at work here analyze culture as a set of lived experiences and social practices developed within asymmetrical relations of power. Culture in this sense is not an object of unquestioning reverence but a mobile field of ideological and material relations that are unfinished, multilayered, and always open to interrogation. This view of culture is defined pedagogically as social practices which allow both teachers and students to construe themselves as agents in the production of subjectivity and meaning. Such a pedagogy transcends the dichotomy of elite and popular culture by defining itself through a project of educating students to feel compassion for the suffering of others, to engage in a continual analysis of their own conditions of existence, to construct loyalties that engage the meaning and importance of public life, and to believe that they can make a difference, that they can act from a position of collective strength to alter existing configurations of power. Such a pedagogy is predicated on a notion of learned hope, forged amidst the realization of risks, and steeped in a commitment to transforming public culture and life: it stresses the historical and transformative in its practice.

In the current debate about the importance of constructing a particular canon, the notion of naming and transmitting from one generation to the next what can be defined as "cultural treasures" specifies what has become the central argument for reforming the liberal arts.[22] For that reason, perhaps, it appears as though the debate were reducible to the question of the contents of course syllabi. The notion of critical pedagogy for which I am arguing provides a fundamental challenge to this position: it calls for an argument that transcends the limited focus on the canon, that recognizes the crisis in liberal arts education to be one of historical purpose and meaning, a crisis that challenges us to rethink in a critical fashion the relationship between the role of the university and the imperatives of a democracy in a mass society.

Historically, education in the liberal arts was conceived of as the essential preparation for governing, for ruling—more specifically, the preparation and outfitting of the governing *elite*. The liberal arts curriculum, composed of the "best" that had been said or written, was intended, as Elizabeth Fox-Genovese has observed, "to provide selected individuals with a collective history, culture, and epistemology so that they could run the world effectively." [23] In this context the canon was considered to be a possession of the dominant classes or groups. Indeed, the canon was fashioned as a safeguard to insure that the cultural property of such groups was passed on from generation to generation along with the family estates. Thus, in these terms it seems most appropriate that the literary canon should be subject to revision—as it has been before in the course of the expansion of democracy—such that it might also incorporate and reflect the experience and aspirations of the women, minorities, and children of the working class who have been entering the academy.

Conceived of in this way, a radical vision of liberal arts education is to be found within its elite social origins and purpose. But this does not suggest that the most important questions confronting liberal arts reform lie in merely establishing the content of the liberal arts canon on the model of the elite universities. Instead, the most important questions become that of reformulating the meaning and purpose of higher education in ways that contribute to the cultivation and regeneration of an informed citizenry capable of actively participating in the shaping and governing of a democratic society. Within this discourse, the pedagogical becomes political and the notion of a liberal arts canon commands a more historically grounded and critical reading. The pedagogical becomes more political in that it proposes that the way in which students engage and examine knowledge is just as important an issue as the choosing of texts to be used in a class or program. That is, a democratic notion of liberal education rejects those views of the humanities which would treat texts as sacred and instruction as merely transmission. This notion of the canon undermines the possibility for dialogue, argument, and critical thinking; it treats knowledge as a form of cultural inheritance that is beyond considerations regarding how it might be implicated in social practices that exploit, infantilize, and oppress. The canons we have inherited, in their varied forms, cannot be dismissed as simply part of the ideology of privilege and domination. Instead, the privileged texts of the dominant or official canons should be explored with respect to the important role they have played in shaping, for better or worse, the major events of our time. But there are also forms of knowledge that have been marginalized by the official canons. There are noble traditions, histories, and narratives that speak to important struggles by women, blacks, minorities, and other subordinate groups that need to be heard so that such groups can lay claim to their own voices as part of a process of both affirmation and inquiry. At issue here is a notion of pedagogy as a form of cultural politics that rejects a facile restoration of the past, that rejects history as a monologue. A critical pedagogy recognizes that history is constituted in dialogue and that some of the voices that make up that dialogue have been eliminated. Such a pedagogy calls for a public debate regarding the dominant memories and repressed stories that constitute the historical narratives of a social order: in effect, canon formation becomes a matter of both rewriting and reinterpreting the past; canon formation embodies the ongoing "process of reconstructing the 'collective reflexivity' of lived cultural experience . . . which recognizes that the 'notions of the past and future are essentially notions of the present.'"[24] In this case, such notions are central to the politics of identity and power, and to the memories that structure how experience is individually and collectively authorized and experienced as a form of cultural identity.

As a historical construct, critical pedagogy functions in a dual sense to address the issue of what kinds of knowledge can be put in place that enable rather than subvert the formation of a democratic society. On one level it authorizes forms of countermemory.

It excavates, affirms, and interrogates the histories, memories, and stories of the devalued others who have been marginalized from the official discourse of the canon. It attempts to recover and mediate those knowledge forms and social practices that have been decentered from the discourses of power. Surely such knowledge might include the historical and contemporary writings of women such as Mary Wolstonecraft, Charlotte Perkins Gilman, and Adrienne Rich, black writers such as W. E. B. Du Bois, Martin Luther King, Jr., and Zora Neale Hurston, as well as documents that helped shape the struggles of labor in the United States. The pedagogical practice at work here is not meant to romanticize these subjugated knowledges and "dangerous memories" as much as appropriate and renew them as part of the reconstruction of a public philosophy that legitimates a politics and pedagogy of difference. On another level, critical pedagogy recognizes that all educational work is at root contextual and conditional: it refuses the totalizing unity of discourses that expunge the specific, contingent, and particular from their formulations. In this case, a critical pedagogy can be discussed only from within the historical and cultural specificity of space, time, place, and context, since it does not arise against a background of psychological, sociological, or anthropological universals but within tasks that are strategic and practical, guided by imperatives which are both historical and ethical.

A critical pedagogy also rejects a discourse of value neutrality. Without subscribing to a language that polices behavior and desire, it aims at developing pedagogical practices informed by an ethical stance that contests racism, sexism, class exploitation, and other dehumanizing and exploitative social relations as ideologies and social practices that disrupt and devalue public life. This is a pedagogy that rejects detachment, though it does not silence in the name of its own ideological fervor or correctness. It acknowledges social injustices, but examines with care and in dialogue with itself and others how such injustices work through the discourses, experiences, and desires that constitute daily life and the subjectivities of the students who invest in them. It is a pedagogy guided by ethical principles that correspond to a radical practice rooted in historical experience. And it is a pedagogy that comprehends the historical consequences of what it means to take a moral and political position with respect to the horror and suffering of, for example, the Gulag, the Nazi Holocaust, or the Pol Pot regime. Such events not only summon up images of terror, domination, and resistance, but also provide a priori examples of what principles have to be both defended and fought against in the interest of freedom and life. Within this perspective, ethics becomes more than the discourse of moral relativism or a static transmission of reified history. Ethics becomes, instead, a continued engagement in which the social practices of everyday life are interrogated in relation to the principles of individual autonomy and democratic public life—not as a matter of received truth but as a constant engagement. This represents an ethical stance which provides the opportunity for individual capacities to be questioned and examined so that they can serve both to analyze and advance the possibilities inherent in all social forms. At issue is an ethical stance in which community, difference, remembrance, and historical consciousness become central categories as part of the language of public life. This particular ethical stance is, as Max Horkheimer has pointed out, one which cannot be separated from the issue of how a socialized humanity develops within ideological and material conditions that either enable or disable the enhancement of human possibilities.[25] It is an ethical stance that moves beyond moral outrage, attempting instead to provide a critical account of how individuals are constituted as human agents within different moral and ethical discourses and experiences. At the heart of such a pedagogy is the centrality of Horkheimer's recognition that it is important to stare into history in order to remember the suffering of the past and that out of this remembrance a theory of ethics should be developed in which solidarity, compassion, and care become central dimensions of an informed social practice.

Central to a critical pedagogy is the need to affirm the lived reality of difference as the ground on which to pose questions of theory and practice. Moreover, such a pedagogy needs to function as a social practice that claims the experience of lived difference as an agenda for discussion and a central resource for a project of possibility. This is a pedagogy that is constructed as part of a struggle over assigned meanings, over the viability of different voices, and over particular forms of authority. It is this struggle that makes possible and hence can redefine the possibilities we see both in the conditions of our daily lives and in those conditions which are "not yet."[26]

A critical pedagogy for the liberal arts is one that affirms for students the importance of leadership as a moral and political enterprise, that links the radical responsibility of ethics to the possibility of having those who are not oppressed understand the experience of oppression as an obstacle to democratic public life; in this sense, critical pedagogy as a form of cultural politics is a call to celebrate responsible action and strategic risk taking as part of an ongoing struggle to link citizenship to the notion of a democratic public community, civic courage to a shared conception of social justice. Chantal Mouffe argues that a critical conception of citizenship should be "postmodern" in that it recognizes the importance of a politics of difference in which the particular, the heterogeneous, and the multiple play a crucial role in the forming of a democratic public sphere:

> The struggle for democratic citizenship is one strategy among others. It is an attempt to challenge the undemocratic practices of neoliberalism by constructing different political identities. It is inspired by a view of politics which assumes a community of equals who share rights, social responsibility and a solidarity based on a common belonging to a political community whose political ends—freedom and equality for all—are pursued in participating institutions. This is a long way from . . . a privatized conception of citizenship that intends to whisk away the notion of political community. Democratic citizenship, on the contrary, aims at restoring the centrality of such a notion.[27]

Central to Mouffe's view of citizenship and my view of a critical pedagogy is the idea that the formation of democratic citizens demands forms of political identity which radically extend the principles of justice, liberty, and dignity to public spheres constituted by difference and multiple forms of community. Of course, this is as much a pedagogical as it is a political issue. Such identities have to be constructed as part of a pedagogy in which difference becomes a basis for solidarity and unity rather than for competition and discrimination.

If pedagogy is to be linked to the notion of learning for empowerment, it is important that educators understand theoretically how difference is constructed through various representations and practices
that name, legitimate, marginalize, and exclude the cultural capital and voices of subordinate groups in American society. As part of
this theoretical project, a "pedagogy of difference" needs to address
the important question of how representations and practices that
name, marginalize, and define difference as the devalued Other are
actively learned, internalized, challenged, or transformed. In addition, such a pedagogy needs to address how understanding these differences can be used in order to change the prevailing relations of
power that sustain them. It is also imperative that such a pedagogy
acknowledge and interrogate how the colonizing of differences by
dominant groups is expressed and sustained through representations:
in which the Other is seen as a deficit, in which the humanity of the
Other is posited either as cynically problematic or ruthlessly denied.
At the same time, it is important for a pedagogy of difference not
only to unravel the ways in which the voices of the Other are colonized and repressed by the principle of identity that runs through the
discourse of dominant groups; there is also a need to understand how
the experience of marginality at the level of everyday life lends itself
to forms of oppositional and transformative consciousness.[28] This is
an understanding based on the need for those designated as the Other
to both reclaim and remake their histories, voices, and visions as
part of a wider struggle to change those material and social relations that deny radical pluralism as the basis of democratic political
community. For it is only through such an understanding that teachers can develop a pedagogy of difference, one which is characterized
by what Teresa de Lauretis calls "an ongoing effort to create new
spaces of discourse, to rewrite cultural narratives, and to define the
terms of another perspective—a view from 'elsewhere.' "[29] This suggests a pedagogy in which there is a questioning of the omissions and
tensions that exist between the master narratives and hegemonic discourses that make up the official curricula of the university, department, or program and the self-representations of subordinate groups
as they might appear in "forgotten" histories, texts, memories, ex-

periences, and community narratives. A pedagogy of difference not only seeks to understand how difference is constructed in the intersection of the official canon of the school and the various voices of students from subordinate groups, but also draws upon student experience as both a narrative for agency and a referent for critique. This suggests forms of pedagogy that both confirm and engage the knowledge and experience through which students author their own voices and construct social identities. In effect, this suggests taking seriously, as an aspect of learning, the knowledge and experiences that constitute the individual and collective voices by which students identify and give meaning to themselves and others by first using what they know about their own lives as a basis for criticizing the dominant culture. In this case, student experience has to be first understood and recognized as the accumulation of collective memories and stories that provide students with a sense of familiarity, identity, and practical knowledge. Such experience has to be both affirmed and interrogated. In addition, the social and historical construction of such experience has to be affirmed and understood as part of a wider struggle for voice, but it also has to be remade, reterritorialized in the interest of a social imaginary that dignifies the best traditions and possibilities of those groups learning to speak from a position of enablement, that is, from the discourse of dignity and governance. In her analysis of the deterritorialization of women as the Other, Caren Kaplan articulates this position well.

> Recognizing the minor cannot erase the aspects of the major, but as a mode of understanding it enables us to see the fissures in our identities, to unravel the seams of our totalities. . . . We must leave home, as it were, since our homes are often sites of racism, sexism, and other damaging social practices. Where we come to locate ourselves in terms of our specific histories and differences must be a place with room for what can be salvaged from the past and made anew. What we gain is a reterritorialization; we reinhabit a world of our making (here "our" is expanded to a coalition of identities—neither universal nor particular).[30]

Furthermore, it is important to extend the possibilities of such cultural capital by making it both the object of inquiry, and by appropriating in a similarly critical fashion, when necessary, the codes and knowledges that constitute broader and less familiar historical and cultural traditions.

At issue here is the development of a pedagogy that replaces the authoritative language of recitation with an approach that allows students to speak from their own histories, collective memories, and voices while simultaneously challenging the grounds on which knowledge and power are constructed and legitimated. Such a pedagogy contributes to making possible a variety of human capacities which expand the range of social identities that students may become. It points to the importance of understanding in both pedagogical and political terms how subjectivities are produced within those social forms in which people move but of which they are often only partially conscious. Similarly, it raises fundamental questions regarding how students make particular investments of meaning and affect, how they are constituted within a triad of knowledge, power, and pleasure, and what it is we as teachers need to understand regarding why students should be interested in the forms of authority, knowledge, and values that we produce and legitimate within our classrooms and university. It is worth noting that such a pedagogy articulates not only a respect for a diversity of student voices, but also provides a referent for developing a public language rooted in a commitment to social transformation.

=====

Another serious challenge of educational reform necessitates that university teachers rethink the nature of their role with respect to issues of politics, social responsibility, and the construction of a pedagogy of possibility. Instead of weaving dreams fashioned in the cynical interests of industrial psychology and cultural sectarianism, university educators can become part of a collective effort to build and revitalize oppositional public spheres that provide the basis for transformative democratic communities. This means, among other things, they can educate students to work collectively to make despair unconvincing and hope practical by refusing the role of the disconnected expert, technician, or careerist, and adopting the practice of the engaged and transformative intellectual. This is not a call for educators to become wedded to some abstract ideal that turns them into prophets of perfection and certainty; on the contrary, it represents a call for educators to perform a noble public service, to undertake teaching as a form of social criticism, to define themselves as engaged, critical, public intellectuals who can play a major role in animating a democratic public culture.[31] Such intellectuals construct their relationship to the wider society by making organic connections with the historical traditions that provide themselves and their students with a voice, history, and sense of belonging. This view resonates with Antonio Gramsci's call to broaden the notion of education by seeing all of society as a vast school. It also resonates with his call for critical intellectuals to forge alliances around new historical blocs.[32]

Educators need to encourage students by example to find ways to get involved, to make a difference, to think in global terms, and to act from specific contexts. This notion of teachers as transformative intellectuals is marked by a moral courage that does not require educators to step back from society as a whole but only to distance themselves from being implicated in those power relations that subjugate, corrupt, exploit, or infantilize. This is what Michael Walzer calls criticism from within, the telling of stories that speak to the historical specificity and voices of those who have been marginalized and silenced.[33] It is a form of criticism wedded to the development of pedagogical practices and experiences in the interest of a utopian vision that in Walter Benjamin's terms rubs history against the grain, gives substance to the development of a public culture which is synonymous with the spirit of a critical democracy.

Central to this task is the need for educators to develop a public language which refuses to reconcile higher education with inequality, which actively abandons those forms of pedagogical practice which prevent our students from becoming aware of and offended by the structures of oppression at work in both institutional and everyday life. We need a language that defends liberal arts education not as a servant of the state or an authoritarian cultural ideology but as the site of a counterpublic sphere where students can be educated to learn how to question and, in the words of John Dewey, "break existing public forms."[34] This is a language in which knowledge and power are inextricably linked to the presupposition that to choose life, so as to make it possible, is to understand the preconditions necessary to struggle for it. As engaged public intellectuals committed to a project of radical pedagogy and the reconstruction of democratic public life, university academics can create forms of collegiality and community forged in social practices that link their work in the university with larger social struggles. This suggests redefining knowledge-power relationships outside of the limitations of the academic specialities so as to broaden the relationship of the university with the culture of public life. In this way academic interventions can provide the basis for new forms of public association, occasions informed by and contributing to moral and political commitments in which the meanings we produce, the ways in which we represent ourselves, and our relation to others contribute to a wider public discussion and dialogue of democratic possibilities not yet realized. This is a call to transform the hegemonic cultural forms of the wider society and the academy into a social movement of intellectuals intent on reclaiming and reconstructing democratic values and public life rather than contributing to their demise. This is a utopian practice that both critiques and transcends the culture of despair and disdain that has characterized education in the age of Reagan/Bush. It is also a practice that provides a starting point for linking liberal arts education to a public philosophy in which the curriculum is not reduced to a matter of cultural inheritance, but is posed as part of an ongoing struggle informed by a project of possibility which extends the most noble of human capacities while simultaneously developing the potentialities of democratic public life.

Notes

1   Of course, a caveat has to be raised here. For many liberal and left academics the university is generally regarded as a site constituted in relations of power and representing various political and ethical interests. On the other hand, some neoconservative educators believe that the true interests of the university transcend political and normative concerns, and that the latter represent an agenda being pushed exclusively by left academics who are undermining the most basic principles of university life. For example, former Secretary of Education, William J. Bennett, has argued that most universities are controlled "by a left-wing political agenda" pushing the concerns of feminists, Marxists, and various ethnic groups. The neoconservative argument is often made in defense of an objective, balanced,

and unbiased academic discourse. The claim to objectivity, truth, and principles that transcend history and power may be comforting to neoconservative spokespersons, but, in reality, the discourse of such groups is nothing more than a rhetorical mask that barely conceals their own highly charged, ideological agenda. The ongoing attacks made by prominent neoconservative scholars against affirmative action, ethnic studies, radical scholarship, modernity, and anything else that threatens the traditional curriculum and the power relations it supports represent a particularized, not a universalized view, of the university and its relationship with the wider society. The most recent example of neoconservative "objectivity" and public conscience was displayed in a meeting in Washington, D.C., of three hundred conservative scholars whose major agenda was to reclaim the universities and to find ways to challenge those left-wing academics, referred to by one of the participants as "the barbarians in our midst" who are challenging the authority of the traditional canon. Underlying this form of criticism is the not so invisible ideological appeal to the "white man's burden" to educate those who exist outside of the parameters of civilized culture: the rhetoric betrays the colonizing logic at the heart of the "reactionary" political agenda that characterizes the new cultural offensive of such groups as the National Association of Scholars. The report on the conservative scholars' conference appeared in Joseph Berger, "Conservative Scholars Attack 'Radicalization' of Universities," *New York Times*, 15 November 1988. For a discussion of the conservative offensive in establishing a traditional reading of the liberal arts and the notion of the canon see William V. Spanos, *Repetitions: The Postmodern Occasion in Literature and Culture* (Baton Rouge, 1987); and Henry A. Giroux, *Schooling and the Struggle for Public Life* (Minneapolis, 1988). Also see Donald Lazere, "Conservative Critics Have a Distorted View of What Constitutes Ideological Bias in Academe," *Chronicle of Higher Education*, 9 November 1988, A52.

2   Philip Corrigan, "In/Forming Schooling," in David W. Livingstone and Contributers, *Critical Pedagogy and Cultural Power* (Granby, Mass., 1987), 17–40.

3   Roger I. Simon, "Empowerment as a Pedagogy of Possibility," *Language Arts* 64 (April 1987): 372.

4   Jacques Derrida, "The Principle of Reason: The University in the Eyes of Its Pupils," *Diacritics* 13 (Fall 1983): 3.

5   Ernst Bloch, *The Philosophy of the Future* (New York, 1970), 86–87.

6   Simon, "Empowerment," 372.

7   Leon Botstein illuminates some of the ideological elements at work in the language of cultural despair characteristic of the educational discourse of the new right:

> In particular, the new conservativism evident in the most influential educational critiques and Jeremiads utilizes the language and images of decline and unwittingly makes comparisons to an idealized American past during which far fewer Americans finished high school. It challenges implicitly (Hirsch) and explicitly (Bloom) the post–World War II democratic goal of American

schooling: to render excellence and equity compatible in reality. In the 1980s, the call for educational reform is not being framed, as it was in the late 1950s (when America was concerned about Sputnik and Harvard's Conant studied the American high school), in terms of what might be achieved. Rather the discussion begins with a sense of what has been lost.

See Leon Botstein, "Education Reform in the Reagan Era: False Paths, Broken Promises," *Social Policy* (Spring 1988): 7. For a critique of the ideology of cultural decline among universities see Jerry Herron, *Universities and the Myth of Cultural Decline* (Detroit, 1988).

8   Simon, "Empowerment."

9   This criticism is more fully developed in Giroux, *Schooling and the Struggle for Public Life*; and Stanley Aronowitz and Henry A. Giroux, *Education Under Siege* (Granby, Mass., 1985).

10   Allan Bloom, *The Closing of the American Mind: How Higher Education Has Failed Democracy and Impoverished the Souls of Today's Students* (New York, 1987); and E. D. Hirsch, Jr., *Cultural Literacy: What Every American Needs to Know* (Boston, 1987).

11   Stanley Aronowitz and I have developed an extensive criticism of Bloom and Hirsch's work in "Schooling, Culture, and Literacy in the Age of Broken Dreams," *Harvard Educational Review* 58 (May 1988): 172–94.

12   This position is more fully developed in Jim Merod, *The Political Responsibility of the Critic* (Ithaca, 1987); Aronowitz and Giroux, *Education Under Siege*; and Frank Lentricchia, *Criticism and Social Change* (Chicago, 1983).

13   Spanos, *Repetitions*, 302.

14   Two classic examples can be found in William J. Bennett, " 'To Reclaim a Legacy': Text of the Report of Humanities in Higher Education," *Chronicle of Higher Education*, 28 November 1984, 16–21; and Lynne V. Cheney, *Humanities in America: A Report to the President, the Congress, and the American People* (Washington, D.C., 1988).

15   Christopher Lasch, "A Response to Fischer," *Tikkun* 3 (1988): 73.

16   Mas'ud Zavarzadeh and Donald Morton, "War of the Words: The Battle of (and for) English," *In These Times*, 28 October–3 November 1987, 18–19. Hazel Carby, in "The Canon: Civil War and Reconstruction," *Michigan Quarterly Review* (Winter 1989), 36–38, is clear on this point and is worth quoting at length:

> . . . I would argue that debates about the canon are misleading debates in many ways. Arguments appear to be about the inclusion or exclusion of particular texts and/or authors or about including or excluding types of books and authors ("women" and "minorities" are usually the operative categories). It also appears as if debates about the canon are disagreements about issues of representation only. . . . Contrary to what the debate appears to be about, talking about the canon means that we avoid the deeper problem. Focusing on books and authors means that we are not directly addressing the

ways in which our society is structured in dominance. We live in a racialized hierarchy which is also organized through class and gender divisions. Reducing these complex modes of inequality to questions of representation on a syllabus is a far too simple method of appearing to resolve these social contradictions and yet this is how the battle has been waged at Columbia and Stanford, to take two examples of campuses engaged in debating the importance of canonical works of western culture. What is absurd about these hotly-contested and highly emotive battles is that proponents for radical change in canonical syllabi are forced to act as if inclusion of the texts they favor would somehow make accessible the experience of women or minorities as generic types. The same people who would argue in very sophisticated critical terms that literary texts do not directly reflect or represent reality but reconstruct and re-present particular historical realities find themselves demanding that the identity of a social group be represented by a single novel. Acting as if an excluded or marginalized or dominant group is represented in a particular text, in my view, is a mistake. . . . Our teaching needs to make connections with, as well as provide a critique of, dominant ideologies and meanings of culture which structure the curricula of departments of English and American studies.

Also see Toni Morrison, "Unspeakable Things Unspoken: The Afro-American Presence in American Literature," *Michigan Quarterly Review* (Winter 1989): 1–34.

17　This particular quote is cited in Frank Hearn, *Reason and Freedom in Sociological Thought* (Boston, 1985), 175. The classic statements by Dewey on this subject can be found in John Dewey, *Democracy and Education* (New York, 1916), and *The Public and Its Problems in the Later Works of John Dewey, 1925–1927*, ed. Jo Ann Boydston (Carbondale, 1984), 2: 253–372.

18　See for example, *Power, Politics, and People: The Collected Essays of C. Wright Mills*, ed. Irving Louis Horowitz (New York, 1963), especially the "Social Role of the Intellectual" and "Mass Society and Liberal Education."

19　For a liberal treatment of this issue, see Robert N. Bellah et al., *Habits of the Heart: Individualism and Commitment in American Life* (Berkeley, 1985). For an excellent analysis and criticism of American life and the decline of community as portrayed in *Habits of the Heart*, see Fredric R. Jameson, "On Habits of the Heart," in *Community in America*, ed. Charles H. Reynolds and Ralph V. Norman (Berkeley, 1988), 97–112.

20　A number of representative essays which deal with pedagogy as a form of cultural production can be found in *Popular Culture and Critical Pedagogy*, ed. Henry A. Giroux and Roger I. Simon (Granby, Mass., 1989).

21　Roger Simon, "For a Pedagogy of Possibility," *Critical Pedagogy Networker* 1 (February 1988): 2.

22　The next two pages draw from Henry A. Giroux and Harvey J. Kaye, "The Liberal Arts Must Be Reformed to Serve Democratic Ends," *Chronicle of Higher Education*, 29 March 1989, A44.

23 Elizabeth Fox-Genovese, "The Claims of a Common Culture: Gender, Race, Class and the Canon," *Salmagundi* 72 (Fall 1986): 133.

24 Gail Guthrie Valaskakis, "The Chippewa and the Other: Living the Heritage of Lac Du Flambeau," *Cultural Studies* 2 (October 1988): 268.

25 The issue of ethics and schooling is taken up in detail in Giroux, *Schooling and the Struggle for Public Life.*

26 Henry A. Giroux and Roger I. Simon, "Critical Pedagogy and the Politics of Popular Culture," *Cultural Studies* 2 (October 1988): 294–320.

27 Chantal Mouffe, "The Civics Lesson," *New Statesman and Society*, 7 October 1988, 30.

28 Nancy Hartsock, "Rethinking Modernism: Minority vs. Majority Theories," *Cultural Critique* 7 (Fall 1987): 187–206.

29 Teresa de Lauretis, *Technologies of Gender* (Bloomington, 1987), 25.

30 Caren Kaplan, "Deterritorialization: The Rewriting of Home and Exile in Western Feminist Discourse," *Cultural Critique* 6 (Spring 1987): 187–98.

31 On this point, see Russell Jacoby, *The Last Intellectuals* (New York, 1987); and Terry Eagleton, *The Function of Criticism* (London, 1984).

32 Antonio Gramsci, *Selections from the Prison Notebooks* (New York, 1971).

33 Michael Walzer, *Interpretation and Social Criticism* (Cambridge, 1985).

34 Boydston, ed., *Later Works of John Dewey*, 2: 253–372.

Eve Kosofsky Sedgwick

Pedagogy in the Context of an Antihomophobic Project

Contemporary discussions of the question of the literary canon—among those of us for whom the canon is a living question—tend to be structured *either* around the possibility of change, of rearrangement and reassignment of texts, within one, overarching, master canon of literature (the strategy of adding Mary Shelley to the Norton Anthology) *or*, more theoretically defensible at the moment, around a vision of an exploding master canon whose fracture would produce, or at least leave room for, a potentially infinite plurality of mini-canons, each specified as to its thematic or structural or authorial coverage: francophone Canadian or Inuit canons, for instance, clusters of magical realism or national allegory, the blues tradition, working-class narrative, canons of the sublime or the self-reflexive, African-Caribbean canons, canons of Anglo-American women's writing.

In fact, though, the most productive canon effects that have been taking place in recent literary studies have occurred not from within the mechanisms of either the master canon or a postfractural plurality of canons, but through an inter-action between these two models of the canon. In this interaction, the new pluralized mini-canons have largely failed to dislodge the master canon from its empirical centrality in institutional practices like publishing and teaching, although they have made certain spe-cific works and authors newly available for inclusion in the master canon. Their more important effect, however, has been to challenge, if not the empirical centrality then the conceptual *anonymity* of the master canon. The most notorious instance of this has occurred with feminist studies in literature, which by on the one hand confronting the master canon with alternative canons of women's literature, and on the other hand reading rebelliously within the master canon, has not only somewhat rearranged the table of contents for the master canon but more importantly given it a title. If it is still in important respects *the* master canon, it nevertheless cannot now escape naming itself with every syllable also *a* particular canon, a canon of mastery, in this case of men's mastery over, and over against, women. Perhaps never again need women—need, one hopes, anybody—feel greeted by the Norton Anthology of mostly white men's literature with the implied insolent salutation, "I'm nobody. Who are you?"

This is an encouraging story of female canon formation, working in a sort of pincers movement with a process of feminist canon *nam-ing*, that has been in various forms a good deal told by now. How much the cheering clarity of this story is indebted to the scarifying coarseness and visibility with which women and men are, in most if not all societies, distinguished publicly and once and for all from one another, emerges however only when attempts are made to ap-ply the same model to a very differently structured though closely related form of oppression, modern homophobia. If I may continue for just a minute more with this analysis of feminist criticism: one of the greatest heuristic leaps of feminism has been the recognition that categories of gender—and hence oppressions of gender—can have a structuring force for nodes of thought, for axes of cultural discrimi-nation, whose thematic subject isn't explicitly gendered at all. We have now learned as feminist readers that dichotomies in a given text of culture as opposed to nature, public as opposed to private, mind as opposed to body, activity as opposed to passivity, etc., etc., are, under particular pressures of culture and history, likely places to look for implicit allegories of the relations of men to women; more, that to fail to analyze such nominally ungendered constructs in gender terms can itself be a gravely tendentious move in the gender-politics of reading. This has given us ways to ask the question of gender about texts even where the culturally "marked" gender (female) is not present as either author or thematic. It is through this mechanism that feminism has had so magnetic an effect on the very insides as well as on the surround of the male and masculist canon. Coming of age at the same time as, and in a synergistic relation to, deconstruction, feminist reading became richly involved with the deconstructive understanding that categories presented in a culture as symmetrical binary oppositions—male/female as well as culture/nature, etc.—actually subsist in a more unsettling and dynamic tacit relation according to which, first, term B is not symmetrical with but subordinated to term A; but, second, the ontologically valorized term A actually depends for its meaning on the simultaneous subsumption and exclusion of term B; hence, third, that the question of priority between the supposed central and the supposed marginal category of each dyad is irresolvably unstable.

The dichotomy heterosexual/homosexual, as it has emerged through the last century of Western discourse, would seem to lend itself peculiarly neatly to a set of analytic moves learned from this deconstructive moment in feminist theory. One has perhaps only to remind oneself that the deviant category "homosexual" actually antedates the supposedly normative "heterosexual": conceptually by something over a decade, and lexically, in America, by at least two years.[1] In fact, heterosexual/homosexual fits the deconstructive template much more neatly than the dichotomy male/female itself does, and hence, importantly differently. The most dramatic difference between gender and sexual orientation—that virtually all people are publicly and unalterably assigned to one or the other gender, and from birth—seems if anything to mean that it is rather sexual orientation, with its far greater potential for rearrangement, ambiguity, and representational doubleness, that would offer the apter deconstructive object. An essentialism of sexual object choice is far less easy to maintain, far more visibly incoherent, more visibly stressed and challenged at every point in the culture, than any essentialism of gender. Indeed, the unbudging conceptual deadlock over the last hundred years between minoritizing views of homosexuality as the fixed trait of a distinct small percentage of the population, and universalizing views of it as a widely diffused potential in whole populations whom only its pointed repression renders heterosexual, answers to the deconstructive analysis of the particular instability of binary oppositions with a congruence that may prove telling on both sides. Thus, the positioning of homosexuality as the thing that is both inside the heart of the normative cultural canon, and at the same time the distinctive and structuring exclusion *from* it, ought to be peculiarly strong.

It is, most historians agree, only recently—and, I would argue, only very incompletely and raggedly, although to that extent violently and brutally—that a combination of discursive forces has carved out, for women or for men, a possible though intensively proscribed homosexual identity in Euro-American culture. Different readers have made claims to be able to trace such a homosexual identity back perhaps a hundred years for both women and men, perhaps as much as two hundred years for men. To the extent that such an identity is traceable, there is clearly the possibility, now being realized within literary criticism, for assembling alternative canons of lesbian and gay male writing *as* minority canons, as a literature of oppression and resistance and survival and heroic making. This modern view of lesbians and gay men as a distinctive minority population is of course importantly anachronistic in relation to earlier writing, however; and even in relation to modern writing, it seems to falter in important ways in the implicit analysis it offers of the mechanisms of homophobia and of same-sex desire. It is with these complications that the relation between lesbian and gay literature as a minority canon, and the making salient of homosocial, homosexual, and homophobic strains and torsions in the already existing master canon itself, becomes an especially revealing process.

It's a revealing process only, however, for those of us for whom relations within and among canons are living and active relations of thought. From the keepers of a dead canon we hear a rhetorical question—that is to say, a question posed with the arrogant intent of maintaining ignorance. Is there, asks Saul Bellow, a Tolstoy of the Zulus? Has there been, ask the defenders of a monocultural curriculum, not intending to stay for an answer, has there ever yet been a Socrates of the Orient, an African-American Proust, a female Shakespeare? And however assaultive or fatuous, in the context of the current debate the question hasn't been unproductive. To answer it in good faith has been to broach inquiries across a variety of critical fronts: into the canonical or indeed world-historic texts of non-Euro-American cultures, to begin with, but also into the nonuniversal functions of literacy and the literary, into the contingent and uneven secularization and sacralization of an aesthetic realm, into the relations of public to private in the ranking of genres, into the cult of the individual author and the organization of liberal arts education as an expensive form of masterpiece theater.

Moreover, the flat insolent question teases by the very difference of its resonance with different projects of inquiry: it stimulates or irritates or reveals *differently* in the context of oral or written cultures; of the colonized or the colonizing, or cultures that have had both experiences; of peoples concentrated or in diaspora; of traditions partially internal or largely external to a dominant culture of the latter twentieth century.

What, from the point of view of a relatively new and inchoate academic presence—the gay studies movement—what distinctive soundings are to be reached by posing the question our way, and staying for an answer? Let's see how it sounds.

> Has there ever been a gay Socrates?
> Has there ever been a gay Shakespeare?
> Has there ever been a gay Proust?

Does the Pope wear a dress? If these questions startle, it is not least as tautologies. A short answer, though a very incomplete one, might be that not only have there been a gay Socrates, Shakespeare, and Proust but that their names are Socrates, Shakespeare, Proust; and, beyond that, legion—dozens or hundreds of the most centrally canonic figures in what the monoculturalists are pleased to consider "our" culture, as indeed, always in different forms and senses, in every other.

What's now in place, on the other hand, in most scholarship and most curricula is an even briefer response to questions like these: Don't ask. Or less laconically: You shouldn't know. The vast preponderance of scholarship and teaching, accordingly, even among liberal academics, simply neither asks nor knows. At its most expansive, it offers a series of dismissals of such questions on the grounds that

(1) Passionate language of same-sex attraction was extremely common during whatever period is under discussion—and therefore must have been completely meaningless. Or

(2) Same-sex genital relations may have been perfectly common during the period under discussion—but since there was *no* language about them, *they* must have been completely meaningless. Or

(3) Attitudes about homosexuality were intolerant back then, unlike now—so people probably didn't do anything. Or

(4) Prohibitions against homosexuality didn't exist back then, unlike now—so if people did anything, it was completely meaningless. Or

(5) The word "homosexuality" wasn't coined until 1869—so everyone before then was heterosexual. (Of course, heterosexuality has always existed.) Or

(6) The author under discussion is certified or rumored to have had an attachment to someone of the other sex—so their feelings about people of their own sex must have been completely meaningless. Or

(7) (under a perhaps somewhat different rule of admissible evidence): There is no actual proof of homosexuality, such as sperm taken from the body of another man or a nude photograph with another woman—so the author may be assumed to have been ardently and exclusively heterosexual. Or

(8) (as a last resort): The author or the author's important attachments may very well have been homosexual—but it would be provincial to let so insignificant a fact make any difference at all to our understanding of any serious project of life, writing, or thought.

These responses, of course, reflect some real questions of sexual definition and historicity. But they only reflect them and don't reflect *on* them—the family resemblance among this group of extremely common responses comes from their closeness to the core grammar: *don't ask, you shouldn't know.* It didn't mean anything; it doesn't have interpretive consequences; it didn't matter; it doesn't make any difference. Stop asking just here; stop asking just now; we know in advance the kind of difference that could be made by the invocation of *this* difference; it makes no difference; it doesn't mean. The most openly repressive projects of censorship, such as William Bennett's literally murderous opposition to serious AIDS education in schools on the grounds that it would communicate a tolerance for the lives of homosexuals, are, through this mobilization of the powerful mechanism of the open secret, made perfectly congruent with the smooth, dismissive knowingness of the urbane and the pseudo-urbane.

And yet the absolute canonical centrality of the list of authors about whom one might think to ask these questions—What was the structure, function, historical surround of same-sex love in and for Homer or Plato or Sappho? What then about Euripides or Virgil? If a gay Marlowe, what about Spenser or Milton? Shakespeare? Byron? But what about Shelley? Montaigne, Leopardi . . . ? Leonardo, Michelangelo, but . . . ? Beethoven? Whitman, Thoreau, Dickinson (Dickinson?), Tennyson, Wilde, Woolf, Hopkins, but Bronte? Wittgenstein, but . . . Nietzsche? Proust, Musil, Kafka, Cather, but . . . Mann? James, but . . . Lawrence? Eliot? Joyce?—the very centrality of this list, and its seemingly almost infinite elasticity, suggest that no one *can* know *in advance* where the limits of a gay-centered inquiry are to be drawn, or where a gay theorizing of and through even the hegemonic high culture of the Euro-American tradition may need or be able to lead. The emergence, even within the last year or two, of nascent but ambitious and fascinating programs and courses in gay and lesbian studies, at schools like Yale, CUNY, Berkeley, and Amherst, may now make it possible for the first time to ask these difficult questions from within the heart of the empowered cultural institutions to which they pertain, as well as from the marginal and endangered institutional positions from which, for so long, the most courageous work in this area has emanated.

Furthermore, the violently contradictory and volatile energies that every morning's newspaper proves to us are circulating even at this moment, in our society, around the issues of homo/heterosexual definition, show over and over again how preposterous is *anybody's* urbane pretense at having a clear, simple story to tell about the outlines and meanings of what and who is homosexual and heterosexual. Jeffrey Weeks points out the thoroughgoing, coercive incoherence of the homophobic etiological models that prevail in our culture, according to which homosexuality is classified at the same time as "sin" *and* as "disease," "so that you can be born with [it], seduced into [it] and catch [it], all at the same time."[2] Antihomophobic analysis has the same divided conceptual heritage: the most current theoretical form in which this conflict is visible is in the debate in gay studies between "social constructionist" and "essentialist" understandings of homo/heterosexual identity. The conflict, within both homophobic and antihomophobic ideologies, has a long history; it is the most recent link in a more enduring chain of conceptual impasses, a deadlock between what I have been calling more generally *universalizing* and *minoritizing* accounts of the relation of homosexual desires or persons to the wider field of all desires or persons. Universalizing discourses are those that suggest that every person has the potential for same-sex, as for opposite-sex, desire or activity; minoritizing ones are those that attribute each of these desires to a fixed, unchangeable segment of the population. Each kind of account can underpin both virulently homophobic and supportively antihomophobic ideological formations.

Historical narratives since Foucault have seemed to show universalizing paradigms, such as the terribly influential Judeo-Christian proscription of particular *acts* called "sodomy" (acts that might be performed by anybody), as being displaced after the late nineteenth century by the definition of particular kinds of *persons*, specifically "homosexuals." A classically based but enduring honorific subtradition of durable and significant pedagogic/pederastic *bonds* between men of different ages was also seen as having been displaced by the new, minoritizing view of homosexual identity. The truth seems to be rather that since the late nineteenth century the different understandings, contradictory though they are, have coexisted, creating in the space of their contradiction enormous potentials of discursive power. We have just at the moment a perfect example of this potent incoherence in the anomalous legal situation of gay people and acts in this country: while the Supreme Court in *Bowers v. Hardwick* has notoriously left the individual states free to prohibit any *acts* that they wish to define as "sodomy," by whomsoever performed, with no fear at all of impinging on any rights safeguarded by the Constitution —at the same time a panel of the Ninth Circuit Court of Appeals ruled last spring (in *Sergeant Perry J. Watkins v. United States Army*) that homosexual *persons*, as a particular kind of person, *are* entitled to Constitutional protections under the Equal Protection clause. To be gay in this system is to come under the radically overlapping aegises of a universalizing discourse of acts or bonds and at the same time of a minoritizing discourse of kinds of persons. Meanwhile in the discourse of Christianity, the subtle constructivist argument that sexual aim is not, at least for many people, a hard-wired biological given but rather a social fact deeply embedded in the cultural and linguistic forms of many, many decades is being degraded to the blithe ukase that people are "free at any moment to" (i.e., must immediately) "choose" to subscribe to a particular sexual identity (say, at a random hazard, the heterosexual) rather than to its other. In the double binds implicit in the space overlapped by universalizing and minoritizing models, the stakes in matters of definitional control are extremely high: dignity, employment, health care, custody of children, stigma, possible incarceration, artistic and intellectual authority, permission to worship or to teach, and, especially given the politics of AIDS research and treatment, and the astronomical recent rise in reports of gay-bashing, life itself.

These definitional contests can occur, moreover, only in the context of an entire cultural network of normative definitions—definitions themselves equally unstable but responding to different sets of contiguities and often at a different rate. The master terms of a particular historical moment will be those that are so situated as to entangle most inextricably and at the same time most differentially the filaments of other important definitional nexuses. In arguing that homo/heterosexual definition has been a presiding master term of the past century, one that has the same, primary importance for all modern Western identity and social organization (and not merely for homosexual identity and culture) as do the more traditionally visible cruxes of gender, class, and race, I would suggest that the now chronic modern crisis of homo/heterosexual definition has affected our culture through its entanglement with particularly the categories secrecy/disclosure, knowledge/ignorance, private/public, masculine/feminine, majority/minority, natural/artificial, whole-ness/decadence, urbane/provincial, health/illness, same/different, active/passive, in/out, cognition/paranoia, art/kitsch, sincerity/sentimentality, and voluntarity/addiction.

Obviously, this analysis suggests as one indispensable approach to the traditional Euro-American canon a pedagogy that could neither dismantle it (insofar as it was seen to be quite genuinely unified by the maintenance of a particular tension of homo/heterosexual definitional panic) nor, on the other hand, ever permit it to be treated as the repository of reassuring "traditional" truths that could be made matter for any true consolidation or congratulation. Insofar as the problematics of homo/heterosexual definition, in an intensely homophobic culture, are seen to be precisely internal to the central nexuses of that culture, this canon must always be treated as a loaded one. Considerations of the canon, it becomes clear, while vital in themselves cannot take the place of questions of pedagogic relations within and around the canon. Canonicity itself then seems the necessary wadding of pious obliviousness that allows for the transmission from one generation to another of texts that have the potential to dismantle the impacted foundations upon which a given culture rests.

I anticipate that to an interlocutor like William Bennett, such a view would smack of the sinister sublimity peculiar to those of us educated in the dark campus days of the late sixties. And I must confess that this demographic specification is exactly true of me. Indeed, I can be more precise about where I might have acquired such a view of the high volatility of canonical texts. At the infamous Cornell of the infamous late sixties, I was privileged to have teachers who invested in both texts and students their most trenchant passions. Like a lot of intellectually ambitious undergraduates, for instance, I gravitated into the orbit of Allan Bloom; my friends and I imitated, very affectionately and more than superficially, his infusion of every reading project with his own persona and with "p-p-p-passion"—his tattoo on the plosive consonant, part involuntary, part stagecraft, all riveting, dramatizing for us the explosive potential he lent to every interpretive nexus. It was from Bloom, as much as from more explicitly literary and deconstructive theorists, that I and some others of that late sixties generation learned the urgencies and pleasures of reading against the visible grain of any influential text. The so-called conservative practical politics that, even then, so often seemed to make his vital cross-grained interpretive interventions boil down to a few coarsely ugly stereotypes and prescriptions wasn't quite enough, at least for awhile, to eclipse the lesson that the true sins against the holy ghost would be to read without risking oneself, to write or utter without revealing oneself however esoterically, to interpret without undergoing the perverse danger of setting in motion all the contradictory forces of any only semidomesticated canonical text.

Now, reading *The Closing of the American Mind*, the splendid pedagogic charms of this great popularizer (of this great teacher) come flooding back to me. Along with feeling gratitude for his enablement of outrageous but central projects of reading, I more specifically recognize in retrospect the actual outlines of what have been for me antihomophobic canonical reconstructions. For Bloom, that is, as also for a particular gay studies project within the traditional canon, the history of Western thought is importantly constituted and motivated by a priceless history of male-male pedagogic or pederastic relations. In a climactic chapter beguilingly entitled "Our Ignorance," for instance, Bloom encapsulates Western culture as the narrative that goes from the *Phaedrus* to *Death in Venice*. The crisis of Aschenbach's modern culture is seen as the deadeningness of the readings that are performed within its intrinsically explosive canon. As Bloom explains,

> As Aschenbach becomes more and more obsessed by the boy on the beach, quotations from the *Phaedrus* . . . keep coming into his head. . . . The *Phaedrus* was probably one of the things Aschenbach was supposed to have read as a schoolboy while learning Greek. But its content, discourses on the love of a man for a boy, was not supposed to affect him. The dialogue, like so much that was in the German education, was another scrap of "culture," of historical information, which had not become a part of a vital, coherent whole. This is symptomatic of the deadness of Aschenbach's own cultural activity.[3]

Bloom is frightened by the petrification of these passions within the tradition. The other danger that, in Bloom's view, threatens cultural vitality, however, is not that these desires might be killed but that they might be expressed. For Bloom, and in this I believe he offers a startlingly faithful and candid representation of Western hegemonic culture, the stimulation and glamorization of the energies of male-male desire (and who could deny that he does an irresistible job of glamorizing them) is an incessant project that must, for the preservation of that self-contradictory tradition, coexist with an equally incessant project of denying, deferring, or silencing their satisfaction. With a mechanistic hydraulicism more reductive than the one he deprecates in Freud, Bloom blames the sexual liberation movements of the sixties—all of them, but of course in this philosophic context the gay movement must take most of the blame—for dissipating the reservoirs of cathectic energy that are supposed to be held, by repression, in an excitable state of readiness to be invested in cultural projects. Instead, as Plato's "diversity of erotic expression" has been frittered away on mere sex, now supposedly licit, "the lion roaring behind the door of the closet" has turned out "to be a little, domesticated cat." In Bloom's sad view, "sexual passion is no longer dangerous in us"; "the various liberations wasted that marvelous energy and tension, leaving the students' souls exhausted and flaccid."[4]

So Bloom is unapologetically protective of the sanctity of the closet, that curious space that is both internal and marginal to the culture: centrally representative of its motivating passions and contradictions, even while marginalized by its orthodoxies. The modern, normalizing, minoritizing equal rights movement for people of varying sexual identities is a grave falling-off, in Bloom's view, from the more precarious cultural *privilege* of a past in which "there was a respectable place for marginality, bohemia. But it had to justify its unorthodox practices by its intellectual and artistic achievement."[5] The fragile, precious representational compact by which a small, shadowily identified group both represented the hidden, perhaps dangerous truths about a culture to itself, and depended on its exiguous toleration, is by this account exactly like the position of Socrates, and by extension of the ideal philosopher/teacher—of any uncoverer of the explosive truths within the body of a culture, to a transient young audience whose own hunger for such initiations is likeliest to be, at the very most, nothing more than a phase they are going through. "He is, therefore," Bloom poignantly writes,

> necessarily in the most fundamental tension with everyone except his own kind. He relates to all the others ironically, i.e., with sympathy and playful distance. Changing the character of his relationship to them is impossible because the disproportion between him and them is firmly rooted in nature. Thus, he has no expectation of essential progress. Toleration, not right, is the best he can hope for, and he is kept vigilant by the awareness of the basic fragility of his situation and that of philosophy.[6]

Socrates within the life of the Greeks, like the individual vessel of same-sex desire within the homoerotic tradition of homophobic Western high culture, depends for his survival on the very misrecognitions that his prestige comes from his having the power to demystify. Furthermore, the compact between the philosopher and youth is held together not only by love but by the perhaps necessarily elitist community formed of mutual contempt. He is allowed to despise them for not, he thinks, seeing him for what he is ("Crito, the family man, thinks of Socrates as a good family man. Laches, the soldier, thinks of Socrates as a good soldier.")[7] Meanwhile, they are allowed to condescend to the spectacle of a certain final, irreducible difference from themselves. It's no wonder that such tight knots of desire-laden self-congratulation at one another's expense should be difficult to untie.

What Bloom offers is eloquent as an analysis—if indeed it is meant to be an analysis—of the prestige, magnetism, vulnerability, self-alienation, co-optability, and perhaps ultimately the potential for a certain defiance that inhere in the canonical culture of the closet. However, it is far from being the whole story. One of the things that can be said about the post-Stonewall gay movement, for instance, is that, to the extent that it posited gay women and men as a distinct minority with rights comparable to those of any other minority, it served notice that at least some people were in a position to demand that the representational compact between the closet and the culture be renegotiated or abrogated. And this move has been absolutely indispensable. It is heartbreakingly premature for Bloom to worry, at least with regard to homophobic prohibition, that the times are now such that anything goes, that "sexual passion is no longer dangerous in us." Our culture still sees to its being dangerous enough that women and men who find or fear they are homosexual, or are perceived by others to be so, are physically and mentally terrorized through the institutions of law, religion, psychotherapy, mass culture, medicine, the military, commerce and bureaucracy, and brute violence.

I am surprised, too, that someone who claims to be as intimately attuned as Bloom is to his students would have failed to notice that the area over which homophobic prohibition maintains the most unyielding grasp is precollege education. What professor who cares for her students' survival, dignity, and thought can fail to be impressed and frightened by the unaccustomed, perhaps impossible responsibilities that devolve on college faculty as a result of the homophobia uniformly enjoined on teachers throughout the primary and secondary levels of public school—where teachers are subject to being fired, not only for being visibly gay, but, whatever their sexuality, for providing any intimation that homosexual desires, identities, cultures, adults, children, or adolescents have a right to expression or existence. A few exemplary news stories from the past year:

> A ninth grade teacher in rural Cambridge, N.Y., . . . allowed a group of students at Cambridge Central School to read . . . a booklet about homosexuality. . . . The school board . . . responded by rescinding her tenure.[8]

Another report:

> In Utah, teachers are not allowed to talk about same-sex intercourse as a method of [AIDS] transmission. In Florida, state law requires that parents write permission notes before their children can be told about AIDS.[9]

Another report:

> A [public] junior high school principal in Toronto burned several hundred copies of a local teen magazine because they carried

an advertisement [offering telephone numbers] for a counseling program conducted by . . . a gay youth group.[10]

Another report:

New Hampshire conservatives are outraged by sympathetic treatment of gays in a federally financed sex education curriculum manual developed by a Strafford County family planning clinic. . . . About three pages of the 45-page booklet are devoted to problems faced by gay youth. . . . The manual encourages educators to empathize with gays when dealing with any issue of adolescent sexuality. . . .

The federal Department of Health and Human Services asked state officials to "take whatever action is necessary" to stop distribution of the manual. . . . State officials demanded the clinic turn over names of the recipients of the manual . . . and hand over copies remaining from the 500 originally printed. They threatened to withhold state funds from all the clinic's programs.

The Strafford County Board of Commissioners, meanwhile, froze $39,000 in funding earmarked for low-income mothers and infants in the clinic's prenatal program.[11]

Another report:

[California] Assembly Republicans have threatened to withhold new state funding for the Los Angeles Unified School District unless it stops a high school teacher from counselling gay students.[12]

Another report:

High school officials [in Appleton, Wisc.] said they gave [a] teacher a reprimand for not informing parents in writing prior to [a talk by a] gay man.[13]

Another report:

A school [Superintendent] in Radford [Virginia] recently canceled a play by a traveling theater group because the group had once performed with people with AIDS. . . .[14]

Another report:

> A drop-in support center and counseling service for Syracuse-area gay youth—established with a small grant from New York State—opened May 1 [1987]. As the gay nature of the project became widely known, however, a political controversy erupted. . . . The youth bureau reluctantly decided not to seek renewal of the grant for fear of having much of the bureau's other funding also cut off by the legislature.
>
> As a result of that decision, the program's funds will run out at the end of this year.[15]

And another:

> In Bangor, Maine, the school district cancelled a proposed "Tolerance Day"—organized after three students killed a gay man—because one of the scheduled speakers was a lesbian.[16]

Obviously, the place where this society has drawn its official limit of "tolerance," where "don't ask" throws down its mask of urbanity to reveal itself as "don't exist," is in the teaching of children—that is to say, in the place where not only attitudes but mind, self, self-esteem, trust, aptitude, courage, acceptance, and the whole braid around them of cognitive pleasures and challenges that go into the creation of adult people, can be fostered or refused fostering. I don't know of any child who has considered or attempted suicide at the intimation that she or he might be heterosexual. Yet such recollections are well known to be commonplace among gay people who discovered this sexuality early—that is, among the ones who had the vitality and courage to survive into adulthood. I genuinely can't imagine how anyone could perceive the culture's refusal to intervene on—never mind its legal enjoinment of—such a scene of institutional denial, repudiation, eradication, as anything short of legally mandated child abuse, in the very place set aside as sacred to children and their fostering. To the credit of their guts and professionalism, both of the major public-school teachers' unions are now considering ways of trying to bring this situation to an end, but it will be difficult, especially as there is essentially no support in American law for teachers who wish to speak other than denigratingly to their classes about gay desires or people.

Political progress on these and similar life-and-death issues, at any rate, has depended on precisely the strength of a minority-model gay activism: it is the normalizing, persuasive analogy between the needs of gay/lesbian students and those of black or Jewish students, for instance, and the development of the corresponding political techniques, that enables progress in such arenas. And *that* side of the needed progress cannot be mobilized from within any closet; it requires very many people's risky and affirming acts of the most explicit self-identification as members of the minority affected.

So, too, at the level of the canon. The invaluable forms of critique and dismantlement within the official tradition, the naming as what it is of a hegemonic, homoerotic/homophobic male canon of cultural mastery and coercive erotic double binding, can be only part of the strategy of an antihomophobic project. It must work in the kind of pincers movement I have already described with the re-creation of minority gay canons from currently noncanonical material. Most obviously, this would be necessary in order to support lesbian choices, talents, sensibilities, lives, and analyses at the same level of cultural centrality as certain gay male ones: as women of every kind are tangential to the dominant canons of the culture, so *gay* women are, and at a terrible price to the vibrance and wealth of the culture. Men who write openly as gay men have also often been excluded from the consensus of the traditional canon, and may operate more forcefully now within a specifically gay/lesbian canon. Within every other minority canon as well, however, the work of gay/lesbian inquiry imperatively requires to be done. We can't know in advance about the Harlem Renaissance, any more than we can about the New England Renaissance or the English or Italian Renaissance, where the limits of a revelatory inquiry are to be set, once we begin to ask— as it is now beginning to be asked about each of these renaissances— where and how the power in them of gay desires, people, discourses, prohibitions, and energies were manifest. We know enough already, however, to know with certainty that in each of these renaissances, they were central. No doubt that's how we will learn to recognize a renaissance when we see one.

Notes

Parts of this essay appeared in the Winter 1989 volume of *SAQ*. The essay is part of my book, *Epistemology of the Closet* (Berkeley: University of California Press, 1990).

1 Jonathan Ned Katz, *Gay/Lesbian Almanac: A New Documentary* (New York, 1983), 145–50.
2 Jeffrey Weeks, *Sexuality and Its Discontents* (London, 1985), quoted in Simon Watney, "The Rhetoric of AIDS," *Screen 27* (January–February 1986): 77.
3 Allan Bloom, *The Closing of the American Mind: How Higher Education Has Failed Democracy and Impoverished the Souls of Today's Students* (New York, 1987), 236.
4 Ibid., 237, 99, 50–51.
5 Ibid., 235.
6 Ibid., 283.
7 Ibid.
8 *The Advocate*, 19 July 1988, 27.
9 Ibid., 13 September 1988, 10.
10 Ibid., 30 August 1988, 30.
11 Ibid., 21 June 1988, 16–17.
12 Ibid., 26 April 1988, 24.
13 Ibid., 26 April 1988, 30–31.
14 Ibid., 1 March 1988, 27.
15 Ibid., 8 December 1987, 20.
16 A. Damien Martin, "Young, Gay, and Afraid," *New York Times*, 1 September 1988.

Alexander Nehamas

Serious Watching

Traditionalist critics of recent developments in American universities are fond of comparing the current situation to the past—that is, in most cases, to their own student days. Gertrude Himmelfarb, for example, recalls a time when, in contrast to today,

> it was considered the function of the university to encourage students to rise above the material circumstances of their lives, to liberate them intellectually and spiritually by exposing them, as the English poet Matthew Arnold put it, to "the best which has been thought and said in the world."[1]

Nostalgia has colored not only Professor Himmelfarb's perception of the past, but also her recollection of Arnold, who actually wrote that the "business" of criticism is "to know the best that is known and thought in the world."[2] We can dismiss Himmelfarb's other inaccuracies, but we cannot overlook her replacement of Arnold's present-tense "is" by the perfect-tense "has been." For this allows her to appeal to Arnold's authority in order to insinuate, if not to argue outright, that the university's concern is with the past and that the present, at least in connection with the humanities, lies largely outside the scope of its function.

Such emphasis on the past does not exclude attention to contemporary works of fine art or philosophy, which can generally be shown to be part of what is often in this context called "the" tradition. But it does disenfranchise present-day cultural products that cannot readily be connected with that tradition. This is especially true of works of popular art, particularly television. These are either totally overlooked, as is the case in our philosophy of art, or disparaged, not only by highbrow critics like Allan Bloom but also by the very people whose livelihood depends upon them.[3] In this way, J. R. Ewing, the hero/villain of *Dallas*, "the man everybody loves to hate," turns out to be the perfect metaphor for the medium that sustains him.

But though it is devoted to the past, this approach is historically blind. Its adherents consider Plato, Homer, and the Greek tragic poets equally parts of the tradition, but they fail to realize that Plato's uncompromising exclusion of the poets from the perfect state of the *Republic* proceeds from exactly the same motives and manifests precisely the same structure as their own rejection of contemporary popular culture. The paradigms of one age's high culture often began their life as entertainment for the masses of another.[4] Our seemingly unified tradition is significantly more complex and inconsistent than we tend to believe. And examining the popular artworks of our day is crucial for understanding the operations by means of which they are invested with value and the conditions under which they too can come to be assimilated (as some always are) into the fine arts and into high culture.

Such considerations aside, however, highbrow critics of television can also be answered in their own terms. This is the point of my essay: television rewards serious watching. Serious watching, in turn, disarms many of the criticisms commonly raised against television.

The common criticisms of television, though they are united in their disdain for the medium, come from various directions and have differing points. Wayne Booth, for example, expresses a relatively traditional preference for primarily linguistic over mainly visual works:

It is hard to see how anyone can eliminate the fundamental difference between media in which some kind of physical reality has established a scene *before* the viewer starts to work on it, and those like radio and print that can use language only for description—language that is always no more than an invitation to thought and imagination, never a solid presentation or finished reality. . . . The video arts tell us precisely what we should see, but their resources are thin and cumbersome for stimulating our moral and philosophical range.[5]

It is worth pointing out, but necessary to leave aside, the ironic and twisted connection between this view and the famous passage of the *Phaedrus* in which books are criticized for lacking, in comparison to the spoken word, just the features for which Booth praises them:

You know, Phaedrus, that's the strange thing about writing, which makes it truly analogous to painting. The painter's products stand before us as though they were still alive, but if you question them, they maintain a most majestic silence. It is the same with written words; they seem to talk to you as though they were intelligent, but if you ask them anything about what they say, from a desire to be instructed they go on telling you just the same thing forever.[6]

This parallel is very important in its own right and should be studied in detail.[7] But what concerns me now is simply Booth's claim that the video arts are inherently incapable of addressing serious "moral and philosophical" issues.

A related criticism is made by John Cawelti, whose celebrated study of the arts of popular culture, particularly of formulaic literature, has led him to conclude that

formulaic works necessarily stress intense and immediate kinds of excitement and gratification as opposed to the more complete and ambiguous analyses of character and motivation that characterize mimetic literature. . . . Formulaic works stress action and plot.

He also considers that "a major characteristic of formulaic literature is the dominant influence of the goals of escape and entertainment."[8] The contrast here is one between the straightforward, repetitive, action-oriented, and entertaining formulaic works which by
and large belong to popular culture—works which include the products of television—and the ambiguous, innovative, psychologically
motivated and edifying works of high art.

Finally, Catherine Belsey, who has approached the study of literature from a Marxist point of view, following the work of Louis
Althusser, draws a contrast between "classic realism, still the dominant popular mode in literature, film, and television" which is characterized by "illusionism, narrative which leads to closure, and a
hierarchy of discourses which establishes the 'truth' of the story,"
and what she calls "the interrogative text." The interrogative text,
she writes,

> may well be fictional, but the narrative does not lead to that
> form of closure which in Classical Realism is also disclosure. . . .
> If it is illusionist it also tends to employ devices to undermine the
> illusion, to draw attention to its own textuality. . . . Above all,
> [it] differs from the classical realist text in the absence of a single
> privileged discourse which contains and places all the others.[9]

It would be easy to cite many other similar passages, but the main
themes of the attack against television, to which those other passages would provide only variations, are all sounded by these three
authors: (1) given its formulaic nature, television drama is simple
and action-oriented; it makes few demands of its audience and offers
them quick and shallow gratification; (2) given its visual, nonlin-
guistic character, it is unsuited for providing psychological and philosophical depth; and (3) given its realist tendencies, it fails to make
its own fictional nature one of its themes. It is therefore self-effacing
and constructs an artificial point of view from which all its various
strands can appear to be put together and unified; it thus reinforces
the idea that problems in the world can be solved as easily as they are
solved in fiction and it domesticates its audience. These reasons are
taken to show that television does not deserve serious critical atten-

tion—or that, if it does, it should only be criticized on ideological grounds.

And yet there are reasons to be suspicious of this view, which can all be based on a serious look, for example, at *St. Elsewhere*—a television drama that appears straightforward, action-oriented, and realistic.

My discussion of *St. Elsewhere* often concerns individual episodes or scenes. Nevertheless, my main concern will be with the series as a whole. As I have already argued elsewhere, the object of criticism in broadcast television drama is primarily the series and not its individual episodes.[10] But, of course, individual episodes are all we ever see, and it is by watching them in sufficient numbers that we become familiar with the series as a whole. A large part of the dissatisfaction with television drama, I think, is due precisely to a failure to appreciate this point. By concentrating exclusively on individual episodes, the critics of television are incapable of seeing where, as it were, the impact of the medium occurs and are therefore unable to be affected by it. Character, for example, is manifested through particular occurrences in particular episodes; but each manifestation is thin and two-dimensional, until we realize that thickness and depth are added to it if (and only if) it is seen *as* a manifestation of character which can be understood and appreciated only over time and through many such manifestations. In this respect, television is not unlike the comic strip, in regard to which Umberto Eco has written:

> a structural fact that is of fundamental importance in the understanding of comics in general [is that] the brief daily or weekly story, the traditional strip, even if it narrates an episode that concludes in the space of four panels, will not work if considered separately; rather it acquires flavor only in the continuous and obstinate series, which unfolds, strip after strip, day after day.[11]

There are, in fact, many similarities between cartoons and at least some television series, especially those filmed before an audience, and this is in my opinion partly responsible for the low regard in which many high-minded critics hold the latter. The stiffness of the poses held by the television actors, the necessity of their half-facing the camera, the inability of the television image to give great detail and its lack of visual texture, the narrow angles and small groups which it can only accommodate, and the staccato rhythm in which lines are often delivered with pauses for laughter or applause are all features that make of television shows cartoons that are animated in a literal sense of the term.

=======

Whatever its connections to the cartoon, television has always been thought to be inherently realistic, not only by high-culture intellectuals but by its own creators as well. During the first years of broadcast television, documentation seemed absolutely essential for drama as well as for comedy. For example, *Medic*, the very first medical show, was, according to a recent discussion, a "highly realistic examination of surgery. The program sought to document medical case histories and used some actual hospital usage."[12] *Medic* was written by Jim Moser, a friend and ex-collaborator of Jack Webb, whose show, *Dragnet*, was also supposedly based on "actual files of the L.A.P.D."; the connection was responsible for *Medic* coming to be known as "Drugnet." The very first situation comedy, *Mary Kay and Johnny*, which opened in 1947, starred an actual married couple, whose child, born after the show was already on the air, was incorporated into the plot and thus set the pattern made famous by Lucille Ball as well as by the Nelsons in *The Ozzie and Harriet Show*. The episodes of the police show *Gangbusters* were based on "actual police and FBI files"; they concluded by airing a photograph of one of FBI's "most wanted" criminals with instructions to call the FBI or the show itself with information about them, thus anticipating the current mania for interactive programs of this sort.[13] Finally, in one of the most absurd cases of the search for verisimilitude, *Noah's Ark*, produced by Jack Webb and featuring a "messianic veterinarian," was based on "actual cases" from the files of the Southern California Veterinary Association and the American Humane Society.

Whether such a mixture of documentation and fictional narrative produces or undermines realism is a complex question. For the moment, I simply want to point out that in the 1960s and 1970s such obvious attempts to incorporate reality into television gave way to a more straightforward melodramatic mode. The mythical quality of melodrama, however, was soon infected with reality once again: a new realism from two new directions, which resulted from the intervention of two very different television authors.

Now the term "author" may well seem inappropriate here, for, among all the arts, television seems to be the most authorless. Most dramatic series are written by different people, or groups of people, each week, and it is very difficult to know precisely who is to receive the credit or the blame for a show's success or failure. In an effort to determine who is finally responsible for the character of each program, Todd Gitlin has argued that while in the film (as Bazin and others have claimed) this role, the *auteur*, belongs to the director, in television the relevant role is played by the producer, perhaps the only person who provides continuity in a show and who determines the overall look of the program.[14] This view is at least partly correct: *Hill Street Blues* (Gitlin's primary concern) and *L.A. Law* are indeed Steven Bochco's creatures, as *Miami Vice* belongs to Michael Mann. If this is a view we accept, then we can say that a crucial factor in the development of American television was the work of Norman Lear, who was responsible for the nature and success of shows like *All in the Family*, *Maude*, *The Jeffersons*, and *Mary Hartmann, Mary Hartmann* (which was actually so parodic that not even he could sell it to the networks). In his various shows, Lear introduced acute social commentary and thematized complex social and political issues through the previously innocuous format of the classic situation comedy. A particularly interesting feature of Lear's work was that it was very difficult to tell where exactly his shows' sympathies lie: "Liberals and radicals tended to interpret *All In the Family* as a left-liberal critique of bigotry and conservatism, while conservative audiences tended to identify with Archie Bunker and to see the series as a vindication of Archie's rejection of his 'meathead' son-in-law's liberalism."[15] This indeterminacy of television is to a great extent dictated precisely by the medium's immense popularity and its need to appeal to an extremely heterogeneous audience. It argues against the facile charge that television "totalizes" its narrative point of view, for, in order to be susceptible to such varying interpretations, the television "text" must be essentially incomplete and open to radical interpretation on the part of its audience (which thereby shows itself to be much more active in its reaction to the medium than our stereotypes often suggest).

Another realistic element in recent television drama is associated not with a person but with a whole production company, MTM Productions, which is behind shows like *The Mary Tyler Moore Show, Rhoda, Phyllis, The Bob Newhart Show, Lou Grant, WKRP in Cincinnati, Hill Street Blues,* and *St. Elsewhere.* MTM Productions was headed by Grant Tinker, but Tinker was not associated with the character of his many shows as directly as Lear was with his. In a serious way, credit for these programs goes to the production company rather than to any individual. And this in turn raises the interesting possibility that the television author need not only *not* be an individual but also that it need not always be an object of the same ontological order: both a concrete individual and an abstract entity—a company —can play the relevant role. Three features of MTM productions are relevant to my account.

First, these shows shifted in many cases the location of the situation comedy from the home, where the genre had been truly at home, to the workplace. But the MTM workplace—a television station, a doctor's office, a police precinct, a country inn, an inner-city hospital—always operates as the locus of an extended family within which individual characters face, defer, or resolve innumerable personal problems. The humor of these shows is less biting, less abusive, and less overtly political than the humor of Norman Lear. Part of their overall message seems to be that one's most real family consists not so much of the people with whom one lives but rather of the people with whom one works. Many characters have restrained personal lives; many are unhappy at home; and happy families, as in both of Bob Newhart's shows, are continuous with the family of the workplace.

Second, in contrast to earlier television drama and following the precedent established by *M*A*S*H*, many of these shows allow for, and depend upon, character development. Characteristically, during the opening season of *The Mary Tyler Moore Show*, the program's title song asked of its heroine "How will you make it on your own?" In later seasons, this was changed to "You're gonna make it on your own," and eventually, in line with Mary Richards's increasing independence, any reference to this issue was dropped altogether.[16]

Finally, other MTM shows followed the lead of *Hill Street Blues*, which was in this respect influenced by the conventions of daytime soap operas and introduced multiple story lines in individual episodes. These stories would often be carried over a number of episodes but, contrary to the situation in soap operas, they would always be resolved. The possibility of containing multiple plot lines naturally depends on the existence of a relatively large cast. Accordingly, programs like *Hill Street Blues* and *St. Elsewhere* ceased to function around a single central figure and developed into "ensemble shows" featuring many actors, each one of whom has relatively little time in front of the camera.[17]

With these ideas in mind, we can now turn to *St. Elsewhere*, which concerns life in a large inner-city hospital in Boston. The show seems straightforward, action-oriented, and realistic. It is full of local color. It is a serious program, addressing complex medical and moral issues (it was the first television show, for example, to present a series of episodes concerning AIDS) in the liberal manner of *M*A*S*H* and *Lou Grant*, but it is also bitingly, parodically funny. For example, during a title sequence a group of hospital personnel are shown hurrying a life-support machine down a corridor in what clearly seems an urgent situation. Now television doctors do occasionally fail their patients: even Dr. Welby lost a few. But, traditionally, these were always cases of nature asserting itself over technology. Here, however, the attempt fails because, in all their dispatch and intensity, the interns clumsily stumble and end up, along with their machine, sprawled across the hospital floor. The fact that this is a scene in the title sequence, and that it is repeated week after week, fixes it in the mind of the program's audience and allows the incident to manifest a feature not only of St. Eligius but of hospitals in general, so that the scene appears realistic as well as funny: things like that do happen, more often than we like to think, in hospitals.

St. Elsewhere lacks the unrelenting technological and humanistic optimism of *Marcus Welby, M.D.* Patients die there, and often there are no lessons in their deaths. The physicians not only help but also cheat and seduce each other. None of the ultimate positions of power in the hospital is occupied by a woman. This, in fact, becomes one of the show's themes, especially when a woman—and a Vietnamese refugee at that—replaces the obnoxious, racist, sexist but technically superb chief of surgery, Mark Craig, when he smashes his hand in a fit of pique and self-doubt. Craig's sexism, which causes a breakdown in his marriage, is consistently addressed in the show, along with his wife's efforts to find a job, a life, and a voice of her own. One of the residents is a former nurse who realized that she could do a physician's job as well as or even better than many of the men who practice medicine. The program features a very successful black doctor, a *summa cum laude* graduate of Yale and chief resident at St. Eligius; a highly motivated black orderly who moves up to paramedic and then to physician's assistant before he realizes that that is as far as he can go; and a friend of his who is content to remain an orderly. For these and many other similar reasons, *St. Elsewhere*, compared to *Marcus Welby, M.D.*, *Dr. Kildare*, or *Ben Casey*, appears to be much more accurate to life within the medical profession.

It is imperative, however, to note the terms of this comparison. The realism of *St. Elsewhere* is measured by comparing it not to life within a hospital, of which most of us know almost nothing, but to the standards and features of earlier shows on the same general subject. On the other hand, there does seem to be something inherently more realistic in a show that features a hospital not in some idealized suburban setting but in the middle of Boston. The fact that the Red Line runs right next to St. Eligius, moreover, places the hospital in the location of the Massachusetts General Hospital, which adds a further touch of verisimilitude—until one realizes that far from being based upon the latter, St. Eligius is constantly being contrasted with it under its fictional name of "Boston General." St. Eligius, in fact, seems modeled on Boston City Hospital. Boston is a real presence—a character—in this program: the governor of Massachusetts appears in one episode, the city's racial conflicts are often addressed, Harvard looms large. And yet this is a very peculiar Boston. For one thing, it contains a bar named "Cheers." And, on one occasion, the show's three patriarchal figures go to this bar, whose fictional existence also involves a very "real" Boston, to drink and talk things over. To complicate matters further, in one episode a resident of St. Eligius passes by the actual bar in Boston which advertises itself as the place which inspired "Cheers," and takes his little son in after asking him, in an allusion to the theme song of that show, whether he wants to eat "where everybody knows your name."

This is, then, an impossible Boston, however realistic its representation appears. Realism in a case like this is indeed measured not by proximity to reality but by distance from fiction whose conventions we have come to see as conventions. At the time, of course, the conventions of the early medical shows were invisible, just as many of the conventions of *St. Elsewhere* will only become visible in the future, and the shows certainly seemed realistic. But even here the situation is complicated: the relationship between program and reality may be more ambiguous, and the television audience may be more aware of this ambiguity, than we are apt to suppose.

George Gerbner and Larry Gross, for example, report that over the first five years of Dr. Welby's television practice the show received roughly 250,000 letters, most of them requesting medical advice.[18] Their conclusion is that viewers consider television characters "as representative of the real world." But consider the fact that people still write letters to Sherlock Holmes at 221B Baker Street (in fact, the firm that occupies that address employs someone just to answer them); yet surely no one aware of Holmes believes that he is an actual person: rather, it is more plausible to suspect that the people writing Holmes engage in a game that exploits Holmes's ambiguous status, his fictional genius and his "actual" address. The same idea is also suggested by the practices of television fan magazines, which explicitly mix information about the various characters of the soap operas with information about the actors who portray them in such a way that it is difficult to separate one from the other. The television audience seems to be enjoying the equivocal interpenetration of fiction and reality. As John Fiske writes in regard to the fan magazines,

> we must be careful not to let the "cultural dope" fallacy lead us to believe that the soap fans are incapable of distinguishing between character and player. . . . This is an intentional illusion, a conspiracy entered into by viewer and journalist in order to increase the pleasure of the program. . . . The reader [is encouraged

into] the delusion of realism not just to increase the pleasure of that delusion, but also to increase the activeness and sense of control that go with it.[19]

If the Boston of *St. Elsewhere* contains both the Red Line and the Red Sox on the one hand and Cheers on the other, it is and it is not a real city. And if this is so, then it is difficult to agree with Belsey's view that "illusionism" and lack of self-awareness are deeply characteristic of television drama. In fact, *St. Elsewhere* mixes fiction so thoroughly with life and is so sensitive to what is now being called "intertextuality" that only ignorance of the medium of television could ever have suggested that the program is naively and straightforwardly realistic. This becomes even more obvious when we realize that only someone familiar with television—a literate viewer—can understand that Cheers is explicitly fictional and that the realistic episode involving the bar and its character is doubly impossible.

═══

Pierre Bourdieu, who objects to paying television "serious" attention, argues that aesthetic approaches to the medium mystify its cultural role and conceal its real importance. In all popular entertainment, as opposed to the fine arts, Bourdieu writes,

> the desire to enter into the game, identifying with the characters' joys and sufferings, worrying about their fate, espousing the hopes and ideals, living their life, is based on a form of *investment*, a sort of deliberate "naivety," ingenuousness, good-natured credulity ("we're here to enjoy ourselves") which tends to accept formal experiments and specifically artistic effects only to the extent that they can be forgotten and do not get in the way of the substance of the work.[20]

Similarly, Herbert Gans writes that members of lower "cultural taste groups" (to which the television audience by and large is supposed to belong) choose their form of entertainment "for the feelings and enjoyment it evokes and for the insight and information they can obtain; they are less concerned with how a work of art is created."[21] Such reactions to entertainment, according to Bourdieu, are the very opposite of the detachment of the aesthete who . . . introduces a distance, a gap—the measure of his distant distinction—*vis-à-vis* "first-degree" perception by displacing the interest from the "content" . . . to the "form," to the specifically artistic effects that are only appreciated *relationally*, through a comparison with other works which is incompatible with immersion in the singularity of the work immediately given.[22]

Based on this distinction between "investment" and "distance," between "immediacy" and "relationality," Bourdieu repudiates aesthetic interpretation and criticism because he considers them self-deceptive:

> Specifically aesthetic conflicts about the legitimate vision of the world . . . are political conflicts (appearing in their most euphemized form) for the power to impose the dominant definition of reality, and social reality in particular.[23]

But Bourdieu's distinction between the immediate enjoyment of popular art by the lower classes and the comparative attitude of the distant aesthete cannot be maintained. The television audience is highly literate (more literate about its medium than many high-culture audiences are about theirs) and makes essential use of its literacy in its appreciation of individual episodes or whole series. Its enjoyment, therefore, is both active and comparative. Consider the following case.

A regular secondary character on *St. Elsewhere* during the 1985 season was an amnesiac, referred to as John Doe. Having failed to regain his memory and find out who he is, Doe, who is a patient in St. Eligius's psychiatric ward, turns obsessively to television. But though his conversation is riddled with lines derived from commercials, his real interest is in the news programs: "Newscasters—*they* know who they are," he insists to his psychiatrist, Dr. Weiss. Weiss, who is concerned with Doe's state of mind, finally tells him not to watch the news any longer: "It's too depressing. I want you to watch shows that lift your soul and put a smile on your face."

Another character on this particular program is the passive-aggressive Mr. Carlin, who loves to torture Doe. Mr. Carlin, portrayed by the same actor, was a regular character in *The Bob Newhart Show*, in which Newhart, a psychologist, was treating him for his (at the time) milder disorder. But Bob apparently failed, and Mr. Carlin has been committed, finding himself in a hospital in a different show.

Doe and Mr. Carlin fight over the television set in the ward lounge, incessantly switching channels. Doe finally gets reconciled to fictional shows, and even tells Carlin that television is "filled with real people." "And they're only *this* tall," Carlin replies, placing his thumb and forefinger six inches apart. "Television is the mirror of our soul," Doe insists; "we look in and we see who we really are." And as he switches from one famous program to another, he catches for a moment the very end of *The Mary Tyler Moore Show* and the logo of MTM Productions (itself a parodic reference to MGM's famous trademark, and, in its substitution of a kitten for MGM's lion, a whole parable of the relationship between film and television). MTM Productions, of course, is responsible not only for *The Mary Tyler Moore Show* but also for *The Bob Newhart Show* as well as for *St. Elsewhere*. As soon as he sees the MTM kitten, John Doe loudly claims that he now knows who he is: he is Mary Richards, Mary Tyler Moore's character. He instantly goes into character, dons a beret like Mary's, identifies various patients and physicians with characters from that show (Mr. Carlin, for example, becomes Rhoda, Mary's friend, though he nastily refuses to play along; Dr. Weiss, naturally enough, is Mr. Grant; Dr. Auschlander, the senior figure in the hospital and quite bald, becomes Murray, and so on), and develops, like Mary, a profound devotion to his new extended family for whom, in Mary's manner, he immediately prepares a party: "Sometimes the people you work with aren't just the people you work with," he tells Dr. Weiss, echoing the main theme not only of *The Mary Tyler Moore Show* but also of *St. Elsewhere*.

Auschlander is worried about Weiss's decision to go along with Doe's fantasy, and seems to be slightly embarrassed at having to appear at Doe's party as Murray. He is disdainful of the television audience in general, echoing at least some of the complaints I have introduced into this discussion. "People sit in front of their televisions," he says, "believing the characters they see there actually exist, eat, breathe, sleep." But when Weiss asks him which character *he* would like to be if he had the choice (which of course he doesn't, since he already is one), he unhesitatingly replies that he would like to be Trapper John, M.D.—a doctor with a reassuring manner who invariably saves his patients, the very kind of doctor *St. Elsewhere* will not allow to exist within its own fictional space and which, from within its own fiction, is thereby asserted to be more "real" than its competitors.

As part of an independent subplot, an astronaut is being treated in St. Eligius for a case of paralysis. The astronaut, however, has also announced that on his next space mission he will walk hand in hand with God. The Navy has sent one of its medical officers to bring the astronaut to earth and to Bethesda. This Navy doctor, who has already appeared in an earlier, unrelated episode of *St. Elsewhere* and who has thus established her "independent" identity, is portrayed by Betty White. As she is on her way to visit Dr. Weiss, she runs into Doe, who immediately exclaims, "Sue Anne! The Happy Homemaker!", recognizing the actress Betty White as the character she was in *The Mary Tyler Moore Show*. Betty White, naturally, responds with a blank stare and a vague "I am afraid you have me confused with someone else."

Doe's party turns out to be a success, but this causes him to start doubting his new identity: "Mary always throws lousy parties," he confesses; "maybe I am not Mary." At that point, Mr. Carlin gets into a fight with another patient, and Doe runs to help him out, attacking this other patient, whom he identifies as "Mr. Coleman," the station manager who, when *The Mary Tyler Moore Show* was cancelled, was supposed to have fired its main characters. "I've committed a violent act," Doe says. "Mary would never do that." Carlin, moved by Doe's friendship, abandons his nastiness and decides to play along with him: "Call me Rhoda," he suggests. But Doe responds (in a way that still mixes fiction and life), "No. I am not Mary. We've just been cancelled."

The next morning, Doe goes for a walk with Dr. Auschlander, who reassures him that his many friends will help him find out who he is. At the hospital's main entrance, Doe, calm, peaceful, and happy, says "I'm gonna make it after all," and in an exact parallel to the final shot of the title sequence of *The Mary Tyler Moore Show*, tosses his beret in the air, replicating Mary in word and deed in the very process of liberating himself from her. Television and reality, fiction and life, character and person are intermixed through and through.

Only a literate and active audience could ever appreciate or even get the point of this ingenious use of intertextuality. Its point is not necessarily deep, though it does ask whom television characters are supposed to resemble, to what reality they correspond, and to whom —actor or character—one is responding in watching and enjoying a program. All these are questions important to ask and difficult to answer, and they make of this episode as "interrogative," self-conscious, and self-reflexive a work as any high-culture critic might possibly wish. But to be part of the high culture is not necessarily to be cultured, and to know much about literature is not necessarily to be literate.

St. Elsewhere lives by confounding fiction and life. During one of the show's last seasons, in an effort to improve ratings, its producers seemed to have decided that the old-fashioned hospital's seedy beige-and-brown background was failing to attract an audience getting used to the pastels made popular by shows like *Miami Vice*. They brought the look of their show in line with that of other high-profile programs by means of a brilliant move: they had the problem-ridden St. Eligius bought by a private hospital chain. And the first thing the chain did was to renovate the building, which provided the show with a postmodernist set and a whole new narrative dimension.

The fictional hospital company was called "Ecumena" and was immensely interested in artificial heart transplants. The Humana Corporation, on which Ecumena was obviously based, objected to the whole idea, especially because Ecumena was depicted as a cold, impersonal, profit-obsessed enterprise. They succeeded in getting a disclaimer added to the closing credits, and they finally won an injunction against the use of the word "Ecumena." The name had to go. *St. Elsewhere* characteristically responded by mixing fact and fiction. Within the show, a nameless hospital company sued Ecumena on the grounds that their name was too close to theirs and won. The chain is renamed "Weiggert Hospitals" and as the Ecumena sign is being removed from the entrance to St. Eligius, it slips from the workers, falls to the ground, splinters into countless fragments, and almost kills the hospital administrator, a devoted and often heartless employee of the chain, who looks in disgust and mutters, echoing the show's producers, "It's been that kind of day from the beginning."

═════

In order to know where to look in order to locate the psychological power of broadcast television, we must concentrate on two features on account of which the medium has often been criticized. The first is that broadcast television works by repetition. We meet the same characters in the same general circumstances though in varying specific situations week after week over a long period of time. The second is that the television camera can cover only a small visual angle and this, together with the low resolution of the television image, requires a large number of close-up shots. For many, this is equivalent to saying that television is visually elementary and intellectually boring.

And yet some of the medium's greatest achievements depend on these two features. For the first allows us to become acquainted with television characters gradually and over a long period of time and the second enables us to come, in an almost physical sense, very close to them. And this closeness is not only physical. Our continuous exposure to these characters also brings us close to them in a psychological sense. Just as the characters of *St. Elsewhere* interact with one another every fictional day, so the audience comes to know them slowly, routinely, in a more or less controlled situation, not unlike the way in which they know the people they themselves work with. To a serious extent the relationship of the characters to one another replicates the relationship of these characters to their audience and the relationship of many members of that audience to the people they in turn work with. We come to know these characters, and many of the characters of television drama generally, *intimately*—in both a physical and a psychological sense. But to say that we come to know them intimately is not to say that we come to know them deeply. Their innermost nature, unlike the nature of the characters of novels, is not exposed; better put, television characters have no innermost nature. And yet, I want to suggest, the intimacy with which these not deep characters are revealed is one of the medium's glories.

Many of the people we know best in life often move or infuriate us by some particular gesture or action the significance of which is very difficult to communicate to others because, as we say, "it has to be seen in context." The same is often the case when we try to recount a funny, moving, or nasty moment in a television program to someone who is not familiar with it. In one episode of *St. Elsewhere*, for example, Donald Westphall, St. Eligius's chief of medicine, gets fired by the company representative. Mark Craig, who has always derided Westphall for being weak, boring, a do-gooder, and stubborn, continues to mock him for not apologizing and asking for his job back. When Westphall asks him why he cares whether he leaves or not, Craig, who is at the point of leaving the room, stops, turns, and, in a tone as supercilious as it is confessional, replies, "I'll miss you. Ridiculous as it may sound, you're the best friend I have." This is a moving and poignant moment, but it is difficult to say why, precisely because it is a *moment*, a small part of a complex relationship, and it is only within that relationship that it acquires whatever significance it has.

St. Elsewhere works through the accumulation of such moments, and allows its audience to come to know its characters intimately but not deeply—just as these characters themselves know one another in the extended familial space of their workplace. Such knowledge can be extremely fine-grained, but it depends essentially on long exposure. One must have learned, over time and through a large number of isolated incidents, precisely what a prude Westphall is in order to understand exactly what he does when, just before leaving the hospital and upon being told that he can have his job back provided he becomes a "team player," he turns his back and drops his pants in the face of the hospital administrator.

We might be tempted to say that even without knowledge of Westphall's character we do know what he does, though we may not know exactly what it means. But this is misleading, because it suggests that there is one level on which his action is described and another on which it is interpreted, because it separates description from interpretation. It is much more nearly correct to say that we literally do not know what Westphall does on this occasion unless we see it in light of everything else he has ever done. Television, because of its serial character, highlights the essential interconnection of human actions—a psychological point—and the interdependence of their description and interpretation—a philosophical issue: Is it really true to say that it is "thin and cumbersome in stimulating our moral and philosophical range"?

The serial unfolding of character and the ability of individual characters (at least in some programs) to change and develop with time have an important consequence. They render character ambiguous. By this I do not mean that television characters are difficult to understand. Rather, the point is that television can present various aspects of its characters without offering a single, all-encompassing judgment about their ultimate nature or worth. This is another sense in which television characters have no depth.

Mark Craig, the chief of surgery at St. Eligius, for example, is a terrific surgeon and a horrible sexist. *St. Elsewhere* does not account for his sexism in any way that justifies it. Craig is also brusque, selfish, insensitive, and competitive, but also fiercely loyal to, and proud of, his residents. He is, in addition, insecure and more in need of others than he could possibly admit. He both loves and detests his son, who was addicted to drugs, married beneath him, and got killed in a car accident. We learn all this, and more besides, about him over a long period of time in a way not unrelated to that in which we come to know many of our friends and acquaintances. The net result of this gradual accumulation of detail is that there is no net result about Craig's character. It is difficult, perhaps impossible, and certainly not fruitful to say of him, or of most of the characters in this program, whether we like or dislike him. We may be devoted to him in the sense of wanting to know what he will be doing in the next episode, but approval or disapproval are not at issue. Do I *like* him? How can I, given his sexism, his crassness, his lack of sensitivity? Do I *dislike* him? No, because I do like his clipped manner, his pride in his work, his frightening straightforwardness. His character has too many sides for me to make a general evaluation of it. But where I see the absence of "totalization," others may not. And they may well like or dislike Craig, often for exactly the same reasons in each case. The television text is, in this sense, indeterminate. It allows its viewers to focus on different aspects of the characters it depicts and to see the same character in radically different ways depending on their own preferences and values. It is, as John Fiske, echoing Roland Barthes, characterizes it, a "producerly" text—subject to various operations on the part of its viewers.

Similar things can be said about the show's female characters. Nurse Papandreou, for example, can be an absolute terror, nasty and full of invective. She is also unquestionably a superb nurse. She terrifies the obnoxious Victor Ehrlich, but she also brings out the best in him (the little of it there is) when she relaxes in his company at a Greek feast, invites him up to her apartment afterward, and eventually marries him. And, once married, she shows a perceptive and mature side in her relationship to him which, precisely because it does not carry over into her other interactions, makes it impossible— for me, at least—to make a general judgment about her. Is she a good or a bad character? What about most of the people with whom we live and work on a daily basis? We live and work with one another, and toward most of them we have no single unequivocal reaction.

Classical realism, according to Catherine Belsey, always creates an overarching point of view from which all the pieces of each story can be seen to fall together. I have just argued that, at least on a psychological level, *St. Elsewhere* undermines any effort to occupy such a point of view. And just for this reason, *St. Elsewhere* reveals that its medium has the resources for presenting unusual aspects of human character—unusual enough to pass completely unnoticed if we are not willing to watch seriously.

Is *St. Elsewhere*, however, realistic in the further sense that its aim is to achieve "closure," to provide on a narrative level a final settlement of all the details of its plot and to put its viewers in the comfortable position of having finished *with* the story as well as simply having finished it? Jane Feuer has argued that *All in the Family* aimed at that goal: "The Lear family, however much they were divided along political lines, would each week be reintegrated in order that a new enigma could be introduced."[24] In fact, however, this was not quite true of *All in the Family*. Often the show's episodes end with an extreme close-up of Archie Bunker, who has just been rendered speechless by losing an argument. But speechlessness is not accommodation. And the look on Archie's face—part admission of defeat, part stubborn reassertion of his inner conviction that he is always right—allows viewers of different political orientations to draw their own different conclusions about the very nature of the episode they have just watched.

St. Elsewhere, however, appears to provide just the kind of closure Belsey associates with classical realism. The program was cancelled at the end of the 1987–88 season. Since this was known in advance, the show's final four episodes were devoted to constructing a complete resolution of its various subplots and to disposing properly of every single one of its regular characters. Manifesting a remarkable and unusual single-mindedness, *St. Elsewhere*, with the exception of those who died, created a future for all its characters and left absolutely no loose ends. Or so it seemed until the show's final scene.

Throughout the last episode, which is supposed to occur in the spring, the characters keep remarking that the temperature is dropping and that it is about to snow. At first these remarks are so out of place that they pass unnoticed until their cumulative weight makes them as impossible to ignore as they are to understand. Indeed, snow begins to fall. We see the hospital in the middle of a snowstorm, and the camera pans in order to take in the whole building—a shot which strongly disposes us to expect that the show has come to its end. But as the pan continues, and the building gets progressively smaller, it also, inexplicably, begins to shake. And suddenly we realize that what we are seeing is not at all the "real" hospital but only a cardboard cutout enclosed in a glass paperweight and surrounded by "artificial" snowflakes.

Whose toy is this? It belongs to Tommy, Dr. Westphall's autistic son, who was looking at the snowfall from inside the hospital in the scene immediately preceding. Tommy, completely absorbed, is sitting on the floor shaking the paperweight. But can this be Westphall's son? He is sitting in a shabby room and not in Westphall's suburban house, and he is being watched over by Dr. Auschlander—who cannot be Dr. Auschlander, since Dr. Auschlander died of a stroke earlier on in the episode. At that point, Westphall enters: he wears a hardhat and carries a lunch box. But, of course, this is not Westphall either: he turns out to be a construction worker and the son of the man we had known as Auschlander up to that point. Having greeted his father,

"Westphall" looks at his son and says, "I don't understand this autism thing, Pop. . . . He sits there all day long, in his own world, staring at that toy. What's he thinking about?" He then lifts the boy, places the toy exactly in the middle of the top of the television set, and leaves the room. The camera now closes in for the truly final shot of St. Eligius, encased—frozen—in its glass container.

Turning a story into a dream or a fantasy at the last moment is one of the most uninteresting ways of accounting for loose ends that could not be coherently pulled together. In this case, the whole show we have been watching for five years or so is made the content of the mind of an autistic boy—but only after every single one of its strands has been carefully, obsessively pulled tight. It is impossible for a story of such complexity to have been conceived by an autistic eleven-year-old. The ending is unbelievable. And it is also, since no loose ends had remained, unnecessary. Why, then, is it there?

It is there, I think, as a final reminder that the story was after all a fiction, as much a fiction as the fiction that an autistic boy could ever spin such a fiction. It is a reminder that just as the story of the boy's spinning such a fiction cannot be true, so every part of the show itself, everything that we have seen has been fiction, though it was fiction that, as we have seen, took its shape, its colors, its plot, and its very end—its death—from the demands of life. What is real, this ending asks, and what is fiction?

And the toy in which the boy was absorbed, left on top of the television set, now emerges as a metaphor for television and for its viewers' relation to it. It is not very flattering, if one does watch television, to see oneself described as an autistic eleven-year-old. Yet this character, the show tells us, is the show's creator, and is acknowledged as such by the other characters' awareness of the snow for which the boy is directly responsible. Who is it, this ending asks, who, along with life, gave the show its shape, its colors, and its end? How much has the viewer contributed? Is it a good or a bad thing to watch television, and to be part, and in part a creator, of its fiction?

These are heady questions, and there are many others like them. The fact that they are raised by a program like *St. Elsewhere* shows that the literate opponents of the popular media have no monopoly on literacy, and that the very notion of literacy needs to be examined anew. "Whoever begins at this point, like my readers," Nietzsche wrote, "to reflect and pursue his train of thought will not soon come to the end of it—reason enough for me to come to an end"—and for me as well, but not before I cite one more attack on his time by an author who considered it "an age, wherein the greatest part of men seem agreed to convert reading into an amusement, and to reject every thing that requires any considerable degree of attention to be comprehended."[25] Thus David Hume. But Hume's complaint is both older and more recent: it was first made by Plato and is being repeated today by countless educated people who are unaware of its provenance. It suggests that even those with the greatest knowledge of history are not necessarily the most historical of people, and that the gesture of rejecting "every thing that requires any considerable degree of attention to be comprehended" is not peculiar to "the greatest part of men"—or, rather, that it is, except that the greatest part of men, and women, includes us all.

Notes

1   Gertrude Himmelfarb, "Stanford and Duke Undercut Classical Values," *New York Times*, 5 May 1988.

2   Matthew Arnold, "The Function of Criticism at the Present Time," in *Critical Theory Since Plato*, ed. Hazard Adams (San Diego, 1971), 588.

3   Allan Bloom, *The Closing of the American Mind: How Higher Education Has Failed Democracy and Impoverished the Souls of Today's Students* (New York, 1987), 58. An article in *Applause* (February 1987), the magazine of the public television station in Philadelphia, plugging Patrick McGoohan's series *The Prisoner*, which WHYY was about to air again, closes as follows: "Watch the show when you get the chance. It's not perfect—the fashions, for example, are horribly dated. But it's very good. And for a television show, that's saying a lot" ("*The Prisoner* Returns," 23).

4   The argument for this view, stated dogmatically here, can be found in my "Plato on Imitation and Poetry in *Republic* 10," in *Plato on Beauty, Wisdom, and the Arts*, ed. J. M. E. Moravcsik and Philip Temko (Totowa, N.J., 1982), 47–78; and, with more immediate relevance for this paper, in "Plato and the Mass Media," *The Monist* 71 (Spring 1988): 214–34.

5   Wayne Booth, "The Company We Keep: Self-Making in Imaginative Art," *Daedalus* 111 (Fall 1982): 42.

6   Plato *Phaedrus* 275D, trans. Roy Hackforth (Cambridge, 1952).

7   Nehamas, "Plato and the Mass Media," 221–22.

8 John Cawelti, *Adventure, Mystery, and Romance* (Chicago, 1976), 14, 13.

9 Catherine Belsey, *Critical Practice* (London, 1980), 68, 70, 92.

10 Nehamas, "Plato and the Mass Media," 228–30.

11 Umberto Eco, "On 'Krazy Kat' and 'Peanuts,'" *New York Review of Books*, 15 June 1985.

12 Robert S. Alley, "Media Medicine and Morality," in *Understanding Television*, ed. Richard P. Adler (New York, 1981), 231.

13 David Marc, *Demographic Vistas* (Philadelphia, 1984), 73.

14 Todd Gitlin, *Inside Prime Time* (New York, 1983), 273–324.

15 Steven Best and Douglas Kellner, "(Re)Watching Television: Notes Toward a Political Criticism," *Diacritics* 17 (Summer 1987): 104.

16 On this and other instances of character development in MTM shows, see Jane Feuer, "The MTM Style," in *Television: The Critical View*, ed. Horace Newcomb (New York, 1987), 60–62.

17 See Thomas Schatz, "*St. Elsewhere* and the Evolution of the Ensemble Series," in Newcomb, ed., *Television*, 85–100.

18 George Gerbner and Larry Gross, "The Scary World of TV's Heavy Viewer," *Psychology Today*, April 1976, 44.

19 John Fiske, *Television Culture* (London, 1987), 121, 123.

20 Pierre Bourdieu, *Distinction: A Social Critique of the Judgment of Taste* (Cambridge, Mass., 1984), 32.

21 Herbert Gans, *Popular Culture and High Culture* (New York, 1974), 79.

22 Bourdieu, *Distinction*, 34.

23 Pierre Bourdieu, "The Production of Belief," in *Media, Culture and Society: A Critical Reader*, ed. R. Collins et al. (London, 1986), 154–55.

24 Jane Feuer, "Narrative Form in American Network Television," in *High Theory/Low Culture*, ed. Colin MacCabe (Manchester, 1986), 107.

25 Friedrich Nietzsche, *On the Genealogy of Morals*, trans. Walter Kaufmann (New York, 1969), 1: 17; and David Hume, *A Treatise of Human Nature*, ed. L. A. Selby-Bigge (Oxford, 1888), bk. 3, pt. 1, sec. 1, 456.

Elizabeth Kamarck Minnich

From Ivory Tower to Tower of Babel?

While many of us have been hard at work trying to bring about some of the changes in liberal arts education that have indeed taken place, others have made it evident that they would prefer to return to earlier times, to the days in which, as they like to say, "Educated men could converse together." Among the immediate causes for concern of the educated men is, of course, the opening of their club to a motley lot of others not only as students but as active professionals, and not only as professionals but as subject matter worthy of serious study. Those who were, at best, occasional objects of past restricted conversations are now speaking, constituting their/our own status and meaning as subjects. To those who are not prepared to hear us, that seems to mean not only that conversation is breaking down, but also that what they took to be the basic and "proper" relation between subject and object is threatened.

We deal here with a contemporary situation, but it has older and deeper roots. In 1951, Karl Jaspers wrote:

In all past history there was a self-evident bond between man and man, in stable communities, in institutions, and in universal ideas. Even the isolated individual was in a sense sustained in his isolation. The most visible sign of today's disintegration is that more and more men do not understand one another, that they meet and scatter, that they are indifferent to one another, that there is no longer any reliable community or loyalty. Today a universal situation that has always existed in fact assumes crucial importance: That I can, and cannot, become one with the Other in truth; that my faith, precisely when I am certain, clashes with other men's faith; that there is always somewhere a limit beyond which there appears to be nothing but battle without hope of unity.[1]

Jaspers suggests, in regard to the present context, that the malaise of those troubled by changes in the liberal arts curriculum, who fear the transformation of the ivory tower into the tower of Babel, can be seen as a manifestation of a broader malaise of our times: "this age of unprecedented ruin and of potentialities that can only be darkly surmised."[2] It is no surprise that, in such times, some cling to old certainties as if they had not vanished. But Jaspers also suggests that this historicized unease touches "a universal situation"—"that I can, and cannot, become one with the Other." That is, we are capable of apprehending, even at times perhaps comprehending, difference but not of overcoming its most fundamental expression as *alteritas*, as otherness. On that basic level, where we encounter not any particular difference but the simple fact that we, and any certainties we hold, are particular—that no one is everyone or everything—a desire we may all share for authentic communication that moves through the given boundaries between us can emerge. Those of us who were not part of earlier culture-constituting conversations and so in some ways (but by no means all) benefit from—have desired, even, and worked for —the breaking up of homogeneous communities, also know what it means to run into limits "beyond which there appears to be nothing but battle without hope of unity."

Our goal, then, as we engage the present national conversation about the liberal arts, need not be to establish who wins and who loses. It is not to reclaim old certainties, nor to reject them all and proliferate new perspectives, but, rather, to recognize that which Jaspers claims is the aim of philosophy, in which "all its other aims are ultimately rooted": *authentic* communication.

In the friction between our differing reactions to the opening of liberal arts conversations to ever more members of our polity, something very important has been generated—a great and widespread public interest in higher education. That interest is entirely appropriate. There is a critically important relationship between democracy and education. But, of course, just what that *means* is not a simple question. There are layers and layers of sedimented meanings here that are by no means coherent or consistent. More critically, there are layers and layers of differing ways of understanding how we think, how we know, how we comprehend. We have not only agreed and differed on the relationship between democracy and education, and on what those concepts and sets of practices mean. We have agreed and differed philosophically, especially (and again appropriately, considering that we deal here with education) on the level of epistemology. What we wish to discuss together is, then, by no means presented to us simply or clearly.

That could be daunting; it can also be liberating. If there is no one meaning for *democracy*, and no one meaning, either, for *liberal arts education*, then we can at least clarify the meaning of boundaries that are inadequately drawn, find passages through any that have become too impermeable.

The framers of the United States Constitution and form of government, following the Greco-Euro-Anglo male tradition, created a singular, apparently general (if not universal) abstraction—the people —which, because it was faulty, not because it was an abstraction, not because it was a general term, functioned to privilege similarity of a particular kind, similarity to a particular group of men, over difference. The new inclusiveness of the New World had exclusion built into it, not just as all inclusion does—any circle creates an outside just as it encloses an inside—but in a way that was, and is, particularly difficult to see clearly, and hence to undo. When a few members of a category are defined as the category itself—when a particular group of males become "men," and men become Man, the *singular* exemplar of Mankind—thinking about men in their plurality and difference becomes difficult, thinking about humans who are not male becomes very difficult indeed, and authentic communication among the wonderfully diverse members of humankind becomes impossible.

We are all familiar with the long history of struggle to extend the political provisions grounded in the principle that "all men are created equal" to all adult males and to any adult females. That that struggle has needed to be continued in *all* areas of the dominant culture was for a long time far less evident. In academia, it was believed, equality could pertain only to *access*. Once women and nonprivileged men were admitted to the gentlemen's club, it was believed, equality would have its due. The liberal arts themselves were concerned with knowledge, not politics; they dealt with universals, or, at least, with the disinterested quest for them of minds capable of transcending their times, their contexts. We know better today. We are ready to recognize that the dominant tradition is built not only on abstractions, generalizations, but—and this, as simple as it appears to be, is what matters—on *faulty* generalizations. The few were taken to be, and/or to be adequately representative of, all. Thus, those who were defined as different by the same dominant culture became and remain to a striking extent today not just different, but Other. What, after all, are we to do with people who are not included in "the people"? What *are* they, if they are not "people"?

There is an emblematic study that catches the effects of such foundational yet faulty abstractions all too well. The Brovermans asked one hundred clinical psychologists, psychiatric social workers, and psychologists (male and female) to describe a "normal" human, a "normal" man, and a "normal" woman. They found that the definitions of "normal" for a man and for a human coincided, while the definition of a "normal" woman differed from both. Thus, by the operative definitions of practicing psychologists, a woman can be a "normal" woman only if she is an "abnormal" human, and a "normal" human only if she is an "abnormal" woman.[3] Examples of this absurdity, which is by no means only conceptual, can be multiplied in all fields of the liberal arts. Hull, Scott, and Smith caught it very well in the title of a book they published on Black Women's Studies: *All the Women Are White, All the Blacks Are Men, But Some of Us Are Brave.*[4]

The hold and power of inadequate definitional acts—as crude as they are, once seen—are evident even in our efforts today to be inclusive. Consider the phrase, "women and minorities," by which we are supposed to understand a special subset of the citizenry. The phrase does not indicate a subset or a minority, of course. Women constitute 51 percent of humankind, and, with the male members of "minority" groups, constitute a significant majority even in this country, and certainly in the world. In terms of the curriculum, the Alice in Wonderland reversal that turns the majority into "minorities" surfaces in the odd notion that Women's Studies is less inclusive, more specialized, less essential, more partial, more politicized, less significant than studies, classes, programs that conflate a small group of Euro-American males with "mankind," and "mankind" with humankind.

We do not mean to be so sloppy in our thinking. The problem is that our thinking is in thrall to old definitional acts and their complementary politics. When a particular history, a particular strain of philosophy, a particular literature, is called History, Philosophy, Literature, the exclusions built into the founding and continuing definitions of fields as of professions do not show. Unprefixed, "History" sounds as if it refers to the thing itself; "Women's History" sounds like a particular kind of history; "African-American Women's History" sounds like a still more particular kind of history. "Euro-American Men's History"—or Literature, or Philosophy—listed without the particularizing, contextualizing prefixes attached to all other groups' studies, takes on the mantle of the universal.

But in particularizing History, or Philosophy, or anything, we seem, to some, to be particularizing *everything* such that no words, concepts, theories that claim generality, let alone universality, can be used anymore. Given that we cannot speak at all without using words that reflect a generalizing abstraction, we seem to be left speechless. *Can* we particularize without creating de novo a language unfounded on generalizations? We cannot even conceive of what that might mean. So, are we paralyzed? Of course not. We have the ability to think about our own thinking—to see, in this case, universals *as* universals, and hence to see them as a particular kind of category rather than as the limit of all thought. Universals are not the same as other categories, but insofar as we think them, they are still categories of—within—thought. And experience, including the experience of thinking, in William James's words "exceeds, surrounds, and overflows" *all* words, all concepts, all categories.[5]

There is always a *more* to what is apprehended by any human, always a slippage between experience and thought, thought and concept, concept and category. Humpty Dumpty, who tried to marshall words and make them do what *he* wanted, had a great fall. And if appeals to William James's pragmatism and to Lewis Carroll's playing with logic do not help, consider that there are already many languages in the world. We need not make up a new one if ours seems to trap us. As Walter Benjamin observed, the act of translation—if nothing else—reminds us that in "all language and linguistic creations there remains in addition to what can be conveyed something that cannot be communicated; depending on the context in which it appears, it is something that symbolizes or something symbolized" and is not ever finally or fully *in* any one language.[6]

We can move, then, from undoing faulty abstractions, to particulars which are themselves also always abstractions, albeit of a different order, to the horizon of meaning, to the *more* that is always beyond any one perspective, any thought, any word, any theory—if we will risk the always incomplete journey. Only those who are fearful need remain within the meanings created by what James calls "privative" concepts, although the fearful will find no safety by staying on only one side of the looking glass, locked into only one historical language, one hegemonic discourse because there is always more to be said, and there are always those to say it, in many tongues. But they need not be fearful: to question the limits of supposedly general or universal terms is not to destroy the *possibility* of universality, any more than opening conversations to those who were excluded destroys the possibility of communication. Quite the contrary: it expands the realm of possibility, which is essential to the expansiveness of human freedom.

There is always contradiction, ambiguity, ambivalence to remind us of the terror and joy of possibility experienced in its present mode of uncertainty and incompleteness. We need not move off entirely into philosophy, poetry, or theology to remember that. Consider some observable aspects of education as a set of practices, ideas, institutions in the United States. Education is, by its nature, conservative, or conservationist. But education in democracies, at least, is also supposed to be one of the main provisions for an independent-minded and always plural citizenry, and one of the main routes of access to leadership and privilege. The men who established this form of government did not intend to undo either sex/gender or racial hierarchies; they did, however, want at least to make more permeable the Old World class divisions. Liberal arts education was to allow motivated and talented young white men to "rise," as the language then would have it, as high as their abilities could take them. Thus that which was intended to function to exclude some of us was also designed to increase in some ways, and that dedication to inclusiveness, to plurality and to change, was enshrined in the founding principles of education as of the polity. Later educators and reformers did not have to make up a wholly new language to open education to the rest of us. So faulty abstractions leave room for correction precisely as they claim generality: their power resides in their claim of generality, even universality, but so does the possibility of correcting them. After all, by definition, universality cannot be achieved in any particular form.

═════

In 1892, the great American educator Anna Julia Cooper, thinking about the need for her political work for all women and her educational work for black Americans, wrote against the kind of thinking, and politics, and education, built on oppositional dualisms:

> It is not the intelligent woman vs. the ignorant woman, nor the white woman vs. the black, the brown, and the red.—It is not even the cause of woman vs. man. Nay, 'tis woman's strongest vindication for speaking that the world needs to hear her voice. . . . The world has had to limp along with the wobbling gait and the one-sided hesitancy of a man with one eye. Suddenly the

bandage is removed from the other eye and the whole body is filled with light. It sees a circle where before it saw a segment. The darkened eye restored, every member rejoices with it.[7]

Cooper realized, it seems, that our problem is actually *not* so much with divisive dualisms as it is with invidious monism—the error of taking a part to be the whole such that all else, everyone else, must be forced into similarity with it, or considered similar but lesser, or locked utterly outside it as the Other. The invidious monism she diagnosed so well is itself culturally powerful, perhaps more so than dualism. It provided Augustine with an influential "solution" to the challenge of Manichean dualism. Following the Neoplatonists, he denied Evil any separate, if opposite, existence, defining it, simply, as a lack of goodness. Thus has Woman been defined, not as Man's equal opposite, but as a failed man (Aristotle), as only imperfectly in the category, Man. Cooper knew this to be monocular vision (as, much later, did the feminist historian Joan Kelly). And her binocular insight, which gives us not two separate entities but convergence of particularities into an articulated whole, is closely akin to Kant's recognition that "logical egoism," "thinking without regard for others," constitutes "Cyclopean thinking." Kant put such deprived thinking on a continuum with madness, opposing its deprivation to the *sensus communis* that develops from as it reaches toward the possibility of being able to think in the place of all others. That, of course, is radically different from modes of thought that create, in Hegelian terms, the Master and the Slave, a subject locked in struggle with a subject it is determined to turn into an object out of a tragic need to be recognized without recognizing.

Invidious monism leaves stranded those who would be the defining One, or few, in a realm in which authentic conversation is impossible, in which conversation may be no more than echoes of one voice or the spurious harmony of group prejudice. Divisive dualism turns conversation into crossed monologues. Neither achieves for us the authentic communication we desire.

Although we could continue from here to critique what has constituted itself as philosophy in the dominant Western tradition, my point is also that, in choosing to be in some genuine sense *for* democracy in almost any of its many meanings, one is also choosing to be committed to an ontology that grounds an epistemology able to inform education that can support democracy. That is, we need a coherent, democratic philosophy of education. Anna Julia Cooper, like John Dewey and Hannah Arendt (among others), believed that such a philosophy needs to be built on a kind of radical pluralism founded on an understanding of equality that does not confuse it with sameness. They understood equality as the essential political guarantor of difference—egalitarian difference, not that which defines it on an Augustinian scale, moving downward from the fullness of being to that which is fallen, nor oppositional dualistic difference. Put it this way: as long as Man cannot recognize the full implication of his being with other men and with women, so long will he struggle not with the malaise of encountering *alteritas*, but with his own faulty definitions, which turn the given of our differences into the falsely constructed and fearful Other—the barbarian at the gates.

In most of its meanings, democracy is a rejection of the notion of sovereignty in which the sovereign is defined in contradistinction to subjects, here understood as those who suffer subjection. "Rule by the people" smuggles sovereignty in again; even if "the people" rule, the problem is not solved, but only mightily confused. What can it mean for all to rule all? If all rule, no one rules—which betrays that few were indeed thinking of *all* ruling. "But representatives of all can rule," you may say. No; representatives, of course, *represent*. "Then they are ruled by the people." No; that is impossible if we remember, as we keep trying to do, that "the people" is a vastly diverse group. Again, at least as long as there is any freedom, there will always be more than any representative can represent. Thought will be required, and interpretation, and judgment, all informed by ongoing open conversations. There is no rule as there is no certainty in democracy, as in freedom. Hannah Arendt, who wished to convince us that *only* democracies can be genuinely political—because only they can allow plurality to appear in public—wrote that the "famous sovereignty of political bodies has always been an illusion, which, moreover, can be maintained only by the instruments of violence, that is, with essentially non-political means. Under human conditions, which are determined by the fact that not man but men"—and not men, but people—"live on the earth, freedom and sovereignty are so little identical that they cannot even exist simultaneously. . . . If men wish to be free, it is precisely sovereignty they must renounce."[8]

If that is so, then we also require a different understanding of power to break out of the old tangle of errors. If we take power to have as its root meaning *potential*, the "ability to do or effect something or anything" that all subjects have, rather than *mastery, or dominance*, which turns some subjects into objects, we are freed to think of the specifically relational, *communicative* capacities of speech and action as fundamental to the political realm. We begin to see human beings as creatures that have in common, as Arendt put it, being unique in each being unlike any other that has ever "lived, lives, or will live."[9] What we have in common, then, is our uniqueness, not our samenesses defined by notions and standards set by the few, but our capacity to differentiate ourselves, to actualize our special capacity to become unique in interaction with each other. And here we encounter yet again *alteritas*, now as it can be experienced under conditions of political and educational equality. We can fear and flee the mystery of Otherness, but we can also celebrate it as the ground of possibility for the wonder of uniqueness.

Thus, the kind of distinctions we make intellectually and in practice is what matters. We are not refusing to make distinctions when we refuse the old divisions, any more than we are refusing to generalize when we question the old generalizations. We are simply struggling to learn to think freely so we may understand freedom.

Thinking, as Arendt understood it, actualizes the basic human abilities to question, to think even about thinking itself, to see things from many different perspectives, to move between languages. That is, the activity of thinking—and not any of its products—keeps us from submitting to our own conceptual and/or political constructions (or those imposed on us by others). That this troublesome activity is political we ought to know. Socrates was put to death for corrupting the youth of Athens. Thinking is insubordinate; political systems that depend for their continuance on closed and unchanging categories, on abstractions that lock in divisions, will always fear it. That is so not only because thinking refuses the closed, finished nature of any of its own constructs, but because, like democracy, it depends on and helps actualize the human plurality which cannot be recognized in tyrannies that turn the people into one subjected subject. Thinking is profoundly related to action, which takes place in public with others. We may remove ourselves from the world we share with others when we actually think (we "stop and think" as Arendt liked to say, delighting in the cliché), but as we think, we think with others. An education that does not emphasize thinking but, rather, systems of knowledge and information, produces scholars who can converse with one another—but not with others. They have been prepared to study others as objects, and to think of governance as rule (preferably by "experts" informed by knowledge).

Those who have not encountered the differences among people in ways that interrupted their certainties do not make good thinkers; they also make poor citizens of democracies. Insofar as our education limits the others in whose place we learn to think, it limits our thinking, and thus also our political abilities. But the dominant tradition in the United States has for too long excluded too many, while hiding that exclusiveness behind partial universals. The "liberal arts," be it remembered, were defined in contradistinction to the "servile arts," the skills of those who were not allowed into the "highest education," the "education worthy of a free man." The "liberal arts" were indeed considered liberating, but not in the sense we use the term today. They were the arts to be cultivated by those men who did not need to work, who were "liberated" from the necessities of labor— productive, reproductive, and nurturant. All the rest of us became the conditions for the liberation of the few; we worked, we cared for them, we served them that they might be free, precisely, to know and to rule.

That is hardly the vision of freedom that is suggested by the understanding of democracy in its relation to thinking I have been exploring in the light of a quest for open conversation, for authentic communication. It is enough to make one who desires an egalitarian democracy turn from the tradition of the liberal arts in despair. But, as you have of course noticed, I refuse to yield possession of the whole complex tradition. What we need is *not* to choose between "the traditional" and "the innovative," the canon of Great Books on the one hand, and the works, and people, so long excluded on the

other. We are not stranded on a thin wire between the Ivory Tower
and the Tower of Babel. What we need, I am suggesting, is to think
together about thinking—to think in the company of all who can
help us, past and present, as we can in an egalitarian democracy and
education. For that effort, Arendt recommended to us a special kind
of thinking, a particular attitude toward the past:

> [T]his thinking, fed by the present, [may work] with the "thought
> fragments" it can wrest from the past and gather about itself.
> Like a pearl diver who descends to the bottom of the sea, not to
> excavate the bottom and bring it to light but to pry loose the rich
> and the strange, the pearls and the coral in the depths, and to
> carry them to the surface, this thinking delves into the depths of
> the past—but not to resuscitate it the way it was and to contrib-
> ute to the renewal of extinct ages. What guides this thinking is
> the conviction that although the living is subject to the ruin of
> the time, the process of decay is at the same time a process of
> crystallization, that in the depth of the sea, into which sinks and
> dissolves what once was alive, some things "suffer a sea change"
> . . . as though they waited only for the pearl diver.[10]

No one, and no group, owns our very complex, multicolored, multilayered cultures. In them are the strands of the Ariadne's thread we
are trying to find to help us enter and return safely from the Minotaur's lair of the liberal arts.

═════

Socrates tells us that he learned his method, his love of wisdom and a
way of living by its inspiration, from a wise woman named Diotima.
She taught him, he says, the method of question and answer, a con-
versational method that is animated by Eros, a powerful love for that
which we do not *and cannot* possess. Jung took up that meaning of
Eros to indicate that not the genital sex drive but Eros as human relat-
edness is fundamental to our psyches. Those concerned with equality
remember that relations between two subjects depend on undoing
any dominance that turns one into an object, and those concerned
with peace continue to struggle to undo the construction of differ-

ence into the kind of Otherness which is not *alteritas*, but one of its most dangerous stand-ins, The Enemy.

Feminist and multicultural scholarship remembers in transformative ways such strands from within and from outside the dominant tradition, weaving them into nets with which we can go pearl diving. That does not mean, as I noted at the beginning, that we simply add new gems to the old—that, having refused the old exclusivities, we simply proliferate new particularities. What it means is that we, citizens of a democracy premised on equality, can approach the past as equals, converse with it as equals, and, in so doing, unlock it from its own exclusions so that all that was always also there can now be seen and heard as it, as we, speak for ourselves at long last.

It is time we released ourselves, recognized that the dominant tradition has, among its pearls, traps, mistakings of many sorts, and that forgetting gender is prime among them. The poet, Muriel Rukeyser, writes:

> Long afterward, Oedipus, old and blinded, walked the roads. He smelled a familiar smell. It was the sphinx. Oedipus said, "I want to ask one question. Why didn't I recognize my mother?" "You gave the wrong answer," said the Sphinx. "But that was what made everything possible," said Oedipus. "No," she said. "When I asked, What walks on four legs in the morning, two at noon, and three in the evening, you answered Man. You didn't say anything about woman." "When you say Man," said Oedipus, "you include women too. Everyone knows that." She said, "That's what you think."[11]

Oedipus, we might say, did *not* think when he answered the Sphinx's riddle. He gave a conventional answer, and thereby earned a kingdom. But the plague came to his kingdom, forcing the king back into conversation, into the asking of questions, questions that revealed to him who his mother was. He ceased being a king and took up wandering with his sister/daughter Antigone until he died in a grove sacred to the "daughters of darkness and mysterious earth." There, and no longer a king, he became a blessing.

We have no answers to the riddles of our time. But perhaps we know enough of the Sphinx's powers that those who give only the conventional answers will not, this time, win the kingdom by insulting her with their thoughtlessness. Maybe by now we have learned to send no one person to speak with her; maybe by now we know enough to prepare to meet her question with our own, to draw her, the frightening Other, into ever-widening democratic conversation. The world —the whole diverse, polyglot world, and the earth on which it depends—is still the home of plagues, still calls on us as in Oedipus's time to give up our partialities and attachment to rule. Our survival as well as our freedom may depend upon our doing so.

Notes

1 Karl Jaspers, *Way to Wisdom, an Introduction to Philosophy*, trans. Ralph Manheim (New Haven, 1960), 25.

2 Ibid., 24.

3 Inge K. Broverman et al., "Sex-Role Stereotypes and Clinical Judgments of Mental Health," *Journal of Consulting and Clinical Psychology* 34 (1970): 1–7.

4 *All the Women Are White, All the Blacks Are Men, But Some of Us Are Brave: Black Women's Studies*, ed. Gloria T. Hull, Patricia Bell Scott, and Barbara Smith (New York, 1982).

5 Jacques Barzun, *A Stroll with William James* (New York, 1983), 128.

6 Walter Benjamin, *Illuminations* (New York, 1969), 79.

7 Anna Julia Cooper, *A Voice from the South* (New York, 1988), xiv. See also John Dewey, *Democracy and Education* (New York, 1966). Dewey criticizes theories of knowledge which "state or imply basic divisions, separations, or antitheses, technically called dualisms," whose origin "we have found in the hard and fast walls which mark off social groups and classes within a group; like those between rich and poor, men and women, noble and baseborn, ruler and ruled" (333).

8 Hannah Arendt, *Between Past and Future: Eight Exercises in Political Thought* (New York, 1968), 164–65.

9 Hannah Arendt, *The Human Condition* (Chicago, 1958), 8.

10 Hannah Arendt, Introduction to Benjamin, *Illuminations*, 50–51.

11 Muriel Rukeyser, "Myth," in *The Norton Anthology of Literature by Women: The Tradition in English*, ed. Sandra Gilbert and Susan Gubar (New York, 1985), 1787–88.

Bruce Kuklick

The Emergence of the Humanities

Some of the learned in the humanist tradition in America either claim (or live their lives in such a way as to suggest) that higher learning is a good in itself, to be pursued without regard for anything but its own supposed intrinsic merits. Learned endeavor, in this view, has a transcendent and eternal value that needs no further justification. On the other hand, there have been repeated demands made for what we today call the application of the humanities to other more "relevant" or practical fields of endeavor. Still other members of the tradition have persistently affirmed the role of learned discourse as the study that should suffuse life. In this last formulation, which reconciles the first two positions, learned understanding is not irrelevant to practical affairs but only indirectly relevant. Its insights are not applied to everyday affairs because they are the background of educated involvement in life; they are not so much goods in themselves, irrespective of their function in the world, as necessary to all worldly good.[1]

Strains among these three approaches have persisted in America over three centuries, but the form in which the strains are expressed changes. Different elite groups carry these impulses at different times and express them differently. And the social context in which the elites operate alters so that the ways in which the tensions are resolved differ in different periods. Our present conception of the humanities is temporally bound, a recent invention. At the same time, in American cultural history of the last 350 years, there is a set of enduring issues—the interest in the connection or lack of connection between the worldly and the otherworldly. Our present-day humanities derive from this interest.

In the American colonies during the seventeenth and eighteenth centuries, learned ideals were incarnated by the Puritan religious groups of New England. The dissemination of their work required not just a grasp of divinity, of Calvinist theological ideas, however much they have been stressed, but also an understanding of the ministry as a social group. Religious leaders had to meet the practicalities of the active pastorate, and they had to mediate conflicts between philosophic doctrine and these practicalities. Calvinists in America negotiated issues between the preacher and his flock as well as between the authority of an individual congregation and the religious establishment. The church stood between the demands of the faith and the realities of the world.[2]

The American Puritans established themselves intellectually by criticizing what they saw as the Aristotelian logic chopping of the scholastics. Philosophy had to be made the guide to life, and the scholastics, so the Puritans held, in concentrating on certain aspects of Aristotle's logic, had removed philosophy from human affairs. On the contrary, Puritan leaders urged, rhetoric had to be elevated to an equal place with logic; people would then have the ability not only to grasp the truth but also to convince others of it. This so-called "dialectic" was a mode of analysis that enabled the learned to grasp the structure of certain propositions that reflected the structure of the world, and a compelling way of expressing these truths to achieve practical results.[3]

The dialectic was the philosophic backbone of Protestant religion in the New World. Ministers put classical learning to use in a religious framework. The ancient authors were an adjunct to Biblical study. In a strict sense, then, the clergy were the preservers and transmitters of the classical heritage in America. But the perusal of the classics as an adjunct to the Bible was designed to explicate the appropriately ideal life for man to lead and to convey the point of leading such a life. The ministers did not just expound higher truths. They were pastors concerned with the members of their congregations, absorbed in the needs of the church as a temporal institution as well as their parishioners' lives in the world. The Bible, as well as Calvinist theology, had to be made to fit the world, and vice versa. The clergy found its vocation in interpreting the sacred to the profane.

In the eighteenth century the life of Jonathan Edwards illustrates a central point I want to make about this tradition. During his early career, Edwards was a practical evangelist whose job was, as he conceived it, to save souls. Later, during the Great Awakening, he wrote to defend his ideas of saving souls. By the end of his life Edwards was writing philosophic tomes about the Calvinist worldview. Clergymen in New England did not all have careers that transversed these three positions—the practical, the theoretical, and the combination of the two. But Edwards's life does convey how the clergy in early America variously developed the learned concerns I have specified.

From a narrow point of view the clergy's job was to deal with God, as did Edwards at the end of his life. Or clergy could be intensely worldly—as was Edwards as an active pastor at the start of his ministry. But the pastorate more often than not mediated between humanity and its creator—as did Edwards in the middle of his career. That is to say, the various New England cultural disputes in the seventeenth and eighteenth centuries reveal that, within the context of Calvinist religion, individuals could embrace the "extremes" to which I have pointed. Yet centrally the ministry in its various disputes also tried to adjudicate the demands of this life and those of the life of the spirit.[4]

During much of the nineteenth century the clergy still defended the learned tradition but did so in an altered social environment. In the eighteenth century the clergy's role was diffuse; in the nineteenth century it was fragmented and specialized. The model active pastors in the nineteenth century were never also theologians but simply eloquent preachers. The nineteenth century was the era of American oratory; a new sort of divine emerged who swayed large audiences with watered-down homilies.[5] The teachers of this pastorate were those in control of the burgeoning system of divinity schools that grew up in the United States in the first quarter of the nineteenth century, the first professional schools of higher learning in the country. By the middle of the century these men had no knowledge of the clergy's daily rounds but were able to devote themselves entirely to the enterprise of systematic theology. That is, in the nineteenth century, there was a clear separation of responsibilities between the more worldly clerics and the more otherworldly divines.

When theology withdrew from the center of the college to the margin of the academic community in a special school, the constitution of the tiny but growing American university was weakened insofar as it wanted to preserve its continuity with the past and to safeguard the tradition I have been discussing. In the ancient universities theology was responsible for animating schools of higher learning with a sense of their comprehensive calling. The professionalization of theology in America in the nineteenth century, on the one hand, and the disengagement of the active pastorate from speculation, on the other, were early and potent symbols of the fragmentation of knowledge and culture. Divinity-school theologians acquired the social role of speculation, the ministry that of applying this speculation. In between was the religious leadership comprising the college professoriate. Almost all of these men were ordained clergymen, but they did not have their own congregations, nor was their major concern the elaboration of systems of theology.

For the college professoriate, learned impulses were neither merely speculative nor merely applied; rather, they infused the careers of the college teachers. The teachers compromised the otherworldly and the this-worldly traditional extremes now institutionally located in divinity schools and in the popular pulpit. The vagaries of the earlier learned enterprise yielded to specialization in the nineteenth century, but also to a specialist group that trod between the material and the spiritual. Socially located as an entity, the college professoriate functioned to inculcate the dominant values of various local cultures; teachers fortified the norms of the educated classes, the established

moral and religious conventions. Custodians of the truths essential
to civilization, the functionaries of higher education conveyed them
to the young men who would assume leadership in the United States.
The culmination of collegiate training was a senior course in *moral*
philosophy, taught by the college president, always a clergyman, but
one whose expertise was in academic administration and philosophy
(not theology). This class rationalized man's duties and exhorted the
young to carry them out.[6]

Lest I have given the impression that we have discovered the Golden
Age of my American learned tradition, let us also remind ourselves
that this mediating group of clerics has usually been excoriated by
scholarly commentators. As one astute critic has noted, their work
was filled with "the flat metallic taste of facile moralism and unac-
knowledged self-aggrandizement."[7] The collegians actively attended
to public affairs and schooled their students to attend. Believing informed discussion essential to the republic's health, and sanctioned
as spokesmen for the upper middle class, they debated the great issues
of the day. But their perspective on political life was jejune. Although
not removed from the world, the professoriate was not perspicacious
about it. It distinguished between politics and public affairs, offering
learned comment on the world without being of it. The collegians'
own textbook analyses dissociated politics from political life or,
rather, mirrored knowledge of only a narrow, restricted, and genteel
life.[8]

A third era, its formative years being those from the 1880s to the
1920s, extends until the present. It is associated with the rise of
the modern university and the professionalization of all of academic
life. As I have suggested, this view overlooks the professionalizing
drive in theology that occurred in the early nineteenth century. But
the conventional wisdom exposes aspects of intellectual life that are
common to everyone connected with higher learning today.

During the late nineteenth century the university as we understand
it—the social organization defining the modern professoriate—came
into existence. Amateur intellectuals, those without an institutional
base, all but disappeared as the university came to be the sole focus
in the production and distribution of knowledge. Various areas of
study hived off from older and vaguer "departments" of inquiry, and

scholarly disciplines were established as limited fields of knowledge in the university, distinguished by special techniques and an accepted set of doctrines. Academic departments grew up, and disciplinary integrity was defined by the number of positions in a given field the university would finance. Teachers were trained and placed in this field by an intensified apprenticeship leading to the doctorate and appointment as a college professor. The proliferation of universities and the enlargement of a new educational bureaucracy also contributed to the evolution of a novel twentieth-century way of life within which careers could be made. The professional grades centering on the concept of tenure were codified. An arcane disciplinary language, professional associations, and scholarly journals became common. Academics learned to consult, to raise funds, to receive grants, and to inhabit research centers of various sorts that live on the social edge of the university and participate in the culture of expertise.

There were gains and losses in this process. Wealth, family, and gentility became inadequate to guarantee a successful life in the literary and cultural world. Appraisals of merit were more frequently made by a less than personal consensus of experts and came to depend on evaluations of published writing. Ministerial training ceased to be the sine qua non for having something to say about moral and social problems. Newly independent and qualified researchers explored the unknown territories of their terrains of inquiry in detail. On the other hand, professionalization painfully restricted the field of vision—and the visions—of its practitioners. To make a long story short, the revolution in higher education and scholarship provoked the credible lament that we now know more and more about less and less.

I want to consider these developments in the somewhat wider perspective of what I call the ideal of applied science that dominated the emergence of the research university. In this period not only did religious training become inessential for higher learning but the ministry also lost its long control of collegiate education—dating back to the early seventeenth century—to a new breed of academic administrators. Like their predecessors, these administrators believed that higher education served the nation, but their idea of the nation's future was different. Post–Civil War America would be a business culture requiring many kinds of skilled men. As a repository for the knowledge an advancing and complex society would need, the university would train them. The new captains of erudition—symbolized by Charles William Eliot, the M.I.T. chemist who led Harvard for forty years—conceived the modern university as a group of associated schools wherein scholars of diverse interests would prepare students for leadership in American life. Believing that social usefulness and truth seeking were compatible, they asked their publics not to look for immediate returns from universities; but they were convinced that an institution engaged in liberal studies would produce public-spirited, service-oriented men. Modern education would foster open minds and broad sympathies, not detached scholarship. Although the universities would not be practical in a shallow sense, they would be scientific in the sense of wedding theory and practice. The American administrators specifically rejected the German conception of "pure" research; instead, when they imported conceptions of German scholarship they joined them to ideas of cultural serviceability.

The faith in all areas of academic life in this vaguely defined notion of science to solve ethical, social, and political problems was unbounded. This faith was primary to what we today think of as the hard sciences. They were justified not as yielding pure and applied research in the contemporary sense, but as all somehow socially serviceable. Socially serviceable science was the dominant model.[9]

Let me examine how our humanities emerged in this sort of university and what their background was. In the nineteenth century, learned ideals were most interestingly embodied in the academic philosophers who brought together the concerns of the pastor and the theologian. Their central study was called "moral philosophy." Today we would best comprehend this old discipline as an omnibus study of the social sciences conceived as explicitly normative. In the late nineteenth century various of the social science disciplines—economics, political science, anthropology, and sociology—emerged out of the old moral philosophy. The academics who created the new social sciences, however, astutely conceived their scholarly spheres on the dominant model of applied natural science. The social sciences were systematic and objective yet also useful for practical problem solving. What I am saying, then, is that the heart of the nineteenth-century learned impulse is the locus of contemporary social science. But the efflorescence of the contemporary social sciences from the core of the learned areas of collegiate inquiry must also be seen in conjunction with the professional growth of what we now call the humanities.

In an important essay Laurence Veysey has argued that our current conception of the humanities came into existence after World War I when an ill-assorted and ragtag collection of academic disciplines banded together to protect their fields from the encroachment of the much better organized sciences and social sciences. Our current conception of the humanities, says Veysey, must be analyzed socially and politically: it is the product of disciplinary imperatives and social forces at work in the university as well as an unchanging, genteel, elitist, cultural context, exclusivist and socially pretentious.[10] This examination is attractive and compelling, but its refreshing cynicism must be tempered by understanding a larger piece of institutional history and by realizing that it is possible to be too cynical.

Among the salient studies of the mid-nineteenth century was another branch of philosophy called intellectual philosophy—mainly logic, epistemology, and metaphysics. Out of this came psychology —the empirical science of mind *and* what we today call philosophy, the least empirical parts of the philosophical enterprise, centered on epistemology.

History, now also a central part of the humanities, had only a minor belletristic role in the nineteenth-century college curriculum. But as the old moral philosophy fragmented, history grew as an independent discipline, absorbing most significantly those aspects of the study of politics and economics that had a past dimension. Indeed, history's ambiguous status—now categorized as a "humanity," now as a social science—flows from its old association both with moral philosophy and with the minor field of nineteenth-century literary inquiry. The latter belletristic history is contemporary humanistic history; the former moral philosophy is the social science component of history today.

The place of classics in the humanities spectrum is perhaps the most striking illustration of the point I want to make. In the eighteenth century the ancient languages in America were a necessary prerequisite to all learned endeavor: they were the medium in which the West's concern for the connection of the here and now to the abiding was preserved, transmitted, and carried on. In the nineteenth century philology preserved the role of the classics as it emerged in the United States as the scholarly study of ancient languages. Philology was a means of understanding the most accurate and warranted interpretation of the Bible; mastery of Greek, Latin, and Hebrew was the key to comprehending sacred texts that unlocked the meaning of life. Philology was thus a precondition to the work of the American learned tradition. As the study of philology progressed in the nineteenth century, and the learned came to explore the nature of language more complexly, philology's independent status developed and rose. Language was central to grasping man's nature and his knowledge of the physical and moral world, and philology was the principal and most high-powered study of language.[11] So when linguistic studies of various sorts began to be recognized as humanities in our present sense, they were justified because they gave us an entry into an examination of enduring questions. Language was a key to the study of the nature of reality and of human culture.

In short "our" humanities, as they came into existence from 1890 to 1920, composed the least worldly leavings in the university, after the hiving off of the social sciences. The old moral philosophy spawned all those disciplinary studies of the human world that most easily fit the stress of the new universities on applied science. What was left could not be easily applied and was justified as being the home of eternal truths; what was left had no obvious extrinsic value and was often, therefore, legitimated because of its absolute value. Veysey's understanding of the humanities must be supplemented by a grasp of the preeminence of the applied science model *and* a realization that the humanities do have something in common—they aren't very useful, and if they are to be valued at all they must be valued for themselves alone.

The emergence of the humanities in the United States has little to do with the anti-orthodox secular impulse associated with Renaissance humanism. Rather, in America our humanities arose from the stronghold of orthodoxy. The nineteenth-century clergy gave birth to our current social sciences and, almost as an afterthought, to our current humanities.

I originally defined learned impulses in the religious tradition I am surveying as those associated with linking abiding queries to the problems of daily life, and I contended that tension existed between the worldly and the otherworldly. In the United States in the nineteenth century the otherworldly pull existed in divinity schools, the worldly in the pulpit; learned impulses infused life in the work of the clerical professoriate. By the first third of the twentieth century divinity was not an important study, nor was the pulpit a significant public platform. The professoriate in the modern university was still the locus of the learned enterprise, but professionalization and homage to applied science had exacerbated the conflict between claims of relevance and irrelevance. The social scientists took over the relevant aspects of these ideals; what was called the humanities took over the otherworldly. That is, from my perspective learned endeavor today embraces in two separate areas what in the nineteenth century was more clearly one. The social sciences codify the practical, the humanities the eternal dimensions of the old moral philosophy. The impulse to proclaim the purity of scholarship for its own sake became a barricade for humanists to protect themselves; and the claim that social science could resolve practical problems was a barricade for social scientists to protect themselves. The first group justified its claim on the university budget by its intrinsic worth, the second group by its instrumental worth. The view that the aim of the learned tradition should be to infuse life became more difficult to maintain. It was harder, both intellectually and institutionally, to yoke the enduringly spiritual to the day-to-day material. The blunted sensibility of the social scientist matched the pompous arrogance of the humanist.

This is not to deny that within the contemporary social sciences and humanities the missing impulse does not develop. The connection of social science to the social order in terms of both research agenda and cognitive content appears to me undeniable. But many social scientists stalwartly affirm a belief in a "value-free" social science: they believe in a discipline that might theorize about culture but, in crucial ways, be independent of culture. Social scientists have a yen for the otherworldly in the sense of an objective realm free of the mark of social contamination. Social workers, public policy professionals, and so on might apply the results of social science, but these results, many argue, are transtemporal and transcultural. On the other hand, the desperate recent attempts by the humanities to appear relevant is another aspect of the same institutionalized dilemma. They are the less worldly disciplines but have a yen to be more worldly.

I think it is clear that the dominant push in the American learned tradition has always been conservative—to defend reigning tendencies in the culture and to justify the world's being as it is. Although I have not spoken about this, I would also add that, so far as I can tell, both academic conservatives and their critics have been peripheral as causal agents to whatever social changes do occur. Moreover, I think that a full understanding of this intellectual tradition requires a grasp of the self-aggrandizing character of the learned. Ideas may be believed and promulgated because they are true; but one always has to see the quest for truth in a context that is also a quest for preservation of the power of those engaged in developing the higher learning.

I interpret the ferment in literary studies today from this perspective. The emphasis on methodology and theory reflects an interest in establishing a "scientific" basis for literary studies, a basis that would eventually make them more like the social sciences, more practical in character. Although distinctive, more theory-driven humanistic disciplines might take their places among the applied sciences, making progress and advancing to new insights. The (unfortunate) chronic reinterpretation of texts might then yield to genuine, useful knowledge that would assist in social change.

But there is always change. Each of the eras I've discussed has its own sacred texts and canonical works. There were always disputes about the interpretation of these books and the wisdom of studying them. Attention has time and again shifted from some to others. In the most striking case the Bible effectively dropped off the list of required reading toward the end of the nineteenth century. But I should conclude as a historian that noting alteration is not to endorse it. Questions about the reality of changes should not be mixed with questions of their value, just as the truth of my story should not be confused with whatever moral the story might have.

Notes

1 This paper is a sibling of my "Professionalization of the Humanities," in *Applying the Humanities*, ed. Arthur L. Caplan, Daniel Callahan, and Bruce Jennings (New York, 1985), 41–54. Here the material in the older essay is placed in a different context.

2 See David Hall, *The Faithful Shepherd: A History of the New England Ministry in the Seventeenth Century* (Chapel Hill, 1972).

3 See Elizabeth Flower and Murray G. Murphey, *A History of Philosophy in America* (New York, 1977), 1: 14–45.

4 For the width of interpretations see Patricia Tracy, *Jonathan Edwards, Pastor* (New York, 1980); and Sang Hyun Lee, *The Philosophical Theology of Jonathan Edwards* (Princeton, 1988).

5 See Donald M. Scott, *From Office to Profession: The New England Ministry, 1750–1850* (Philadelphia, 1978); Ann Douglas, *The Feminization of American Culture* (New York, 1977); and Daniel Calhoun, *The Intelligence of a People* (Princeton, 1973).

6 See Bruce Kuklick, *Churchmen and Philosophers: From Jonathan Edwards to John Dewey, 1746–1934* (New Haven, 1985); Donald Meyer, *The Instructed Conscience* (Philadelphia, 1972); and H. Wilson Smith, *Professors and Public Ethics* (Ithaca, 1956).

7 Robert Charles Post, "Studies in the Origins and Practice of the American Novel: Social Structure, Moral Reality, and Aesthetic Form" (Ph.D. diss., Harvard University, 1980), 19.

8 Meyer, *Instructed Conscience*, 103–7, 114; Smith, *Professors*, 25–27.

9 These issues are discussed in relation to philosophy in Bruce Kuklick, *The Rise of American Philosophy* (New Haven, 1977). But there is an entire literature on professionalization, a good bibliography for which (through 1975) is given in Carol S. Gruber, *Mars and Minerva: World War I and the Uses of the Higher Learning in America* (Baton Rouge, 1975), 10–45, 261–81. For some doubts about the idea and further references see the essay by Laurence Veysey cited below.

10 Laurence Veysey, "The Plural Organized Worlds of the Humanities," in *The Organization of Knowledge in Modern America, 1860–1920*, ed. Alexandra Oleson and John Voss (Baltimore, 1979), 51–106. Veysey pays lip service to a more complex intellectual analysis, but its substance is missing in this essay.

11 Jerry Wayne Brown, *The Rise of Biblical Criticism in America, 1800–1870* (Middletown, 1969); for the later period see the discussion and citations in Ferenc M. Szasz, *The Divided Mind of Protestant America, 1880–1930* (University, Ala., 1982), 14–41.

Phyllis Franklin

The Academy and the Public

My assignment is to consider one of the "emerging conditions" likely to affect liberal arts education in the late twentieth century: namely, heightened public interest in the academy. We have just experienced a period of national blue ribbon commission reports, which succeeded in doing what such reports are meant to do: focus public attention on the academy and "make things happen" within it.[1] Indeed, the authors of a recent book on blue ribbon commissions and higher education chose as their subtitle *Changing Academe from the Outside*. I call your attention to this particular "condition" because academics have had difficulty presenting their case to the public and because people who study these matters predict more commission reports in the years ahead and therefore more public interest in higher education.[2]

Working at the Modern Language Association has given me an unusual vantage point and allowed me to see how some things seem to happen at the national level. Like all perspectives, mine is limited by what I have been able to see and biased by my values and by my commitment to those whose interests I represent. Having issued this disclaimer, I offer several observations about how those of us in the academy might help the public get a fairer view of us and of higher education.

I should say at the outset that I see nothing wrong with the public's interest in the academy. I subscribe to Edward Shils's view of the relation between the academy, the principal place intellectuals are likely to congregate in our society, and those outside it, particularly those in positions of influence. Perhaps a useful way to distinguish between the two groups Shils calls the intellectuals and the powers is to say, as Shils does, that while intellectuals (or academics) concern themselves with long-term questions and values, those in positions of power must deal with the immediate problems of life.[3] Like Shils, I assume that relations between those in the academy and those outside, whether the larger public or people in positions of power, are inevitably—and appropriately—complex and strained, as each group goes on being what it is and doing what it is supposed to do. Public interest in the academy is normal—even encouraging, since it recognizes that the academy matters. Tension between the two groups is also normal. The truth is, society needs the academy to keep its unique commitments, and the academy cannot function in a vacuum. Shils notes that within "extreme and impossible alternatives, a wide variety of forms of consensus and dissensus in the relations of the intellectuals and the ruling powers of society have existed. The discovery and the achievement of the optimum balance of civility and intellectual creativity are the tasks of the statesman and the responsible intellectual."[4] (By "statesman," I take Shils to include women as well.)

Now to my first observation. We need to recognize that certain kinds of statements in national reports about the way we do our work require a response because they are potentially damaging. Any charge of failure that mistates or distorts facts or uses faulty reasoning must be corrected, even if the charge seems peripheral to the main point of a report. Because national blue ribbon commissions are expected to issue reports that lead to change in government policy, legislation, or funding, assertions of failure are likely to be followed by attempts to correct what is wrong or to eliminate support for ineffective activities. Consequently, identifying errors in a report that aims at influencing public policy or the expenditure of public funds is not small-minded. When, as is likely, facts are incomplete, unclear, or contradictory, and more than one interpretation is reasonable, the problem must be spelled out in as fair a way as possible, so that those who make decisions will have the best information and analyses of the facts before them. I reached this conclusion as a result of the following experiences.

In the summer of 1985, the MLA had reservations about the appropriateness of the appointment of Edward Curran as the head of the National Endowment for the Humanities (NEH). Our reservations led us to urge the members of the Senate Subcommittee on Labor and Human Resources to hold a serious public hearing on the matter. As I visited the offices of both Democratic and Republican senators, I repeatedly heard the same reason offered for the nomination of someone outside the humanities community to head the NEH, and that reason was the failure of humanities professors. Only an outsider, I was told, someone who was not a member of the higher education community, could straighten out the mess the professors had made. The specific charge of failure stemmed from the decline in the number of students majoring in the humanities during the seventies. In a report issued by the NEH in November 1984, titled *To Reclaim a Legacy*, William Bennett, then head of the NEH, had asserted his belief that the decline in the number of majors was largely the fault of humanities professors. He argued that the professors drove students away from the humanities because the professors were too specialized, taught trivial rather than "great" books, and were politically tendentious.[5]

At the time, those who studied trends in college enrollments were in general agreement that during the seventies students turned away from majors in the social sciences and the natural sciences as well as the humanities because they—and their parents—thought that majoring in practical subjects was the only way to be sure of getting good jobs after graduation. The shift "from traditional liberal arts disciplines to fields with immediate vocational utility" was clear.[6] Although this trend was widely discussed within higher education, no one bothered to correct what was, in the context of the NEH report, a relatively minor point. Instead, members of the academic community joined journalists and the public at large in debating other questions William Bennett posed: the role of Western civilization in general education programs, the books all students should read, and the effects of specialization on teaching.

In large part, the arguments the MLA made in one Senate office after another on the Curran nomination aimed at showing that humanists had not failed. The politics of the Curran nomination and its defeat were far more complex than this statement suggests. Nevertheless, at the level of public discourse, government actions are expected to have publicly acceptable reasons. Consequently, once the charge that the humanities community had failed in its teaching mission was challenged and thereby neutralized, the MLA's request for reassurance about the qualifications of a candidate from outside higher education became publicly acceptable.

This experience taught me how an uncontested charge of failure could be used to influence the thinking of members of Congress. Three months after the NEH published Bennett's report, I saw a different charge of failure used against the academy. In February 1985, the Association of American Colleges (AAC) released *Integrity in the College Curriculum.*[7] This report gained immediate national attention. At the AAC's annual meeting, before representatives of the press, government officials, members of college boards of trustees, and college and university administrators, the authors of the report charged that the college curriculum in the United States was in serious disarray and that faculty members, because of their scholarly orientation and disciplinary commitments, were almost wholly to blame. Joining the authors of the report at the AAC meeting, William Bennett, then Secretary of Education, said that the college curriculum was too important to be left to the faculty, and his audience nodded agreement. Concerned members of college and university governing boards announced their intention to play a more active role in decisions affecting the curriculum.

Although the AAC report dealt with many curricular issues, the only part of it that had a clear and immediate political consequence was the assertion of failure on the part of faculty members, and therefore of academic institutions. Within days of the AAC meeting,

Secretary Bennett reported to Congress that American colleges and universities were defrauding students, and he argued against federal support of student loans.

The point is, people who set up as specialists cannot afford to let inaccurate charges of failure stand, as though they don't matter. One can be reasonably certain that such charges at the national level will be followed by proposals for change or for the withdrawal of support from an activity or group that has been labeled ineffective.

As we all know, it is one thing to talk about the need to respond to misleading charges of failure. It is quite another thing to get a coherent response before the general public. The problems we face are formidable. Not only are the issues we deal with of a kind that make simple, newsworthy statements almost impossible, but we must depend on others to carry our messages. Although we may never be able to present our views with full precision and clarity to the general public, we are in a better position to reach two important groups of opinion leaders so that they can communicate our concerns to policymakers. I have in mind those who work in foundations and those who administer colleges and universities.

For the most part the people who work in foundations come from academe, and so they understand and are generally sympathetic with academic culture and values. Well informed about the academy and related matters, they not only have a good deal to say within foundations about what kinds of scholarly work and educational programs deserve assistance but are also asked to speak regarding federal and private support for scholarly work and higher education.

We need to understand the role we play in shaping their views of the academy. Members of the foundation community form a relatively small network, characterized by considerable consensus about current needs and worthy projects. Not unnaturally, they tend to trust one another's judgments as disinterested, but they also look to academics for formal and informal evaluations of projects and for opinions about intellectual developments. Their impressions of what goes on in the academy are, as you would expect, affected by academics' evaluations of one another's work and by the informal opinions they hear about issues in the disciplines. I have observed that so long as the information the members of the foundation community receive from the academy does not exceed what one might call "normal disciplinary disagreements," they know how to assess it.

However, when disciplinary disagreements become excessive, the members of the foundation community are unable to evaluate information coming from a field. What can even a sympathetic observer think when Group A in a discipline says that the scholars in Group B don't understand what they are doing, and then Group B says that Group A is crazy? Injudicious statements and obviously biased evaluations send a number of different but wholly negative messages about academic integrity. Worse than the possible loss of funds for any specific project is the foundation community's loss of confidence in a field. I have observed this happen as a result of some unusually harsh disagreements about critical theory, the relative value of writing and literature, and the ties between introductory language instruction and literary study.

College and university administrators constitute the second group of opinion leaders we can reach. They too are members of our community and share our culture and values. And they are expected to speak to issues affecting the academy. During the difficult period from the end of November 1984 through 1986, many college and university presidents publicly supported key academic values and endeavored to correct distorted charges against higher education.

In addition to speaking as individuals, college and university presidents and other administrators also participate in national networks. Thirty associations make up the influential American Council on Education (ACE), which acts as the coordinating and convening body for what is called the Washington Higher Education Secretariat. Participating organizations include those representing specific kinds of institutions—for example, the major research universities, state universities and land grant colleges, law schools, and Catholic colleges. Also included are organizations for those who carry out specific administrative functions—for example, graduate school deans, college and university attorneys, and college and university business officers. ACE and other members of the secretariat are well positioned to attract ongoing press coverage, and they regularly represent higher education issues in Congress. Although we do not have direct access to the ACE, we have indirect access through campus administrators, who can bring issues to the attention of the national associations. If we wish the higher education associations, like the foundation community, to help us convey our messages, we have to make sure that these messages are clear and effective.

Which brings me to my final observation: we must maintain basic scholarly values and insist on high standards in our discourse. I receive letters from MLA members commenting on intellectual and professional questions, and some of the authors of these letters ask that I not reveal their names. They fear that colleagues in their departments and in the MLA will treat them badly because of their views. Some of them are right. I have observed occasional exchanges in meetings at our annual convention when participants all but prevented someone who wished to be heard from speaking. In my opinion, actions like this represent a breakdown of norms for discussion in our community. I find the signs of intellectual intolerance troubling not only because of what they say about academic integrity but also because, without respect for one another, we will be unable to sustain the respect of the two communities most likely to speak in our behalf.

The current situation is complicated because we are in a period of heightened public interest in the academy, and so all of our debates —whether on campuses, at foundations and federal agencies, or in scholarly meetings—are public acts that may have unexpected consequences. In making this point, I do not suggest that we withdraw from normal discussions of—and disagreements about—the quality of our courses and programs, the effectiveness of our teaching, or the merit and validity of our work as scholars. But I believe that some ways of arguing are more constructive than others. Since our audience these days is likely to be larger than it has been and to include people who either do not share our assumptions and values or are unfamiliar with them, we probably need to explain more than we normally do in our discussions with one another. For example, complaints about specialization, which arise frequently among us and reflect genuine concerns and genuine difficulties, now require greater specificity. Although we grumble regularly about specialization, few of us, I suspect, think that we can function without it. But outsiders could easily misunderstand, unless we spell out which aspects of our own and others' work we would eliminate or modify and which features of higher education we would change.

We must also face the fact that the broadening of the audience for our discussions is likely to have other consequences. I fear that some academics have already used public interest in the academy as a weapon against those whose ideas they oppose: negative publicity outside the academy instead of careful debate within it. This temptation is dangerous. To borrow (and modify somewhat) Oliver Wendell Holmes's test, when we confront an idea that we "loathe" and we have the opportunity to discredit the idea among people in positions of power, will we take advantage of the opportunity or will we uphold our community's traditional commitment to freedom of inquiry and expression?

As for those in positions of power, perhaps some among us will be able to explain that we accept responsibility not only for conserving and teaching the achievements of the past but also for encouraging innovation, and that we depend on individual academic communities to determine the balance or emphasis appropriate to their institutions' missions. Perhaps we—or those who speak for us—can convey that as "modern" scholars we are specialists, that debates are natural, and that reasonable people in our community can and will disagree on curricular and other matters without reducing the academy to chaos. Perhaps we can also convince them that many if not all of us are committed to—and I use Hazard Adams's phrase—"an ethic that refuses to accept tyranny, particularly intellectual tyranny."[8] I quoted earlier a statement by Edward Shils regarding the role of statesmen and responsible intellectuals in establishing a constructive relation between academics and those in positions of power. In the absence of statesmen—or women—the task of achieving such a relation, clearly, rests with us.

Notes

1   Janet R. Johnson and Laurence R. Marcus, *Blue Ribbon Commissions and Higher Education: Changing Academe from the Outside* (Washington, D.C., 1986), 3.
2   Ibid., xiii.

3 Edward Shils, "The Intellectuals and the Powers," in *The Intellectuals and the Powers and Other Essays* (Chicago, 1972), 3.

4 Ibid., 21–22.

5 William J. Bennett, *To Reclaim a Legacy: A Report on the Humanities in Higher Education* (Washington, D.C., 1984).

6 Phyllis Franklin, "From the Editor," *MLA Newsletter*, Winter 1988, 4.

7 Association of American Colleges, *Integrity in the College Curriculum: A Report to the Academic Community* (Washington, D.C., 1985).

8 Hazard Adams, "The Fate of Knowledge," in *Cultural Literacy and the Idea of General Education*, ed. Ian Westbury and Alan Purves (Chicago, 1988), 67.

George A. Kennedy

Classics and Canons

In the controversy between neoconservatives and postmodernists, teachers of Greek
and Latin have found themselves in a curious
position. Their central texts—the Homeric
poems, Greek tragedy and historiography, the
Platonic dialogues, Aristotle's treatises, Latin
poetry of the Augustan age, Augustine's *Confessions*, and some other works—surely fall
within any definition of "great books"; these
works ask questions and propose hypothe-
ses that are the basis of much of traditional
Western civilization, and as such are revered
by traditionalists. Furthermore, classical philology of the nineteenth century supplied
the paradigm for historicist methods of interpreting texts; it aimed to be "scientific"
and objective, and characteristically sought
to know "the truth" insofar as the evidence
allowed. Its stance was often highly moral,
conditioned by Judeo-Christian values and
by patriotism as understood in the modern
nation. As such, it has continued to appeal to
those who dispense largess from the Old Post
Office Building.

But classical studies in the twentieth century has been more "conservationist" than "conservative." It has more often been motivated by the desire to preserve the great monuments of the Greco-Roman world as things valuable in themselves—like the whale and the redwood—than by an insistence that specific truths are to be found in them. Some of the joy of life would be gone if we could not read the *Odyssey* or the plays of Aristophanes, whose aesthetic experience is more certain than any message they may contain. What has become more clear in the last generation is the complexity and variety of attitudes in the classical world, the irrational forces lying beneath its classic serenity, its tragic sense, its comic laughter at the foibles of mankind, and the life of its marginal groups. To feel oneself vicariously, through reading literary and archaeological texts, a part of a Greek city, where the blood of animal sacrifice steamed on the altars, where slaves did the hard work, where most people were dead by the age of thirty, including men in war and women in childbirth, "respectable" women were sequestered, unwanted babies were exposed to die in the hills, and men made love to boys in the shady corners of the gymnasia, is not quite what the neoconservatives have in mind by studying the classics, but it is perhaps more real, more human, than Plato's ideal city where philosophers are kings. We read the great books rather differently than did previous generations. The *Aeneid* is a case in point, no longer a celebration of war, piety, and patriotism, but a highly ambivalent reaction to the Augustan establishment.

Though "classical" literature is almost by definition canonical, for practical purposes, at least at the level of graduate studies, the classical canon is the entire corpus of surviving evidence of antiquity, from the *Iliad* down to and including the graffiti on the walls of Pompey. It is worthwhile to consider briefly the history of canon formation, its assumptions and uses, for the subject does not seem very well understood by modern students, many of whom cannot even spell the word. Though the Homeric poems were the standard textbooks of Greek schools from an early time and were a unifying intellectual and aesthetic experience for all Greeks, they were repeatedly criticized for their immorality—by Xenophanes for example, long before Plato—and it seems clear that one reason they were used to teach reading was their imaginative appeal to young people. Their devotees, like Ion in Plato's dialogue, also claimed practical wisdom for them, but neither the society nor the religion they describe was that of the classical period, and allegorical interpretation was resorted to at an early time to make their contents palatable to the thoughtful.

The concept of a "canon" originated with the scholars who worked in the Alexandrian library in the third and second centuries B.C., particularly Aristophanes of Byzantium and Aristarchus of Samothrace. The word *kanon* in Greek means "a straight rod," "a ruler," and thus "a standard." None of the Alexandrian scholars believed that the function of poetry was anything other than pleasure; Eratosthenes in particular ridiculed the view that any kind of knowledge of the world could be derived from Homer, only aesthetic knowledge, the enchantment of a great poem.[1] The library at Alexandria attempted to collect all texts that could be found and to use them for literary study, but the scholars there provided guidelines for student readers by listing what they regarded as the best examples in each literary genre: nine lyric poets, for example, headed by Pindar, and including one woman, Sappho. The morality of the contents was of little interest to them, but consistency of characterization was, as well as subtlety of diction and versification, elegance of ornamentation, and imaginative power. Though their salaries were paid by the Egyptian kings, and the poetry written in their time is often propagandistic, their literary standards seem largely untouched by contemporary political considerations.

We know the Alexandrian canon best from the survey of it in the tenth book of Quintilian's *Institutio oratoria*. Quintilian, teaching rhetoric in Rome in the second half of the first century after Christ, created a corresponding Latin canon. He is candid about his objective: to provide a reading list for students that will enrich their feeling for style, supply models to imitate, and provide a knowledge of sources to which they can allude. He was teaching prose composition and oratory, and thus cautions about too free an imitation of poetic devices; in his Roman way, he takes a more moral stance toward contents than did his Greek sources. The canons of the Alexandrians and of Quintilian give primacy to poetry; through ancient times only three prose genres were consistently regarded as "literary" and thus developed canons: oratory, historiography, and philosophical writing of the type seen in the Platonic or Ciceronian dialogues.

Occasionally the literary epistle was regarded as a distinct form. The prose romance, though already developed by Quintilian's time, is simply ignored as nonliterary, and all other publications are "hypomnemata," or *aides mémoires.*

The *Septuagint,* the authoritative Greek text of the Old Testament, was according to tradition also a product of the Alexandrian library, and the concept of a biblical canon was perhaps influenced by the existence of a literary canon, but the standards were different: the authenticity or orthodoxy of the religious teaching of the work was the sole criteria, though allegorical interpretation made it possible to include certain traditionally admired works of literary merit, such as the Song of Solomon. These days the neoconservatives often seem to blur the distinction between literary and doctrinal canons, between a chef d'oeuvre and a sacred text. The reason American young people should read the Constitution of the United States has little to do with its literary merit, and the reason they should read *Paradise Lost* has little to do with its religious doctrine.

Some kind of canon is necessary. Even in the surviving literature of Greece and Rome, not to say in Renaissance and modern literature, there is too much for any student to read. In the extreme case that every student read a totally different set of books, discussion of literature would be almost impossible. Though canon formation in English was much encouraged by the likes of T. S. Eliot and F. R. Leavis, the practical impulse for it was the perceived need to use knowledge of some group of texts as the basis of judgment about admission and financial aid for college applicants and for placement of matriculants within the curriculum. The reading required for admission to liberal arts colleges in the early twentieth century was extremely specific, down to listing what plays of Shakespeare and what poems of Tennyson would be expected. That there was a hidden agenda in the requirements, both political and aesthetic, need not be denied, but a factor in the formation of the canon was also choice of works which the average American student could understand and have some initial sympathy with.

Latin studies long had a rather rigid canon that reaches back at least to the Renaissance and in the case of Virgil to antiquity. After a year of introductory grammar the student read Caesar's *Commen-*

taries. The primary reason was not the inculcation of imperialism, probably more a factor in Britain than in America, but the relative simplicity of the grammar and style, the limited vocabulary, and the fact that the work is an adventure story that might appeal to boys. There was a sexist element certainly. The account of the invasion of Britain was one of the parts regularly read, giving a link to the Anglo-Saxon world, and the *Commentaries* went nicely with Shakespeare's *Julius Caesar*, often read in second-year English. To try to forge interconnections between disciplines seems a worthwhile motivation. In the third year, students read Cicero. The practical reason was to increase their understanding of Latin prose with more complex texts, and to preserve the vestige of a traditional role of the liberal arts as the preparation of a public speaker; but Cicero as the defender of the Republic against Caesar offered a counterbalance to any totalitarian sentiment the student might inadvertently have picked up the previous year. Then the fourth year was committed to Virgil. Again a vivid story, and one with the special titilation of the adventure with Dido in the fourth book, just the right thing to interest teenagers. Some teachers further exploited students' awakening interest in sex with a little (expurgated) Ovid, or even Catullus. In recent years the canon has been somewhat set on its head: war, and thus Caesar, isn't acceptable; sex has moved down into junior high school, and Virgil and Ovid and Catullus (though not yet the homosexual poems) can be read earlier. The college canon in this country was always somewhat less rigid than that taught in secondary schools, but it too has become more flexible. Petronius, long read in the closet by the precocious, has become a regular feature.

In addition to the distinction between a literary and a doctrinal canon, a distinction needs to be made between canons at the various levels of liberal arts education. Given the low level of cultural literacy of American teenagers, it can well be argued that the required reading of secondary schools should begin with texts that have some initial relationship to the students' experience, but that also provide a reasonable challenge to their linguistic and mental abilities, and open up to them varieties of literary forms and techniques. The whole objective should be to encourage reading, and new ways of reading, both as student and adult. Texts by and about women and minorities are obviously important choices because close to the students' experience. Some of the works read should not be modern and some should not be about Americans, in order to enhance students' understanding of the experience of other times and places. Students should also read at least a few "great books," though there are several hundred from which choices can be made. Classicists have long held out Virgil as the author "you will get to read when you know a little more Latin," and students have long deferred gratification and sometimes experienced it. The same can be done with Shakespeare. There is, for the better motivated, the additional gratification of having gone through a rite of passage and reached a goal that society had told them everyone was entitled to. I remember how disappointed I was in my study of German that we never read any German authors I had heard of before.

There are several college and graduate school literary canons which are again related to fulfilling the reasonable expectations of students. Students sometimes complain that they attain no overall grasp of their discipline and the interrelations of its parts. In the study of the national literatures, almost the only structure for a grasp of the whole is the framework of historical development. It has its limitations, but it can be taught both as continuity and discontinuity, with awareness of both ideology and marginality. However it is taught, the history of literature requires some selection of archetypes, and those may be different in different departments or courses, but if the utility of the framework is to go beyond the immediate department or course, there needs to be overlap with what others have regarded as the most seminal texts. In practice, that sometimes means reading a work that the instructor does not regard as very interesting but that others do, and the student should thus know something about. Croce and Eliot, vacuous as they are, are parts of twentieth-century criticism and need to be looked at in a course on its history.

Literary theory has its own canons, the texts which each school of thought finds most interesting and to which its own interpretation best applies. Insofar as literary theory seeks to understand the nature of literariness and the functions of literature in society, the restricted nature of the canon of each movement is a limitation, as inhibiting as the canons of the traditionalists. Deconstructionists seem largely interested in logocentrist texts, and provide no approach for reading that long line of works from Mimnermus of Colophon to Samuel Beckett that come to the reader already deconstructed. The Russian Formalists, in contrast, liked only defamiliarized texts. The canon of the New Critics was perhaps larger, but they preferred texts with unified patterns of imagery, and in common with other schools they ignored whole genres, such as artistic oratory. If classical criticism was obsessed with epic and tragedy, modern criticism is equally obsessed with the novel, the short story, and lyric poetry. Good critical theory should test itself on a wide variety of texts, including some outside the Western tradition. Canons of course exist there as well, in India, China, and Japan, to say nothing of the canons to be found in purely oral cultures.

The desire for a canon is probably a basic human instinct, perhaps related to self-preservation: the assertion of control over chaos, the marking out of one's turf. We each have a canon based on the limits of what we think we may control and what fulfills our own needs. Some of us can live without a clear definition of the limits, just as some of us can live without revealed religion. Most cannot, and we need to share our canon; thus we fall into sects with our own sacred books. The history of literature shows alternating periods of contracting and expanding the canon. The narrow canon of the Middle Ages burst open in the Renaissance, only to be narrowed again in the eighteenth and nineteenth centuries. Today it is opening up again, to the despair of the more insecure. It is likely to contract again in another century or so, whatever the direction of social and political development, if only because we cannot otherwise deal with the proliferation of writing. As the twentieth century ends, the question begins to be asked, What are its permanently great works of literature? For the general public that might be rephrased, What have I missed in the culture of my own time? Since the utility of canons is chiefly educational, it is likely that academics will chiefly furnish the answers, influenced by the social and political powers that provide them the time to do so.

A strength of modern criticism is the energy of its commitment to social values and their implementation. Oddly, the same could be said of the neoconservatives. Politicization is a recurrent phenomenon in the history of criticism and often projected as reform. Plato's banishment of traditional Greek poets from his ideal state was part of an attempt to reform Greek society of his time; in Italy in the last third of the sixteenth century, according to Bernard Weinberg, critical treatises reflecting the Counter-Reformation gave increased prominence to political implications of literature: "the emphasis is less on 'character building' and more on the consequences to the state of the practice of the art of poetry as a whole or of certain of its forms. As a rather surprising corollary, theorists are now less prone to banish or expel the poet from the state and more prone to seek ways in which the practice of his art can be controlled and turned to the advantage of the body politic."[2] The attempts of political and social reform through literature and criticism in the late twentieth century have built into them curious features: conservatives, otherwise often supporters of rugged individualism and deregulation, favor a regulated literary canon; liberals, otherwise often proponents of governmental intervention and regulation, as in conservation of the environmental heritage, resent governmental initiatives to preserve the literary heritage. A weakness of both camps is the shrillness of their rhetoric and their tendency to talk past each other. As Juvenal said of satire, "*Si natura negat facit indignatio versum.*"[3] Even at the conference on the liberal arts in North Carolina, the partisans in the liberal camp were more interested in staking out a position than in listening to one another. As the sessions moved on, speakers, commentators, and questioners repeatedly ignored points already made. The neoconservatives ought simply to be amused, but may lack the wit. A sign of rhetorical shrillness is the tendency of postmodernists to use the word "must" when they mean "should, in my opinion and if my goals are to be obtained." There is no necessity in literary criticism; you can always close a book unread. It was like this, however, in that other exciting period of literary ferment, the Renaissance. Poggio and Trebizond even had a fistfight in the Vatican library. The secret of success of modern literary theory is the pleasure principle, the opening it allows to creativity and inventiveness. That has also been the secret of success of literature, starting with the Homeric poems.

The North Carolina meeting was called a conference on the liberal arts; the liberal arts include the sciences and have since antiquity, but they were only given token attention. But the legitimacy of modern criticism in fact has its basis in the scientific study of linguistics and psychology, which are the two areas of *les sciences humaines* that have made the greatest progress in the twentieth century. Postmodern literary theory would not exist had it not been for the work of Saussure, Benveniste, Jakobson, and others like them. The neoconservatives, including Allan Bloom, have no effective answer to the arbitrary nature of signs, nor are they apparently prepared to challenge the scientific *episteme* that is the paradigm of our culture. They only lament its results and imply that we should keep our knowledge as a kind of academic secret for fear of corrupting the youth. Though relativism and behaviorism are anathemas to them, they ignore the increasing evidence in mathematics, physics, and biology that these are phenomena of nature. It is hardly surprising that they turn out also to be phenomena of language and culture. In the long run, modern literary theory will have the greatest success if it calmly cites the epistemological evidence on which it builds and asserts the need for all scholars to pursue "the truth" to whatever unpleasant conclusion that may lead.

Notes

1   On the critical views of the Alexandrian scholars see Rudolf Pfeiffer, *History of Classical Scholarship* (Oxford, 1968), 87–233.
2   Bernard Weinberg, *A History of Criticism in the Italian Renaissance* (Chicago, 1961), 1: 346.
3   Juvenal *Satires* 1.79: "If nature denies, indignation composes the verse."

Richard Rorty

Two Cheers for the Cultural Left

In the course of our conference, Henry Gates defined the "American Cultural Left" as a "Rainbow Coalition of feminists, deconstructionists, Althusserians, Foucauldians, people working in ethnic or gay studies, etc." The emergence of this left in the course of the last ten years or so is an important event in American academic life. The humanities, and particularly, the departments of literature, are where the action is in the American academy. These are the only places where something is happening which gets widely discussed among the professors, intrigues some of the best students, and upsets the administrators.

Our conference has been, in part, a rally of this cultural left. The audience responded readily and favorably to notions like "subversive readings," "hegemonic discourse," "the breaking down of traditional logocentric hierarchies," and so on. It chortled derisively at mentions of William Bennett, Allan Bloom, or E. D. Hirsch, Jr., and nodded respectfully at the names of Nietzsche, Derrida, Gramsci, or Foucault.

As a Deweyan philosopher who also thinks of himself as a reformist, bourgeois, Dewey-style liberal, I had predictably mixed feelings
about the conference, as I do about the cultural left itself. I agreed
with a lot that was said about Bloom and Bennett, disagreed with a
lot that was said about Hirsch, and was perplexed by the widespread
acceptance of a view about contemporary American society which I
do not share. This is the view summed up in Frank Lentricchia's statement, at the beginning of his *Criticism and Social Change*: "I come
down on the side of those who believe that our society is mainly unreasonable and that education should be one of the places where we
can get involved in the process of transforming it."[1]

I do not see our society as "mainly unreasonable," but as perhaps
the most reasonable society yet developed in a big, rich, culturally
heterogeneous, industrialized country. I have to admit that our country frequently does murderous things, such as waging the Vietnam
War and collaborating with the oligarchies of Latin America. But I
think that it does fewer of these things than most countries, and that
it can often be persuaded to feel guilty about doing them. I also have
to admit that the country seems to be getting increasingly selfish—as
instanced by its apparent willingness to let millions of ghetto children
grow up without hope, a topic to which none of our politicians (with
the single exception of Jesse Jackson) seems willing to speak. But it
still seems to me about as reasonable as societies have so far gotten.

In saying that it is reasonable I mean, for example, that public
opinion is malleable to argument, that a free press prevents the officials from getting away with quite a lot that they would otherwise
attempt, that the youth is still able to make a difference by saying,
with outrage, "what is being done betrays our country's traditions."
It is a reasonable society because, unlike Romania or Paraguay or
South Africa, there are functioning mechanisms of social improve-
ment which rely on persuasion rather than force. It is, in Czelaw
Milosz's phrase, a "moderately corrupt republic," but it is still a republic, and one still capable of an occasional lurch forward (like the
Wagner Act, Social Security, the civil rights movement, the Stonewall
riots).

The difference between saying "our society is mainly unreasonable" and saying "we are betraying our country's traditions" parallels

the difference between speaking, with Lentricchia, of "the transformation of society" and, as I prefer to do, of "the reform of institutions." I take "transformation" to be more or less synonymous with "revolution," and I am not sure that I want to see our society revolutionized, to see our basic institutions replaced. My reason is that, though I would very much like to, I cannot think of any better basic institutions. (When I was younger I thought it might be a good idea to nationalize the means of production—but that has been tried elsewhere, and does not seem to work.) I can think of hundreds of particular ways in which I should like our institutions to be *changed*, but I hesitate to speak of *transformation* because I think the word should be used only by those who have some sort of blueprint for the results of transformation (in the way in which Jefferson and Adams, or Lenin and Trotsky, did, and Abbie Hoffman did not). As far as I can see, the contemporary cultural left has no such blueprint. Its attitude seems to be one which Foucault once expressed, in reply to criticism of his unwillingness to sketch a utopia: "I think to imagine another system is to extend our participation in the present system."[2]

This is the attitude which we reformist types find most alien—one in which the fear of complicity has overcome the fear of impotence. Members of the cultural left spend a lot of time accusing each other of complicity—of "still being under the spell of hegemonic discourse"—and out-de-phallogocentrizing each other. This parallels the old Marxist practice of using the charge of right-wing deviationism as a polemical weapon. When such practices become current within a leftist movement, the movement tends to become less and less socially useful, more and more self-involved. Its tone becomes more and more like that of the Straussians and the Heideggerians: the tone of a saving remnant which despises its opponents too much to argue with them, has become preoccupied with internal doctrinal purity, and finds comfort only in the thought that it may be able to inculcate its ideas in the rising generation. It becomes increasingly difficult for members of such a movement to think of themselves as fellow citizens, to say "we" when they speak of the country in which they live. Instead, it gradually takes on the person-from-another-planet, spectator-of-time-and-eternity tone of voice—the tone common to Strauss and Foucault.

I can make my mixed feelings about our conference more concrete by taking up Hirsch's book. Hirsch is a reformist liberal with whom I have a lot of political (although no philosophical) views in common. He thinks that the current flap about the weakness of American precollege education is a good opportunity for liberals to change education for the better. He thinks that the educationist establishment has let things slide to the point at which students can graduate from high school without being able to read *Newsweek* (or, for that matter, *Mother Jones* or *The Nation*). He has some ideas about how precollege education could be changed so that the high-school graduates will be able to catch the allusions sprinkled through such periodicals. In particular, he wants to make the students pass exams on how many allusions to famous people, events, slogans, and so forth, they can recognize.

His *Cultural Literacy* makes a good case for his description of the present situation, and his ideas seem to have some chance of being adopted.[3] It is true that, as many participants in the conference noted, his ideas are likely to be adopted for a lot of the wrong reasons. Still, if they were adopted they would make things a lot easier for the cultural left in the colleges and the universities. It is, after all, easier to teach Shakespeare in a Stephen Greenblattish, quasi-Foucauldian way to students who recognize the names of Shakespeare's plays, easier to explain possibilities of social transformation to students who know that the French Revolution antedated the Russian, easier to talk about sexism to students who recognize the term "women's suffrage" and the name "Betty Friedan," easier to talk about homophobia to students who have heard of Oscar Wilde, and so on.

Hirsch and I would, I think, agree that the primary and secondary schools should continue to pass along most of the conventional wisdom of the previous generation—to socialize the children by inculcating the standard, patriotic, upbeat, narrative about our society, its history, and its values. In the first place, there is no chance of getting them to do anything else; the system of local school boards insures this, and any other system of control would probably be worse.[4] Even if Henry Giroux someday succeeds William Bennett as Secretary of Education, as I hope he may, he will not be able to prevent precollege education from being nine parts socialization to one part liberation. Nor should he try, since you cannot liberate a tabula rasa; you cannot make a free individual out of an unsocialized child. You can gradually alter patterns of socialization, but cultural revolution, in which the government tries to turn the children against their parents by promulgating a new primary and secondary curriculum, has not proved to be a good idea.

In the second place, as long as the children are told that this is the land of liberty and justice for all, celebrate the Great Emancipator's and Martin Luther King's birthdays, and pick up a story about history as the story of increasing freedom, they will, if they go on to college, be grist for both liberal and radical mills.[5] Reformist liberals in social science and humanities departments have had quite a bit of success, over the past seventy years, in nudging each student generation a little more to the left—in insuring that the college-educated usually favor more liberal candidates than do voters who never went to college.[6] Their radical colleagues have had quite a bit of success in skimming a saving remnant off of each of these generations. Both groups have used the primary school talk about "liberty and justice for all," as well as the narratives of "the growth of liberty" learned in high school, as a basis for their teaching. Both have insisted that America is still betraying its own traditions and ideals—an insistence which does not do much good unless the student has a fairly firm grasp of, and attachment to, those traditions and ideals.[7]

So I would have hoped that the discussion of Hirsch had consisted of remarks like "Hirsch has a point, but . . . ," or "Granted that the kids are culturally illiterate, still . . . ," or "Here's a way to draw up a better list than Hirsch's . . . ," or "Maybe we can piggyback on Hirsch by . . . ," or even "Maybe we can use Hirsch as a Trojan Horse by . . . ." But the typical remark about Hirsch was that he had a hegemonic conception of culture, that his list was biased toward the status quo, and the like. His book was lumped with Bloom's as a symptom of a wave of reaction. It was criticized at a high-theoretical, rather than a low-practical, level. This treatment of Hirsch made me feel that the conference was overphilosophized and underpoliticized, in the sense that it was more concerned with doctrinal purity than in asking what is to be done.

In this it resembles the cultural left as a whole. This left makes even more of a big deal of philosophy than the Marxists used to. Its members tend to think that they have done something politically useful if they have deconstructed a text, or detected totalization at work in it, or shown, in the manner of de Man, the impossibility of reading it. The cultural left seems to me to share with the old-timey Marxists both an instinctive distrust of proposals for concrete, piece-meal reform and the conviction that it is very important to find the "correct theoretical analysis" of a social phenomenon, even if this analysis leads not to proposals for specific changes but only to one more reiteration of the need for transformation. I have lots of doubts about this overemphasis on theory, but since I have set them out elsewhere, I shall not repeat them here.[8]

Instead, I shall end these remarks by adverting, at last, to what I liked best about the conference. Even though I thought that phi-losophy was given too much importance, I agreed with the gist of the philosophical remarks made. The participants tended to take for granted most of the philosophical theses which Foucault and Derrida took over from Nietzsche: truth is a matter of useful tools rather than of accurate representation, the self is a nexus of relations rather than a substance, truth and power will always be inextricably interlocked, there is no point in trying for grand totalizing theories of history ("scientific socialism," for example), there is no such thing as "ratio-nality" other than that contextually defined by the practices of a group, etc. These theses are common to Nietzsche and Dewey, and as a Deweyan I am naturally happy to see them becoming entrenched.[9]

Adoption of these theses has led the cultural left to dismiss Plato-nist talk of "timeless truths" or "eternal values." Dewey, too, tried to get rid of this talk, and urged educators to think more about growth and less about truth. This left is following his advice by changing the canon in various disciplines, not by reference to mythical "stan-dards of excellence" but simply by reference to what it now seems especially important to tell the students about. This is the way in which, in periods of academic freedom, the canon has always been changed. At times of high excitement within a discipline, the canon gets changed faster than usual.[10] This is a time of excitement in the humanities, and the rate of canon change is speeding up. Such changes seem to me all to the good, as long as they do not lead us to give up the very idea of a canon. There is, after all, a good pragmatic reason for overlap in reading lists across time and space: parents and children can communicate more easily if they have read some of the same books, as can, say, graduates of Amherst and of Miami-Dade Community College.

My hunch is that certain specific changes in the canon—those which will help students learn about what it has been like (and often still is like) to be female, or black, or gay—will be the chief accomplishment of the contemporary cultural left. This will be a very important accomplishment indeed. It will not amount to a transformation of society, but it will make life much less cruel for a lot of people, and will make America into a more decent place. Thanks to the trickle-down effect, we can expect *Their Eyes Were Watching God* to turn up in high-school English classes before the end of the century. A little later, it may be followed by *Giovanni's Room* and *Rubyfruit Jungle*. As has happened so many times in the past in our country's reformist history, the books that startled college sophomores will be the books their descendants have to write essays about in high school.

Someday, thanks to the effect of books like Eve Kosofsky Sedgwick's on the current generation of Ph.D.'s in literature, and the effect which those Ph.D.'s will have on the next generation of college graduates, we may have annual commemorations of the Stonewall riots in the high schools, just as we now (to Bull Connor's astonishment, presumably) have annual commemorations of King's birthday. A lot of the participants in the conference are, like Sedgwick, busy saying new and important things which will eventually trickle down, and do a lot of good. Any left that can accomplish that much is worth at least two cheers.

Notes

1 Frank Lentricchia, *Criticism and Social Change* (Chicago, 1983), 2. This is not the place to discuss this very intelligent and powerful book in detail. I cite it because I have a sort of love-hate relation to it. I enthusiastically share a lot of Lentricchia's attitudes (for example, his preference for William James and Kenneth Burke over Paul de Man) while nevertheless finding the book pervaded by a sense of alienation which I find unintelligible.

2 Michel Foucault, *Language, Counter-Memory, Practice: Selected Essays and Inter-views*, ed. Donald F. Bouchard, trans. Donald F. Bouchard and Sherry Simon (Ithaca, 1977), 230.

3 They have this chance in part because Hirsch has gotten his hands dirty: he has done a lot of hard work familiarizing himself with the (rather dismal) literature of the educational establishment, finding out where the levers of power in this estab-lishment are, trying to persuade professional groups and state boards of education of the need for change, raising money from foundations to get sample curricula and tests written, and so on. Except that he wants to reform rather than transform, Hirsch is a good example of what Lentricchia commends: "the *specific intellec-tual* described by Foucault, one whose radical work of transformation, whose fight against repression is carried on at the specific institutional site at which he finds himself and on the terms of his own expertise" (*Criticism and Social Change*, 6).

4 This is not, of course, to say that local schools should be financed out of local taxes. The decision of the New Jersey Supreme Court that such a financing method violates the constitutional rights of the students seems to me a reformist move which deserves more attention than it has received.

5 Half the students will not go on to college—the poorest half. Surely any cultural left which hopes to see change produced by democratic means will want that half to have the recognitional capacities necessary to function as part of the electorate, rather than letting these capacities be reserved for the other, richer, half?

6 I admit, however, that things seem to be changing, since recently a substantial majority of college students have been voting for Reagan, and now Bush. May God forgive them.

7 I enlarge on this point in "Education, Socialization, and Individuation," forthcom-ing in *Dissent*.

8 See my "Thugs and Theorists: A Reply to Bernstein," *Political Theory* 15 (1987): 564–80.

9 A lot of my recent work has been devoted to pointing out analogies between Nietz-sche and William James, Foucault and Dewey, Derrida and Donald Davidson, and so on.

10 See, on this point, David Bromwich, "Canon Bashing," *Dissent* (Fall 1988): 479–81. I agree with Bromwich's point that the cultural left tends to confuse mass culture with democracy and to be suspicious of canons simply on the basis of that confusion. It is true, as Alexander Nehamas has pointed out with reference to Greek tragedy, that what was once mass culture often gets converted, after a lapse of time, into an aesthetic object of interest to high culture. But that is no reason for telescoping the process. One good reason for having a high culture is to provide an alternative set of fantasies to those current in mass culture. If there are no such alternative fantasies, one of the important stimuli to social change—the urge by the intellectual elite to explain to the masses that they do not understand what is really going on—is likely to disappear.

Stanley Fish

The Common Touch, or, One Size Fits All

When Robert Penn Warren died in the fall
of 1989 the *New York Times* printed a lengthy
and admiring obituary in which it was noted,
among other things, that Warren was greatly
influenced by John Crowe Ransom. No doubt
the Ransom influence extended to many matters, but the *Times* chose to highlight only
one. Ransom, it informed us with authoritative solemnity, "once pointed out the impov-
erishment of modern life and the handicap
to a writer in the destruction of commonly
held myths that had been the heritage of the
Western world" (16 September 1989, p. 11).
What is curious is not that Ransom's observation (if it is his; there is no reference) is
remarked, but that it has almost no relationship to what the rest of the article goes on
to say about Warren, and indeed it is only by
way of an obviously strained transition that
the journalist is able to return to his or her
putative subject.

If this is a puzzle, it is a small one that registers only on someone like me who is watching
for signs. The puzzle becomes less puzzling
and the signs more foregrounded when one
turns to another vehicle of high-middlebrow

journalism, the *New Yorker* magazine, and finds in the 21 August 1989 issue two reviews that appear on consecutive pages. The first, by Brad Leithauser, is a review of the fiftieth anniversary reissue of John Steinbeck's *Grapes of Wrath*. The tone is set from the very first sentence when Leithauser reminds us that Steinbeck quarried his titles and epigraphs from the Bible, hymnals, Shakespeare, Milton, Burns, and Blake. This practice is immediately read as a "signal of the grandeur [Steinbeck] self-consciously aspired to," and we are not surprised by the subsequent judgment that this grandeur was seldom if ever achieved. More than a hint of what is to come is provided when the list of Steinbeck's strengths is barely distinguishable from the list of his weaknesses: on the one hand, "sympathy for the disenfranchised, moral urgency, narrative propulsion," on the other, "repetitiveness, simplistic politics, sentimentality."[1] Only the asymmetry of the order in the two lists prevents us from seeing that sympathy for the disenfranchised (strength) is the same as sentimentality (weakness), narrative propulsion the same as repetitiveness, moral urgency the same as simplistic politics.

As it turns out, *any* politics is regarded as simplistic by this reviewer, who tells us, first, that one could aptly describe *The Grapes of Wrath* as a novel about the homeless and, second, that nevertheless it is "old fashioned, especially in its very willingness to tender solutions for the social problems it documents." The apparent paradox of downgrading the book because it is both up-to-date and out-of-date is resolved when these two categories are subsumed under the larger category of "popular fiction," ever up-to-date and therefore soon dated: ". . . how at home the novel would seem on a current *Times* best-seller list, with a blurb reading something like 'Three generations of a dispossessed Oklahoma family head west toward hope.'" In the context of this judgment the fact that "the book remains one of the best selling American novels of all time" reads as an indictment. Mixing faint praise with genteel condescension, Leithauser moves in the following pages to a final assessment: Steinbeck leaves us with "a regretful sense . . . of how much better a writer he might have been"; as it is, his book only "occasionally offers one of the rarest and most gratifying pleasures that literature opens up to us, . . . that little miracle of transformation by which . . . a stick figure becomes an Everyman."[2] This last word says it all: a work rises to the stature of serious literature only if it transcends the local concerns that inspire its author.

If Leithauser's assumptions remain implicit, they are explicitly proclaimed in the book reviewed on the next page, Robert Alter's *Pleasures of Reading in an Ideological Age*. Alter's thesis is in fact adumbrated in his title: the true pleasures of reading—the pleasures of contact with a "transhistorical human community" through the medium of "the common stuff of our human existence"—are opposed to "the explicit ideological commitments" of "political systems."[3] The thesis is warmly approved by the anonymous reviewer, who, with an irony that escapes him or her, calls it "timely": "This timely study takes issue with contemporary schools of literary criticism that maintain that the literary canon is an instrument of domination, or that literary works are no different from other verbal communications, or that a literary text has no meaning."[4]

It is tempting to linger on the inaccuracy of this characterization of the contemporary critical scene, to point out, for example, that a relationship to particular political agendas is only one of the things predicated of the canon by advanced critics, or that typically theorists do not deny the difference of literary works but inquire into the production and revision of that difference by social and political forces, or that it is Alter who deprives literary texts of their meaning by regarding their local contexts of reference as discardable and beside the literary point. But I will resist the temptation and focus instead on the relationship between the two apparently dissimilar reviews, one dismissive of popular or middlebrow culture, the other taking potshots at the alleged absurdities of the high academy. What links them is their joint affirmation of a supposed *common* ground in relation to which popular culture and contemporary literary theory are alike passing fads, deviations from the main path. Both political causes and scholarly agendas constitute mere fashion, and as George Steiner (the author of another book I shall be examining) puts it (he borrows from Leopardi), "Fashion is the mother of Death,"[5] by which he means that what is fashionable—of local and temporary urgency—takes our attention away from what abides, what is central, what is common. So far is Alter from being fashionable that, as the reviewer notes, he declines even to *debate* "Marxism, feminism, structuralism, or deconstruction." As we shall see, this strategy (replicated by the reviewer) is typical of those who oppose the common to the merely ideological, and one can understand why: if what you are affirming is basic to human experience, argument is unnecessary; for the deficiencies of these exotic programs will be obvious to anyone with, as we say, a bit of "common sense." The review of Alter's book (shorter than my analysis of it) ends with the double praise of the author's "lucid and moderate way" and of literature for preserving "from generation to generation" the "diversity, passions and playfulness" of "human beings."[6] The curious—even bizarre— word in this encomium is "diversity." What does it mean? What could it mean? How do you celebrate diversity in a context that affirms the common so strongly?

These and other related questions are raised often in the twelve brief essays that appear in the summer 1989 issue of the *National Forum*. The agenda is set in the introduction by editor Stephen White when he affirms "the notion that we need consensus on some of the things we need to know." He is followed by William Bennett, former Secretary of Education, who laments "the disappearance of a common curriculum in many of the nation's colleges and universities, and the resulting failure of many students to acquire . . . even a rudimentary knowledge of the civilization of which they are both products and heirs." A few pages later Lynne Cheney, head of the National Endowment for the Humanities, offers praise of Columbia University's core curriculum with its "remarkable stability"; Chester Finn, former Assistant Secretary in the Department of Education, concisely summarizes the group concern when he declares that "the foremost job of formal education is to teach our children—all of them—about those things we have in common." From another perspective Elizabeth Fox-Genovese worries that the "extreme claims of feminism . . . risk undermining any aspiration to common standards and a common culture, including a common ideal of justice," and she concludes by warning that "without some semblance of a collective culture and of common ideals, we are left without a common basis from which to defend the claims of the individual against oppression."[7]

No doubt this celebration of the common is intended to be reassuring and even benign, but to these ears at least, phrases like "collective culture" and "common curriculum" have a disconcerting sound, for they suggest the imposing of special and indeed *un*common standards on the very persons whose commonness is supposedly being affirmed. Here we meet in the context of educational policy the familiar problem at the heart of liberal politics: how to reconcile the exercise of authority with the very values—freedom, tolerance, diversity—supposedly protected by that authority. By and large, the contributors to this issue of the *National Forum* evade the problem by assuming its solution in an unexamined invocation of the "common"; that is, in order to get their agenda off the ground they assume that the *content* of the category "common" is uncontroversial; and once this assumption is in place, the claim to be taking account of, and even honoring, diversity can be asserted with apparent coherence. The deep *in*coherence of the claim is embedded in a sentence I have already quoted: "The foremost job of formal education is to teach our children—all of them—about those things we have in common." The question, suppressed by this formulation, is "when?" That is, when do "we" have these things in common? The present tense "have" suggests, indeed insists, that the common is *already* ours, but if that were so there would be no "job" for formal education to do. The sentence fudges the real relationship between its components: education comes first; the common, or rather *some* common, is its product. Our children—"all of them"—do not begin with shared perspectives; they are to be brought to the perspectives common to some of us by a process in which the perspectives they may have shared, had in common, with others of us are either expunged or marginalized.

There is nothing necessarily scandalous about this; the normative and therefore coercive force of education is, or should be, a given. The point is worth making only because Finn and others assume that the category of the common is uncontroversial, a matter of what everyone easily sees, of what is so obvious and perspicuous that only the most skewed perceptions could miss it. This assumption is not argued for but merely asserted in words like "have" in "have in common," for a reason I have already noted: to argue for the common would be to acknowledge that it is *arguable*, a matter of dispute, and as such incapable of serving as the self-evident baseline in relation to which supposedly uncommon views are identified and stigmatized. In place of argument polemicists like Finn render judgments that (in their view) only madmen would gainsay: "Democracy is not just different from totalitarianism; it is better. Freedom of expression beats censorship all hollow, and freedom of worship is preferable both to Inquisitions and to state-enforced atheism."[8] Many of us would agree with these judgments; nevertheless they are not so *indisputably* true as Finn implies. First, the terms are loaded—labels like "totalitarianism" and "censorship" are not the names of practices one is submitting for judgment but of practices that have already been judged; second, even if the terms are not challenged, and censors or inquisitors are willing to identify themselves as such, it would still be possible to debate the value of the actions they perform. Military establishments (including the establishment of the United States) will often insist, and with reason, that censorship is necessary if the nation's defenses are to be maintained; and in times of war inquisitional techniques are engaged in even by democracies. On the other side, democracy has often been derided (in our era, in our country) as mob rule, and in the minds of some feminists, freedom of expression licenses violence against women in the form of pornography.

I am not endorsing any of these positions, but merely pointing out that they can and have been put forward, and put forward by people who are not obviously eccentric or insane. Nor am I denying the possibility of judgment, the possibility of deciding, with William Bennett, that "some forms of government are better than others,"[9] but merely observing that any judgment one might make in that direction is disputable, and disputable by persons no less well *educated* than you or I. The moral is concisely stated by R. T. Smith, another contributor to the *National Forum*, who began, he reports, as a believer in "the test of time," but now realizes that "he had been camping on embattled ground all along."[10] What I want to say is that it is *all* embattled ground and no less so when it is labeled as "common" ground, as something firmly under everyone's feet. Someone who says to you, "This is *our* common ground," is really saying, "This is *my* common ground, the substratum of assumptions and values that produces *my* judgments, and it should be yours, too."

Now this is not an impossible proposition; it could easily happen that you were persuaded to exchange your assumptions and values for someone else's; but in that event, the ground you would then stand on would be no more common, in the sense of being shared by everyone, than the ground you had left behind. The common, in short, is a contested category; its content will vary with the varying perspectives of those who assert it. When Finn declares that the "primary subject matter of public schooling" is "the commonalities, not the differences," he thinks that the difference between the two is easy to tell; and indeed it is, from the particular point of view that Finn (or any particular person) now occupies; but from another point of view the difference will be different; that is, what is the same or common will itself be different and what is different from the differing commonalities will be different. I multiply the differences in such a dizzying way in order once again to make my only point: *it is difference all the way down;* difference cannot be managed by measuring it against the common because the shape of the common is itself differential.

Indeed, the common is differential—relative to the context or interpretive community within which its shape is specified—even when its supposed basis is difference itself. The identification of difference as the common ground on which we all (should) stand might seem to be a powerful and coherent response to the arguments of Finn, Bennett, and Cheney, but it is a response that falls into the very error it would correct. Consider, for example, the essay authored by Gerald Graff and William Cain, "Peace Plan for the Canon Wars," originally published in the *Nation* and reprinted in the *National Forum*. Graff and Cain are expanding on Graff's now familiar directive, "teach the conflicts," by which he means "structuring the curriculum around . . . conflicts." Under current pedagogical conditions, Graff and Cain complain, students see only the preferred unifying project of particular instructors; they are thus "spared the unseemly sight of their teachers washing their dirty linen in public," but the price they pay for this "peace and quiet" is intellectual sterility.[11]

Cain and Graff want us to abandon this form of academic gentility and put conflict at the center of the curriculum. But if conflict is made into a structural principle, its very nature is domesticated; rather than being the manifestation of difference, conflict becomes the theater in which difference is displayed and stage-managed. Once a line has been drawn around difference, it ceases to be what it is— the remainder that escapes the drawing of any line, no matter how generous—and becomes just another topic in the syllabus. By making difference into a new "common" ground Cain and Graff succeed only in evading the lesson of its irreducibility. Strange as it may seem, the effect of bringing difference into the spotlight front and center is to obscure its operation, to hide the fact that the perspective from which one thinks to spy difference is itself challengeable, partisan, conflictual, differential.

Difference is evaded in a different but related way by Betty Jean Craige when, in apparent contrast to Graff and Cain, she counsels "holistic" rather than "oppositional" thinking. "Holohumanists," she tells us, will abandon the dualism of objective versus political points of view, and in the context of a full acknowledgment of the relativity of value, will "teach students to recognize and welcome cultural difference." To that end she urges a curriculum that "would foster a tolerance—and, ideally, an appreciation—of cultural beliefs and behaviors different from our own."[12] This seems admirable, but one must ask from what perspective this recognition of cultural difference will occur, or (it is the same question) from what position the tolerances one is supposed to foster will be identified? Only two answers to these questions are possible and they both subvert Craige's project. If, on the one hand, the perspective from which cultural differences are to be recognized is a perspective shared by everyone—is no *perspective* at all—one would then be claiming for it precisely the objectivity and universality Craige declares "not possible"; and if, on the other hand, the perspective is, in fact, a perspective—shared by some but not by all—the tolerances it encourages one to foster would not be recognized *as* tolerances by the inhabitants of other perspectives. Tolerance, in short, is not an independent value but a context-specific one, and therefore to exercise it is not to avoid oppositional activity but to engage in it. Graff and Cain want to privilege conflict; Craige wants to privilege tolerance. Each fails to see that conflict and tolerance cannot be privileged—made into platforms from which one can confidently and unproblematically speak—without turning them into the kind of normative and transcendental standards to which they are putatively opposed.

In the end, the difference between those who, like Bennett, Cheney, and Finn, would subordinate difference in the name of the common and those who, like Cain, Graff, and Craige, would acknowledge difference by making it into a central value is only apparent, a difference, finally, between different ways of managing (or attempting to manage) difference. (This is not to say that distinctions between these positions cannot be made on other grounds—pragmatic, institutional, humane—and on those grounds the Cain-Graff-Craige position is decidedly more attractive to me.)

The point may become clearer if we substitute for difference—a word that by now must be inducing something akin to seasickness—the notion of the political. It is politics or, as it is sometimes put, ideology that the right-establishment wishes to control, even eliminate; and it is politics that the left-challengers urge us to acknowledge and affirm. But both agendas fail in the same way: on the one side, the control or elimination of politics requires a vantage point which is not itself political, and the impossibility of specifying what is common without provoking a dispute demonstrates that no such vantage point is available; on the other side, the affirmation of politics implies that politics is something one can either refuse or embrace, and that in turn implies a moment when politics is an *option* rather than a name for the condition—the condition of difference—that one can never escape. Those who think they can *choose* politics are no less evading the fact of the political—the fact that point of view and perspectivity are irreducible features of consciousness and action—than those who think they can bracket politics. Politics can neither be avoided nor positively embraced; these impossible alternatives are superficially different ways of *grasping* the political, of holding it in one's hand, whereas properly understood, the political—the inescapability of partisan, angled seeing—is what always and already grasps us.

=====

If we are always in the grasp of the political and can never move either to the high ground of moral certainty or to the even higher ground of a universal tolerance (universals in any direction are what the operation of difference renders unavailable), then the only question is, by what form of the political shall we be grasped? An answer to this question will not be found in the arguments of the opposing sides of the educational debate because those arguments, as we have seen, rest on claims (the claim either to have identified the exclusively normative set of values or to have moved beyond exclusion altogether) that cannot be sustained. It is time therefore to seek an answer elsewhere, not in the nuances of philosophy but in the more material consequences that will follow from the triumph of either agenda. The parties to the debate are telling us, in effect, what will be good for us, and it seems reasonable to ask if the conception of the good they offer is one we would like to embrace.

We will be helped in this inquiry by the growing number of what I call "ethicist" books. The list is an ever-lengthening one, and I can only pause here to rehearse some of the authors (notably male) and their titles: Allan Bloom, *The Closing of the American Mind*, Robert Alter, *The Pleasures of Reading in an Ideological Age*, Wayne Booth, *The Company We Keep*, George Steiner, *Real Presences*, Peter Shaw, *The War against the Intellect*, John Silber, *Straight Shooting*, Page Smith, *Killing the Spirit*, Roger Kimball, *Tenured Radicals*, Charles Sykes, *ProfScam*, James Atlas, *The Book Wars*, Frank Kermode, *An Appetite for Poetry*, Dinesh D'Souza, *Illiberal Education*, Alvin Kernan, *The Death of Literature*, Robert Bork, *The Tempting of America*, Bernard Bergonzi, *Exploding English*, Peter Washington, *Fraud: Literary Theory, and the End of English*. The genre is not a new one (it begins as early as the Book of Jeremiah, chapter 2, verse 7: "ye . . . made mine heritage an abomination"), and the story it tells is always a story of loss, the loss of a time when common values were acknowledged and affirmed by everyone. The villains vary (the devil, the Antichrist, foreigners, immigrants, Jews) but in this latest version of the genre they are moral relativists in general and literary theorists in particular.

The reasoning is simple: by teaching that all norms and standards are specific, contingent, historically produced, and potentially revisable, literary theorists and poststructuralist thinkers, it is said, undo the foundations on which any truly ethical action might be based. After all, the argument continues, if ethical judgments are disputable, and none can ever be grounded in anything firmer than the local conditions of practice, the act of judgment is rendered meaningless and trivial. The response, given many times by many persons but apparently not readily taken in, is that since those who are embedded in local practices—of literary criticism, law, education, or anything else—are "naturally" heirs of the norms and standards built into those practices, they can never be without (in two senses) norms and standards and are thus always acting in value-laden and judgmental ways simply by being competent actors in their workplaces. The poststructuralist characterization of the normative as a local rather than a transcendental realm, far from rendering ethical judgment impossible, renders it inevitable and inescapable. Antifoundationalist thought, properly understood, is not an assault on ethics but an account of the conditions—textual and revisable, to be sure—within which moments of ethical choice are always and *genuinely* emerging; it is only if ethical norms existed *elsewhere* that there would be a chance of missing them, but if they are always and already where you are they cannot be avoided. The counterresponse—that such moments are *not* genuine because they are not rooted in standards and norms that are independently and objectively established—fails when one realizes that were such standards to exist somewhere—in the mind of God or in the totality of the universe—there would be no one capable of recognizing or responding to them. After all, none of us lives in the mind of God or in the totality of the universe; rather, we all live in specific places demarcated in their configurations and in their possibilities for action (including ethical action) by transient, partial, shifting, and contingent understandings of what is and what should be.

But I fear I have slid back into philosophy again so soon after announcing my intention to remove the discussion from its precincts. Let me return the focus to where I promised it would be, on the relationship between the ethicist books and the specification by the educational conservatives of a common good as embodied in a common culture. The relationship is pretty much a straightforward one that proceeds via the story of loss so characteristic of this tradition: if a common cultural heritage has been lost, it must be the case that we have also lost or lost sight of the perspective from which that heritage could be identified and validated; we have lost the perspective of normative ethics, the set of principles that at once underwrites and requires the common. The imperative, then, is to recover and preserve those principles and that is why, in this argument, the maintenance of the traditional literary canon is such a priority; for the canon (again in this argument) is the repository, the ark, of those principles, not only containing them but extending them in the effects it has on its readers.

The process by which this extension occurs is sketched out for us in Robert Alter's book. The first stage rests on a familiar formalist thesis: literary language, unlike ordinary language, escapes the confines of particular, local, historical referents; "densely layered and multi-directional," it provokes "multifarious connections and . . . interpretations," which work against the appeal of "explicit ideological commitments."[13] What literary language works *for* is evidently more difficult to say; Alter attributes to it the very general capacity of "address[ing] reality," and, after acknowledging that " 'reality' is a notoriously slippery term," defines it none too firmly "as an umbrella for the underlying aspects of our being in the world," which in turn is glossed as "the common stuff of our human existence."[14] At this point the line of argument becomes clear: the reader who engages with the language of literature (as opposed to the language of advertising or popular culture) will be immersed in "the common," and by virtue of that immersion will become more and more like it. "Literary texts," Alter tells us, "invite a special mode of attention"[15]—the mode of attending to transhistorical aspects of being—and if the invitation is taken up, that mode will be the mode of *our* existence; we will ourselves be "special"—that is, not special, but universal—in the very same way literature is.

All of this assumes that "literature" is not a descriptive but a normative category, a label applied in approbation and honor and a label withheld from inferior productions like Steinbeck's *Grapes of Wrath* that do not display the proper transcendental qualities. Much of Alter's book is devoted to picking out the works that in his view deserve the label and then presenting them as "the Canon." Once this is done, the paradigm is complete: books made out of transcontextual language point to transcontextual values and thus make their serious readers into transcontextual beings informed by those same (common) values. The entire process is nicely encapsulated in a single sentence from Wayne Booth's *The Company We Keep*, another of the ethicist tracts and in many ways the best of them. Speaking of genuine works of literature like *King Lear, Don Quixote, Bleak House, War and Peace*, etc., Booth says, "When I read [them] . . . I meet in their authors friends who demonstrate their friendship not only in the range and depth and intensity of pleasure they offer, . . . but finally in the irresistible invitation they extend to live during these moments a richer and fuller life than I could manage on my own." [16]

We have all had the experience Booth describes (although perhaps with books different from those he would invoke), but the relation of such "moments" to the strong ethicist argument is problematical. If the truly great works are those that irresistibly invite us to live a richer and fuller life, why have so many readers of the books Alter and Booth list managed to resist the invitation and gone on from reading Shakespeare and Goethe to acts of incredible cruelty? And why, conversely, have readers of works made of supposedly inferior stuff— works of popular and even "low" culture—been moved by their reading to acts of great altruism and service? And why, if the works of the Western canon are the repository of common (in the sense of universal) ethical values, has there been so much argument about the values to be found in them, including the argument that they have nothing especially ethical to teach at all? If what these works "irresistibly" convey to us and convey us to is so common, why is it so much in dispute? And given the dispute, how do we know when the ethical direction we spy in a book is the right one? It would seem that in order to answer these questions one must *already* be in the state of ethical perfection to which the canon is supposed to bring one, which suggests the superfluousness or at least causal irrelevance of the canon to the very values it is said to produce.

At this point an ethicist might respond that the experience of literature does not point us to any particular ethics but to the realm of the ethical in general, and I would respond in turn that the realm of the ethical in general is either empty or full of some contestable set of values that someone or some group wishes to pass off as the general. The point is the same one I have made before: like the "common," the category of the "ethical"—which is, after all, a particular instance of the common—is continually in dispute; it cannot serve as an antidote to politics and ideology, as Alter and others want it to, because it will be, in any form that makes human sense, a political and ideological construction. Another way to put this is to say that the trouble with ethicist arguments is that they don't have an opponent; there are no *non*-ethicists against whom the ethical critic can position himself, for in order to *be* a non-ethicist one would have to stand free of any local network of beliefs, assumptions, purposes, obligations, etc., and such a standing free—necessary both to the moment of pure ethical choice and to the possibility of choosing *against* ethics—is not an option for human beings. Everyone is always and already an ethicist, enacting value in every activity, including the activity of reading.[17] The only question is, which of the many possible ethicisms—ethical stances—should one affirm?

In short, the ethicists are not *the* ethicists, in the sense of being the sole proprietors of a moral vision in a world of shameless relativists; rather, they are the purveyors of a *particular* moral vision that must make its way in the face of competition from other moral visions that come attached to texts no less inherently worthy than the texts recommended by Booth and Alter. In the absence of an exclusive claim to the moral high ground and without the supporting prop of a set of obviously sacred books, the ethicists are left only with the force of their example as displayed in their writings. Is it an example we wish to follow? Is their conception of the common good so compelling that we would wish to embrace it?

On the evidence of their own moral performances, the answer, I think, must be "no." A favorite ploy of these authors is to quote out of context and often without attribution passages or sentences that are presented as self-evident demonstrations of the foolishness, turpitude, stupidity, and absurdity of their opponents. This practice is then justified *ethically*, as when Alter says of examples of what seem to him to be obvious atrocities, "for reasons of simple decency I will not cite the sources or the authors' names."[18] Here is a moment in which the claim of an ethicist to be presenting us with a common moral vision (the word "common" makes many appearances in Alter's book) intersects with the singularity and dubiety of the moral vision informing his practice. In what sense is it "decent" to declare the sentence of another writer "repellent" without in any way acknowledging the large project (whose configurations would include the predecessors to whom he or she was responding) of which the sentence is a part? In what sense is it "decent" to call someone names at the very moment one is depriving the victim of the name he or she has been forthright enough to sign? No doubt Alter would reply that he merely wishes to save his nameless authors from the embarrassment they would suffer were they fully identified; one would think, however, that they might prefer to represent themselves rather than be *mis*represented by a critic who uses the notion of "decency" in order to mask and excuse a form of behavior that many will find *morally* objectionable. (I will not even speak here to the obvious point that Alter's preferred authors—Milton, Henry James, Fielding—would fare no better than his chosen targets were they to be subjected to his procedures.)

The fact that Alter's scholarly practices are ethically questionable does not distinguish him from any number of writers on either side of the debate; but since it is precisely his claim to *be* distinguishable from his less responsible colleagues (who remain nameless), the point is worth making, for it raises in a local, particular form the question I have been asking: do we want such persons to be our *moral* guides? The same question can be put to another self-proclaimed ethicist, Professor Anne Barbeau Gardiner of the John Jay College of Criminal Justice. Writing in the fall 1989 issue of the *ADE Bulletin*, Professor Gardiner is concerned with celebrating the "power of a literary text to convey . . . an ethical point"; "great literary texts of the past are . . . civilization building," she says, and offers as her example a class's experience with Dante's *Inferno*, a must on any ethicist's list. What Professor Gardiner did was describe a number of twentieth-century moral actors—such as the person "who never leaves home without consulting a horoscope"—and then ask her students to assign them to the appropriate circle of hell. She calls the exercise "The 1980s through Dante's Eyes: Name the Circle, Ditch, and Punishment Reserved for These Wrongdoers," and reports happily that "students had no trouble exercising their moral imagination and, after putting themselves in Dante's place, assigning an appropriate level of punishment to each offender."[19] Putting aside for the moment the injustice here done to Dante, whose "place" is surely more capacious than

Gardiner imagines, one is at least uneasy at this display of moral insensitivity in the name of the moral qualities supposedly inculcated by great texts. Are we ready to follow the ethical example of a professor who declares herself pleased to "see that the students enjoyed passing moral judgment"? Is this the training we wish our students to receive? Are these the ethics that underlie our common cultural tradition?

Let me be clear. I would not deny Professor Gardiner her perspective, either on Dante or on the goals and purposes of education. My quarrel is with the assumption, in her writing and in the writings of others, that a few people (self-selected) have a privileged access to common or universal ethical values and that they have this access in part because, unlike their less clear-sighted colleagues, they have identified and bonded with the small set of texts that embodies those values. What the ethicists are saying to us is, "We (not you) are educated, we (not you) are sensitive; therefore you should listen to us." The question again is, should we? and again I look for an answer in the example offered us in the performance of a high ethicist, Martha C. Nussbaum, David Benedict Professor of Classics, Professor of Philosophy, and Professor of Comparative Literature at Brown University. It would seem that if anyone has the proper ethicist credentials for serving as our moral exemplar, it is Professor Nussbaum, who has for some time been conversing with Aeschylus and Virgil (presumably in the original Greek and Latin), engaging strenuously with Plato, Aristotle, Hume, Kant, and others, with ample time, apparently, for serious study of Stendhal, Henry James, and Proust.

The piece of Professor Nussbaum's I have in mind is an admiring review of Wayne Booth's *The Company We Keep*. Nussbaum approvingly rehearses the book's arguments and quotes, among other excerpts, the sentence I have already cited in which Booth pays tribute to literary works that "enable" readers "to live . . . a richer and fuller life than they could manage on their own."[20] Later she offers a discrimination that presumably exemplifies the fuller and richer life *she* is now able to live. Her concern is the difference (slighted, she says, by Booth) between the way one treats a book and the way one treats "a real live person." "Sometimes," she says, "people feel the need for complete numbing distraction, distraction so complete that it blots out all stress and worry." "Consider," she continues, two people in search of such undemanding release. The one hires a prostitute and indulges in an evening of casual sex. The other buys a Dick Francis novel and lies on the couch all evening reading. There must be, I think, a huge moral difference between these people . . . (I say this as someone who reads in just this way whenever I finish writing a paper . . .). The person who hires a prostitute is seeking relief by using another human being; he or she engages in a transaction that debases both a person and an intimate activity. The person who reads Dick Francis is not, I believe, doing any harm to anyone. Surely she is not *exploiting* the writer; indeed, she is treating Francis exactly as he would wish, in a not undignified business transaction.[21]

There is so much wrong with this that it is difficult to know where to begin. Even the most attractive aspect of the passage—the acknowledgment (in the parenthesis) that Nussbaum is talking about herself and is her own chief example—breathes self-promotion and self-dramatization: "Here I am, at this moment, writing a paper that engages the full, rich, and moral me, the very paper you are no doubt admiring me for, at this moment." As for the *argument* of the passage, problems arise at every juncture. Is the moral difference between the two persons Nussbaum imagines as clear as she thinks and in the direction she assumes? Could she be unaware that there is at least an argument for prostitution as a feminist praxis as well as a historical analysis in which the prostitute is the scapegoat category for everything a society cannot bear to confront? And, in any case, will the prostitute be pleased to know that Nussbaum has chosen against him or her and for an evening with Dick Francis? And what of Mr. Francis? Will he be pleased to be the winner of a contest framed in these terms? Does he write, do you think, in order to provide thoughtless distraction for wearily heroic academics? Would he, if given the choice, want Nussbaum for a reader? Would he want to be consumed by a moral being so rarified that she simply discounts whatever serious intentions animate his rather subtle explorations of one aspect of the British character? And what of those of Mr. Francis's readers who are so foolish and morally deficient as to derive from his books something more positive than "numbing distraction," who are not teased out of, but into, thought? And what, too, of all those reviewers who were apparently moved by reading Mr. Francis (perhaps in bed) to speculations about the venerable (even canonical) tradition in which his work appears? And what of the entire world of popular culture, both inside and outside the academy, a world here dismissed without so much as a backward glance? This list of questions could be continued indefinitely, but the answers are less important than the fact that they can be posed with some force, for they speak not merely to Nussbaum's judgment on particular matters of literary culture but to the issue of judgment in general and therefore to Nussbaum's fitness for the role she and her fellow ethicists would play in our society.

One could reply that, after all, there is little danger that the reins of government or even of educational policy will in fact be handed over to Alter, Gardiner, and Nussbaum, and that therefore the thinness of their moral vision is not a matter of great concern. Unfortunately, however, that same vision, similarly thin but politically robust, is now being enacted in the edicts and rulings of highly placed government officials; I am thinking of documents like Lynne Cheney's *Humanities in America: A Report to the President, the Congress, and the American People*. Here, for example, is a key statement from that publication: "The humanities are about more than politics, about more than social power. What gives them their abiding worth are truths that pass beyond time and circumstance; truths that, transcending accidents of class, race and gender, speak to us all."[22] Note that this is a politics that dares not speak its name, but speaks (typically and disingenuously) in the name of the common sense "we" all share. Note also the dismissal of "social power" at the very moment it is being exercised by the head of a socially powerful agency in the form of a publication funded, printed, and mailed by the federal government. This political sleight of hand does considerable work, including the work of eliding questions one might otherwise be moved to ask, questions like "who gets to *say* which are the works that embody 'abiding worth'?" and "who are 'us all'?" The pamphlet itself is an answer: Cheney and her associates will get to say, and what they say will have all the impact and force provided by their relationship to that same federal government. It is also obvious who will *not* get to say, those for whom matters of class, race, ethnicity, and gender are of paramount importance and abiding concern, that is, those who are poor, black, Hispanic, Asian, female, gay, etc.

This is not a characterization that Cheney and company would accept. No polemic issuing from this establishment would be complete without paying lip service to diversity; but more often than not, the recognition is, in itself, an act of marginalization, as in this recommendation near the end of Cheney's pamphlet: "Undergraduates should study texts of Western civilization and should learn how the ideals and practices of our society have evolved. Students should also be encouraged to learn about other cultures."[23] The number of questions begged here is large and familiar: what about the students for whom the word "our" in "our society" is problematical, students for whom the culture made up of texts from fifth-century Athens, first-century Rome, and sixteenth-century England is decidedly "other"? What happens to *their* concerns, perspectives, values, heritages? The answer is that they must learn the "ideals and practices" identified by Cheney. Of course, neither they nor their classmates are *barred* from learning other things; indeed they are "encouraged" to learn them, presumably in the odd or spare moment stipulated in the fifty-hour proposal. After all, secondary and inessential matters must wait their time, even if it never comes.

The work done by Cheney's "also"—"should also be encouraged"— is done elsewhere by what I call the "and Alice Walker" move, performed when you make up a long list of great texts from Plato to T. S. Eliot and then say, "and Alice Walker," thus testifying to your commitment to diversity. Bennett prefers Martin Luther King, Jr., as his token[24] and now has taken to adding Coretta Scott King and Corazon Aquino, a new odd couple pressed into the service of displaying the capaciousness of the former secretary's mind. And Cheney now has kind words (at the end of a paragraph) for Susan B. Anthony and Frederick Douglass. Can Jackie Robinson be far behind?

When pressed on the point that such addenda are obvious afterthoughts, sops thrown to a notion of diversity that is being dishonored in the breach, conservative educators will typically reply, with Chester Finn, that we can't help it if "for a long time [white males] were the principal folks on the planet with the learning, the leisure, and the resources to create literature."[25] This argument, made at length in what the *National Review* (13 October 1989) advertised with melancholy glee as Sidney Hook's "last article" (presumably we are to regard this as deathbed testimony), rests on an assumption that will not survive scrutiny: the assumption that in a world of diverse cultures and subcultures, only those powerful enough to produce their own propaganda in the form of histories, curricula, reading lists, and poet laureateships were creating literature, singing songs, fashioning traditions, having thoughts. The fact that we now know little of the cultures that have been swept into one of history's dustbins hardly seems reason to dismiss them as obviously inferior, unless the reason is the one often given by victors: we won, you lost, now keep quiet! When Hook exclaims, "Of course the culture of the past was created by the elites of the past!" and asks, "Who else could have created it in a time when literacy . . . was the monopoly of the elite?"[26] he doesn't really want to hear an answer; that is, he doesn't want to take seriously his own word "created," for to do so would be to consider the possibility that the creation of a cultural history—of a great tradition—depends on the marginalization and suppression of other traditions and indeed of other elitisms which are now referred to as minor, or ethnic, or regional, or popular, or vulgar, or primitive, when they are referred to at all. Hook, like Finn, wants to take these dismissive labels as natural, even as he acknowledges that he and others of his party have applied them in the act of establishing their own taste as the taste "common to us all." In the end the argument amounts to no more than saying, "We know what's good; what's good is what people like us produce and appreciate, and we are going to see to it that everything else is excluded."

There is a word for this politics and it is "undemocratic"; not because it resists the demand for proportional representation—egalitarianism and democracy are not the same thing—but because it would arrest the play of democratic forces in order to reify as transcendent a particular and *un*common stage in cultural history. This politics would stop time and elevate one set of tastes to a position of privilege from which it could then label all other tastes as vulgar, inessential, and corrupting. Nowhere is the rationale for this political program (which always portrays itself as apolitical and even antipolitical) more clearly in evidence than in George Steiner's *Real Presences*. The first third of Steiner's book is an extended critique of the secondary or parasitic—that which is either a deviation from or unthinking imitation of the genuine, the immediate, the primary, the authentic. Against the endlessly resourceful discourse of the parasitic Steiner opposes "that which the heart knows," for example, that Tolstoy was offering an aberrant judgment when he proclaimed "*King Lear* to be 'beneath serious criticism.'"[27] Of course, the problem (illustrated by Tolstoy) is that not all hearts know the same thing; the problem, once again, is difference. But Steiner knows how to deal with it: the heart that doesn't know or that knows the wrong thing must be disregarded and disenfranchised. "Given a free vote," Steiner laments, "the bulk of humankind will choose football, the soap opera or bingo over Aeschylus." Steiner's strategy is simply *not* to give the bulk of humankind a vote and to refuse it on the basis of a principle that is enunciated as clearly as one might wish: "Democracy is fundamentally at odds with the canonical."[28] In fact, democracy is at odds with the canonic only if the canonic is viewed as a category established for all time; but if canons, in the company of the standards and norms that underwrite them, are always emerging and reemerging in response to historical needs and contingencies, then democracy is simply a name for the canon-making process. It is a process that Steiner (along with Cheney, Bennett, and Finn) would stop in its tracks by declaring, on no obvious authority whatsoever, that after a certain date (it varies from 1490 to 1940) nothing is to be admitted into the curriculum. This is clearly the implication of Steiner's scornful account of recent developments at an unnamed university (we can assume that it is Harvard):

> The bellwether of American universities assigns to its "core curriculum," this is to say, to its minimal requirements for literacy, a course on black women novelists of the early 1980s. [No "and Alice Walker" for him!] Poets, novelists, choreographers, painters of the most passing or derivative interests, are made the object of seminars and dissertations, of undergraduate lectures and post-doctoral research. The axioms of the transcendent . . .

axioms which this essay seeks to clarify—are invested in the overnight.[29]

The moral is obvious and it is drawn: these inferior authors and their texts must be "ruled out of court." Here, in contrast to the cautious timidity of Cheney's core curriculum with its cosmetic concessions to other cultures, races, genders, is the real thing, the authoritative imposition of one group's very particular tastes in the name of the common and the transcendental.

The question is, do we really want it? and if we are to trust the media (a dubious proposition), the answer would seem to be a ringing "yes"! Since 1989, when the *National Forum* published its "canon issue," the questions it raised have been debated with increasing urgency, but the shape of the debate has changed markedly because as things are now only one position is fully represented. In the *National Forum*, pieces by defenders of the traditional curriculum alternate with pieces by advocates of women's studies, minority studies, literary theory, etc.; but in the innumerable essays that have appeared in our major magazines and newspapers in the past two years, these latter groups are given no substantial voice and are introduced only as the excoriated and ridiculed other. Whatever the truth about the relative strength of the warring forces on college campuses, the conservative backlash has certainly won the media battle, so much so that a reader of the 18 February 1991 issue of the *New Republic* (once a respected liberal journal) would have to believe that there was no one on the "multiculturalist" side except a small band of radical-left crazies who had either never encountered or failed to absorb the rigors of the Western tradition. Along with this story, the *New Republic* tells another, contradictory story of a massive subversion which captured the villages and citadels as we slept, leaving only a few brave, beleaguered, powerless souls (like William Bennett, Lynne Cheney, Hilton Kramer, and William Simon) to mount a counterinsurgency. Here is the classically fissured shape of paranoid thought, in which absolute power and absolute vulnerability are simultaneously declared.

But tempting though the pleasures of diagnosis may be, I will forgo them and concentrate on what is for me the significant feature of the *New Republic*'s call to arms: it continues to present the issues in philosophical terms, as a battle between rationality and some darkly terrible alternative. The editor is correct when he observes that "no generation goes by without a 'crisis' in the humanities."[30] In his view, however, these recurring crises trace out a pattern in which the forces of evil reappear in every age to challenge the forces of good: "The most common cause of these recurrent crises has been the demand that the university conform to one orthodoxy or another." My analysis would be less apocalyptic, and I would rewrite his sentence to read: "The most common cause of these recurrent crises has been the resistance of an orthodoxy long in power to orthodoxies just now emerging and experiencing a new strength." Although the attack on multiculturalism and diversity is almost always made in terms of principle, behind it lies something much less grand and more human, a feeling by many older academics that the world they entered so many years ago has changed in ways they find threatening. One gets a glimpse of this feeling in a poignant sentence written by a university teacher in *Academic Questions*, the journal of the National Association of Scholars: "In the more than thirty years that I have been teaching . . . I have observed an increasing drift away from the kind of intellectual-cum-moral consensus I found to obtain . . . when I began my teaching career in 1954."[31] One does not know whether to lament or rejoice for this writer. On the one hand, it is more than thirty years and he is still in the game; on the other, it is not the game he was trained to play, and we can suppose that the very students who should now be presenting him with a festschrift are instead calling into question the assumptions that have guided his work all these years.

The personal distress registered here is real and should not be slighted or diminished (a version of it awaits us all, unless we die young), but neither should personal distress be allowed to read itself as evidence of the triumph of politics over reason. Although it has become fashionable to characterize the debate in these terms, a more accurate characterization would see it as a contest between one kind of politics—derisively called "political correctness"—and another politics—which I would call "political disappointment" or even "political envy." In short, there is politics (and within the differing political frameworks, reason) on both sides, and, as even a cursory reading of Gerald Graff's *Professing Literature* will show, it was ever thus. It has always been the case that the orthodoxy productive of one generation's sense of "the common" (that is, "common sense") is challenged by the concerns and emphases of the next generation; and it has also always been the case that the older generation can only hear the challenge as the emergence of irrationality, the abandoning of standards, the beginning of the end. To the person experiencing it as a diminution of his or her professional authority and influence, change can only be seen as the work of the devil.

I would suggest that we see it simply as change or, to use an even more basic term, as history; for then the arguments against it might begin to seem less heroic than quixotic, deployed not in the service of reason and the American way but as part of a (doomed) effort to stay the replacement of one historically produced "common ground" by its inevitable successor. The question then becomes not, "Will standards and values be subverted by the introduction of new materials and methodologies?" but, "What will be the likely effects of trying to say 'no' to history?" The first question makes sense only if standards and values exist in a realm apart from history where they define the obligations and responsibilities of historically situated actors; but if values and standards are themselves historical products, fashioned and refashioned in the crucible of discussion and debate, there is no danger of their being subverted because they are always and already being transformed.

Transformation, however, is always a painful process, at least for those persons (and I am often one of them) who want things to stay the same, and one can understand the Juvenalian laments ("we are going to hell in a hand-basket") even if one is not moved to echo them. In the end, however, I prefer the quieter tones of pragmatic inquiry: what is to be gained or lost in our everyday lives as students and teachers by either welcoming or rejecting various new emphases and methodologies urged on us by various constituencies? Unlike questions posed in the timeless language of philosophical abstractions, this is a question one can answer. If we harken to those who speak in the name of diversity (and I say again that I myself resist the invocation of diversity as a principle, as a new theology), the result will be more subject matter, more avenues of research, more attention to neglected and marginalized areas of our society, more opportunities to cross cultural, ethnic, and gender lines, more work, in short, for academics. If, on the other hand, we harken to those who would hold back the tide and defend the beachhead won thirty-five or fifty years ago, the result will be more rules, more exclusionary mechanisms, more hoops to jump through, more invidious distinctions, more opportunities to be demeaning and be demeaned, more bureaucracy, more control. I know what I like. In the words of the old song, how about you?

Notes

1   Brad Leithauser, review, *The New Yorker* (21 August 1989): 90.
2   Ibid., 93.
3   Robert Alter, *The Pleasures of Reading in an Ideological Age* (New York, 1989), 76, 54, 270.
4   Review of R. Alter, *The Pleasures of Reading in an Ideological Age, The New Yorker* (21 August 1989): 94.
5   George Steiner, *Real Presences* (Chicago, 1989), 48.
6   *The New Yorker*, 21 August 1989, 94.
7   Stephen White, "Educational Anomie," 2; William J. Bennett, "Why Western Civilization?", 3; Lynne V. Cheney, "Canons, Cultural Literacy, and the Core Curriculum," 11; Chester E. Finn, Jr., "A Truce in the Curricular Wars?", 16, 17; Elizabeth Fox-Genovese, "The Feminist Challenge to the Canon," 34, *The National Forum* (Summer 1989).
8   Finn, *National Forum*, 17.
9   Bennett, *National Forum*, 4.
10 R. T. Smith, "Canon Fodder, the Cultural Hustle, and the Minotaur," *The National Forum* (Summer 1989): 26.
11 Gerald Graff and William Cain, "Peace Plan for the Canon Wars," *The National Forum* (Summer 1989): 9.
12 Betty Jean Craige, "Curriculum Battles and Global Politics," *The National Forum* (Summer 1989): 31.
13 R. Alter, *The Pleasures of Reading*, 28, 27.
14 Ibid., 54.
15 Ibid., 38.
16 Wayne C. Booth, *The Company We Keep: An Ethics of Fiction* (Berkeley, 1988), 223.
17 When I say that everyone is an ethicist I mean more than that everyone is already engaging with books—canonical and noncanonical—in ways that involve ethical commitments; for regarding books as the training ground for moral activity—

which is what Alter and Booth mean by ethical reading—is only one of the many relationships one can have with books, all of them ethical in the only sense of the word that makes sense. Polemical ethicists tend to contrast their life with books with the impoverished life led by those who look to books for leisure (we shall see a stunning example of this in a moment) or information, for advice or political inspiration or sociological data; but these and many other forms of engagement are no less ethical than the engagement with Great Questions demanded by our severe moralists, that is, no less a matter of purposeful behavior in relation to some goal considered (by the actor) to be good. Not only is the ethics of reading a problematical concept because there are any number of possible ethical yields from innumerable literary and nonliterary texts, but the very idea of requiring an ethical yield from our reading is itself a debatable notion, and the alternatives (only partially listed above) are to be found not outside but *within* ethics, which, like difference—indeed the ethical *is* difference—is a realm no one can grasp for one is always and already within it.

18 R. Alter, *The Pleasures of Reading*, 16.
19 Anne Barbeau Gardiner, *ADE Bulletin* (Fall 1989): 24.
20 Martha C. Nussbaum, "Reading for Life," *Yale Journal of Law and Humanities* 1:1 (December 1988): 171.
21 Ibid., 176.
22 Lynne V. Cheney, *Humanities in America: A Report to the President, the Congress, and the American People* (Washington, D.C., 1988), 14.
23 Ibid., 32.
24 William J. Bennett, *National Forum*, 4.
25 Chester E. Finn, Jr., *National Forum*, 18.
26 Sidney Hook, "Civilization and Its Malcontents," *The National Review* (13 October 1989): 31.
27 George Steiner, *Real Presences*, 8, 60.
28 Ibid., 67, 32.
29 Ibid., 33.
30 "Derisory Tower" (Editorial), *The New Republic* (18 February 1991): 5.
31 *Academic Questions* (March 1986): 8.

Francis Oakley

Against Nostalgia: Reflections on Our Present Discontents in American Higher Education

If the friction of constant repetition had not dulled the edge of surprise, most of us, I suspect, would detect something quite odd about the recent spate of critical publications focused on American higher education in general and the American undergraduate experience in particular.[1] The genre is quasi-apocalyptic; the mood, in best American fashion, resolutely masochistic; the cumulative message, in disappointing degree, quite myopic. About this collective jeremiad there is little enough to rejoice; in the contents of the books, articles, and reports which compose it not a great deal to inspire. The line of march pursued is drearily familiar; in its general direction and the staging points that punctuate it, by now, indeed, almost canonical. A golden age of curricular coherence and educational integrity is evoked or implied. If its precise location is no more than foggily determined, that it has since been succeeded by a more or less catastrophic fall from grace is not left in doubt. The recent history of undergraduate education in America is chronicled as a deplorable descent from the realms of gold to our current age of iron, an age distinguished by declining academic standards, curricular incoherence, creeping consumerism, rampant vocationalism, and a wavering sense of mission. The undergraduate college, we are told, is a "troubled institution," often "more success-ful in credentialing than in providing a quality education." And, as for the undergraduate degree, "evidence of decline and devaluation is everywhere." In our own day "a profound crisis" has overtaken under-graduate education, nothing less, in effect, than a "crisis of liberal education" itself—a crisis reflecting (variously) the distortion of our universities and colleges by the research ethos and its concomitant, a "flight from teaching" on the part of the faculty, the fragmenta-tion of knowledge and the attendant growth of hyperspecialization in the academic disciplines, the corrosive inroads of cultural relativism, the intrusion of a marketplace philosophy into the curriculum, its politicization and the subordination of "our studies [accordingly] to contemporary prejudices." Coupled with a "collective loss of nerve and faith on the part of both faculty and academic administrators during the late 1960s and early 1970s" and an abandonment of the old commitment to mediate to successive generations of students the richnesses of the Western cultural tradition, these developments have eventuated, alas, in the decay of the humanities and the "dissolution of the curriculum." In sum, our "educational failures" as a nation are lovingly caressed, a sense of time running out is evoked with an urgency worthy of the Club of Rome, and the compelling need to re-spond to the challenge thus posed is pressed with a vigor redolent of other, less cerebral, realms of discourse.

Anyone even glancingly familiar with the history of American higher education well knows that beneath this current outcropping of discontent lies a veritable geology of alienation, one important stratum of which has been deposited by the academy itself. Some of the worst things said about the American university have been said by university people, and the tone was set right at the start of the century by critics like Thorstein Veblen and Abraham Flexner. What has linked together such academic critics of the academy has been less any shared position than a shared disposition. At its least offensive, that disposition partakes of the angularity and contrasug-gestibility that also leads some of our most gifted students to do their best learning in the teeth of, rather than because of, the curricular arrangements we all labor so hard and so frustratingly to shape. In its more unattractive registers, however, that disposition sounds a note of contempt for the masses of more pedestrian colleagues laboring in the academic vineyard and projects that mood of dyspeptic edginess which led academics themselves, in the aftermath of the turmoil of the late 1960s, to produce a depressing string of books with such arresting titles as *Academia in Anarchy* (1970), *Academics in Retreat* (1971), *Academy in Turmoil* (1970), *Back to the Middle Ages* (1969) (I have never been able to understand why that should seem such a bad idea), *Bankruptcy of Academy Policy* (1972), *Confrontation and Counterattack* (1971), *Death of the American University* (1973), *Degradation of the Academic Dogma* (1971), *Destruction of a College President* (1972), *Embattled University* (1970), *Exploding University* (1970), *Fall of the American University* (1972), and so on. The trail, as Clark Kerr pointed out,[2] could easily be pursued right down through the alphabet.

With a lineage so well established the current harsh vein of commentary could easily be dismissed as simply more of the same old tired stuff. But I myself believe that that would be a mistake. Because of its sources, the publications in which it has appeared, and the remarkable amount of public attention it has commanded, it has, I think, to be taken very seriously. It is part and parcel of the steady drumbeat of negative commentary and critique that, over the past quarter of a century, has led to a marked drop in the public trust and esteem extended to so many of the institutions and organizations upon which the well-being of our society depends. Even if one regards much (though not necessarily all) of this flamboyant criticism of our higher educational system as absurdly inflated, irresponsible, and rhetorically excessive—and I do—one must still give some indication of how one might go about mounting a more balanced appraisal. Criticism, after all, should be the lifeblood of the academy and we can no more afford complacency about the quality of our academic programs than we can about the adequacy of our financial resources.

What, then, is to be said? Well, quite a lot *has* been said, much of it as overheated as the critiques themselves[3] and most of it targeted on the attempts of the critics to vindicate a core curriculum focused on Western civilization and the canon of great books of the Western tradition.

About these well-ventilated issues I have little or nothing to say here. Not because I regard them as unimportant, but rather because I don't see how they can profitably be addressed without first disposing of some perhaps more primitive issues—less theoretical, less grandiose, maybe less interesting. Let me explain what I have in mind by discussing first some general and then some rather specific concerns.

Under the category of general concerns I would like to make a few simple observations about the texture of this recent body of criticism. And perhaps I should add that, in so doing, I have in mind not only the books and articles published by such authors as Allan Bloom, Charles Sykes, Roger Kimball, and Page Smith, but also the reports issued on behalf of the Association of American Colleges, the Carnegie Foundation for the Advancement of Teaching, and the National Endowment for the Humanities by such authors or editors as Mark Curtis, Ernest Boyer, William Bennett, and Lynne Cheney. What strikes me in particular is the comparative lack of interest on the part of most of these authors in statistical data, even when such data are available in overrich abundance. Boyer is very much an exception, of course, but in these writings in general prescription tends to preempt analysis, a sort of disheveled anecdotalism replaces evidence, and a free-fire zone is cleared for eye-catching and sensationalist claims of the type favored by Charles Sykes, who says that "almost single-handedly, the professors—working steadily and systematically—have destroyed the university as a center of learning and have desolated higher education, which no longer is higher or much of an education."[4] Of course, that is utter rubbish, but if one can rely on the blurbs on the book jacket, that fact did not prevent its reviewers in the *New York Times* and the *Washington Post*—struck down, it seems, by a veritable infection of hyperbole—from labeling the book as "an incisive and convincing indictment" or even as "stupendously provocative and important."

Proceeding still under the heading of general observations, let me say that I am struck also by the marked degree to which this critical onslaught is mounted in something of a contextual void both institutional and historical. Few of the critics, that is to say, show any sign of having sensed the sheer size, complexity, and extraordinary diversity of the American system of higher education. No interest is shown in ascertaining how people abroad assess the quality of that system, and, in rendering harsh and peremptory sentence on it, no effort is made to seek comparative leverage by measuring its performance against that of other national systems in the industrialized world. The impact on colleges and universities at home and abroad of the demographic changes that have loomed so large over the past thirty years is hardly noted, despite the fact that these changes almost certainly constitute the single most important set of factors shaping the American undergraduate experience today. Nor (notwithstanding their emphasis on the importance of mediating the cultural heritage) do these critics show much inclination to take a real and unromantic look at either the more distant or the more recent past. As a result, despite the unargued assumption that somewhere and at some time things used surely to be better, the golden age evoked remains, historically speaking, remarkably elusive. Eyes are discreetly averted from the truly enormous gap (evident from the ancient world right down to our own day) between ringing theoretical affirmations of commitment to the plenitude of liberal arts instruction and the fustian realities of what has actually been going on amid the day-to-day confusions and compromises of educational life as it has usually been lived in the pedagogic trenches (a gap very effectively argued and illustrated for the early modern period by such historians as Anthony Grafton and Lisa Jardine[5]). Still less does one detect the presence of any historically informed sense of the range, looseness, variability, and flexibility of the liberal arts tradition itself across the course of its longer history, or of the tensions which have wracked it for centuries and may well account for much of its enduring vitality and strength. That tradition, after all, still bears the marks left by the fateful decision of the early Christian communities in the Greco-Roman world not to establish their own schools but rather to attempt to adapt to their own purposes a robustly pagan educational tradition of essentially Hellenistic provenance. Similarly, historians have detected the continued presence in the tradition of an even older and more enduring tension, that between the rhetorical vision of liberal education as pivoting on the cultivation of the ancient classics or their derivatives and the philosophical-scientific model driven by the urge for critical originality and advancing via the overthrow of received assumptions. The former has traditionally been directed to the development of the skills pertinent to public expression and legal and political persuasion, as well as to the inculcation, in those destined for lives of public service, of the hallowed values and traditions inherited from the past. The latter, instead, has persistently been targeted on the advancement of knowledge and understanding and on the development of critical rationality. Between the hammer and the anvil of these competing approaches little peace over the centuries has been able to grow.

About such things, however, our critics say next to nothing. And if nostalgia is doubtless one of the most distinctively human of emotions, there is little, I believe, to recommend an indulgence in nostalgia for a past that never was. With that in mind, let me turn from the general to the specific and use the remainder of this essay to illustrate the nature of the price these reports and critiques pay for their comparative innocence of evidence and their odd obliviousness to history.

Being by calling a medievalist, my mind turns all too readily to trinities. So I would like to select three topics to focus on: first, the issue of teaching and research; second, the plight of the humanities and its relation to general education; third, the silences of these reports and critiques. And being also a reasonably orderly sort of fellow by disposition, I propose to begin with the first and make my way through to the third, trying in the process to avoid telling you altogether more than you want to know about each of them.

Teaching and Research. First, then, the issue of teaching and research. Or, as the critics would prefer to put it, research *versus* teaching and its corollary, the allegiance of faculty to their academic discipline at the expense of commitment to the particular university or college at which they serve.

At their harshest, the charges are clear enough and are twofold. First, that despite (or because of) the great emphasis the university community places upon research and the mounting surge of publication resulting therefrom, much of what is produced is dull, trivial, pedestrian, or esoteric (or, for that matter, some mind-numbing combination of all four). Second, that teaching is undervalued in the world of higher education, or that the American professoriate is in "full flight from teaching," or even that "the academic culture is not merely indifferent to teaching" but *actively hostile to it.*"[6]

Although the two charges are usually run together on the grounds that academics are shunning teaching in order to mount their oversold and overpriced research effort, they are, in fact, distinct and separable. The first is something of a standard theme in the writings of the more disgruntled in-house commentators on the American academic scene for a century at least, and commentators like Lynne Cheney and Charles Sykes, writing from vantage points outside the academy, have had no difficulty at all in adducing academic authorities of some stature to document their own highly critical accounts of university research.

In his recent book, *Killing the Spirit: Higher Education in America* (another cheery title!), Page Smith, historian and former provost of the University of California at Santa Cruz, concluded after a few pages on the topic "publish or perish"—with some satisfaction and (one has to hope at least) with tongue firmly in cheek—that he had "demonstrated conclusively that the vast majority of what passes for research/publication in the major universities of America is mediocre, expensive and unnecessary, [and] does not push back the frontiers of knowledge in any appreciable degree."[7] Of course, he had done nothing of the sort, nor is it at all clear how anyone in principle could, especially when the method used is, as in these critiques, selectively illustrative and adamantly anecdotal. However amusing at times (and it is), it throws little if any light on the overall quality of the vast amount of scholarship the academy produces. That pretentious rubbish finds its way into print, scholars are in a better position than most to attest. They, after all, are the ones who have to read it. That bad coinage sometimes drives out good in this area, as in others, they would also be the last to deny. But if there is a better way to winnow out the wheat from the chaff than the patient process of peer review, publication, and subsequent scholarly scrutiny—sometimes across long periods of time—no one has been quick to come up with it. Certainly anyone tempted, as is Sykes, to generalize from the Senator-Proxmire-Golden-Fleece-Award approach to the evaluation of research would do well to ponder how often in the course of intellectual history forms of investigation dismissed by contemporaries as uselessly esoteric have in fact borne within them the seeds of future creativity. (I myself think immediately of the ignorance with which Renaissance humanists were prone to deride the disputations in natural philosophy being conducted by contemporary scholastics.)

Fortunately, if we prescind from attempts to judge the overall significance of academic research and the quality of the results it generates, and focus instead on the second charge—that the academy in general overemphasizes research and accordingly undervalues teaching—then we are on more solid ground and capable of supporting a less agnostic appraisal. And some of that ground is statistical. Pointing out recently that the "number of books and articles published annually on Shakespeare grew by 80% between 1968 and 1988," Lynne Cheney simply assumed a direct causal connection between what she called this recent "surge in publications" and "the increased emphasis on research."[8] But, of course, before one accepts that assumption, one has to take into account the enormous increase over those years in the number of potential authors. I do not have the specific numbers for those in English, but between 1965 and 1988, after all, the overall number of faculty members at American colleges and universities came close to doubling.

Moreover, at a less crude level, we have at our disposal quite rich sets of data generated by the Carnegie faculty surveys conducted at regular intervals from 1969 to 1989. They concern the disciplinary and institutional loyalty of faculty, their attitudes toward teaching and research, time devoted to these and related activities, research productivity as measured by the publication of articles, monographs, and books, and so on. Although these data have been studied and added to by scholars like Martin Trow, Howard Bowen, Everett Carll

Ladd, and Seymour Martin Lipset, they have been largely ignored by those alleging the occurrence in the academy of a flight from teaching. And yet they have a good deal to tell us about the subject—some of it quite startling, some a little puzzling, but all of it tending to reshape the teaching/research issue along more complex lines, rendering it less rewarding material for those energized by the joys of polemic.

Statisticians tend in general to be a rather gloomy lot. They are prone to assuming the omnipresent working of a sort of quantitative original sin, constantly predisposing nonstatisticians to the commission of actual sins. And their worry is not altogether misplaced: deductive temptation abounds, the noonday demon seems to be on duty every day, and the fallacious inference waits cunningly to pounce. I am not a social scientist; all I can do with these figures is briefly to elicit, as best I can, the story embedded in them.

And the story that I believe should be told goes something like this. Some facts really stand out and some conclusions seem warranted. First, in response to the 1989 Carnegie survey, no less than 70 percent of faculty overall indicated that their primary interest lay in teaching rather than research. And if you break that global figure down by institutional sector, while it is hardly surprising that 93 percent of faculty at two-year colleges indicated that primary interest, it is quite startling that 33 percent of those at the research universities said the same and 55 percent of those at the doctorate-granting universities (i.e., the institutions in the next echelon down in terms of receipt of federal research funding and numbers of graduate degrees awarded).[9] Second, research productivity as measured by publication activity was broadly consonant with what faculty reported about the primary focus of their interests. Thirty-four percent overall reported in 1989 that they were not currently engaged in any scholarly project; 56 percent had never published or edited a book or monograph alone or in collaboration; 59 percent had published a lifetime cumulative total of five articles or fewer in the professional journals; 26 percent had published none; while a small group of compulsive recidivists—maybe 20 percent overall—were publishing up a storm. Third, although some research activity was evident in all institutional sectors, it was most heavily concentrated in the research universities and least heavily in the two-year colleges. No surprise about that. What is surprising, perhaps, is that the fault line between sectors of higher and lower productivity ran, not between the universities with graduate programs and the four- and two-year colleges, but between the universities and the highly selective liberal arts colleges on the one hand, and the rest of the undergraduate colleges, whether four- or two-year, on the other. And it did so because the profile of research and publication at the leading colleges is, in fact, akin "to that of the smaller universities."[10] Fourth, although there appears to have been a modest increase in the priority given to research overall in the twenty years between 1969 and 1989, the most recent data do not offer much support for the now commonplace assumption that the true allegiance of faculty is to their academic disciplines rather than to their universities and colleges. It is true that only 2 percent overall were willing to admit that their discipline was no more than "fairly important" to them; and that percentage was exactly the same for people at two-year colleges as it was for those at research universities. At the same time, however, 85 percent declared that their college or university was very or fairly important to them (91 percent at the liberal arts colleges, 80 percent at the research universities), and these percentages reflected a significant increase in institutional allegiance over the course of the decade preceding.[11] Fifth, when one talks about faculty commitment to teaching and research, one should not simply assume that some sort of zero-sum game is necessarily involved, that is, that a heavy research commitment is necessarily bought at the price of reduced attention to teaching or institutional service. Our leading liberal arts colleges are justifiably celebrated for the intensity of their commitment to undergraduate teaching. But it turns out that their faculties have succeeded in combining that commitment with comparatively high levels of scholarly engagement and productivity. Similarly, analysis of the pertinent data for our research universities reveals that there is surprisingly little difference between the most active researchers and the rest of the faculty in overall levels of teaching activity and accessibility to undergraduates. It also reveals that the most active researchers are in aggregate "much more likely [than their less active colleagues] to be involved in the administrative processes of their department and their institution." Such people seem to do more of everything, and the crucial variable may well be not differing interests, but differential levels of energy.[12]

What, then, are we to conclude? Two things, I would suggest. So far as the commitment to teaching goes, the first is reassuring, namely, that "the *normative* climate in [American higher education], as reflected in academics' personal preferences, is far more favorable to teaching than most observers would have predicted."[13] "[M]ost college and university professors in the United States do not think of themselves . . . as research people," and their actual behavior reflects that fact. "Their interests lie primarily in teaching-related activities."[14] The second conclusion is less reassuring. It seems clear that, in aggregate at least, the structure of extrinsic incentives and rewards in the academy is tilted markedly in the direction of research. Yet in 1989 over 60 percent of faculty overall indicated their belief that teaching effectiveness rather than research and publication should be the primary criterion for promotion of faculty, and 35 percent felt that the pressure to publish was having the effect of reducing the quality of teaching at their university or college. (If we concentrated on the research universities alone, that figure would go up to 53 percent.)[15] Hence Everett Ladd's conclusion that "an ascendant model in academe, positing what faculty *should be doing,* is seriously out of touch [not only] with what they *actually do,* [but also with what they] *want to do.*"[16] That conclusion calls for thoughtful scrutiny and, if correct, for an appropriate array of responses that would have to be calibrated differentially for the various institutional sectors into which higher education is divided. But it is a far cry from alarmist and punitive talk about a flight from teaching or even a hostility to it, the existence of which the available evidence simply does not support.

The Plight of the Humanities and the Matter of General Education. Nor does it support, to turn now to my second topic, much that has been said about the current plight of the humanities or the pertinence to that plight of an alleged decline in general education. In many of the recent critiques (as a proxy for the precise enrollment figures we do not have) much emphasis has been placed on the decline, over the past two decades, in the number of undergraduates choosing to major in the humanities—and it has, indeed, been quite dramatic. Between 1966 and 1986, as Lynne Cheney has pointed out, despite an increase of 88 percent in the overall number of bachelor's degrees being awarded, the number of those awarded in the humanities declined by 33 percent.[17] And the critics have repeatedly suggested that our universities and colleges must bear the brunt of the blame for this decline because of their high tuition charges and their failure "to reestablish a sense of educational purpose," "to restore the humanities to a central place [in the curriculum]," and "to bring the humanities to life."[18] Roger Kimball, in his book *Tenured Radicals: How Politics Has Corrupted Higher Education* (a sort of Apocalypse II of the genre), attributes the decline, at least in part, to the refusal of students "to devote their college education to a program of study that has nothing to offer them but ideological posturing, pop culture, and hermeneutical word games." He also has great fun at the expense of the authors of the American Council of Learned Societies' response to the critics—entitled *Speaking for the Humanities*—for their rather puzzled efforts to qualify and explain (he would say "explain away") that decline.[19] But a closer look at the statistics suggests that their puzzlement is warranted, that the basic task of *describing* what has been happening is a much more challenging one than people have assumed, and that we had better get *that* right before proceeding to the apportioning of blame or the prescription of reforms in general education. And in attempting to get it right there are a series of things we should be aware of.

First, the decline of undergraduate interest in the humanities, though it is more dramatic, is in fact part of a broader decline of interest in the arts and sciences as a whole, in contrast to a marked growth of interest in preprofessional and vocational studies.[20] And we should certainly be doing a good deal more worrying than we seem to be doing about the natural sciences. The combination of increasing scientific sophistication and decreasing interest in scientific careers among American students strikes me as cause for real concern. Without the extraordinary influx of foreign graduate students and researchers, which we cannot assume will last, the United States would already be suffering from very serious shortages of research personnel in the basic sciences.

Second, when you set out to weigh the significance of statistical trends, you have to be rather self-conscious about the date you choose as your point of departure. Because so many of the pertinent data series were initiated in the late sixties, 1966 or 1970 has usually been chosen as the starting point for measuring these enrollment trends. But if you go back further, as Sarah Turner and William Bowen did last year in a very important article published in *Science*, you find that, after a phase of continued *increase* during the postwar years, the late 1960s marked the high point both in the number of arts and sciences B.A. degrees conferred and in the percentage they constituted of all baccalaureate degrees awarded.[21] It is because the subsequent decline has been from that high point that it stands out as being quite so dramatic.

Third, if you break the figures down by institutional sector, both the earlier rise and the subsequent fall in arts and sciences enrollments have been concentrated to a marked degree not in the research or doctorate-granting universities but in the state colleges and comprehensive institutions. This is also the sector of higher education that underwent the greatest expansion earlier on as overall enrollments swelled. These institutions had been heavily oriented toward professional and preprofessional programs, had responded to surging applications by upgrading themselves academically and strengthening their curricular offerings in the arts and sciences, and then reversed themselves in the 1970s when the competition for students became acute, expanding their vocational and preprofessional programs of study at the expense of the arts and sciences. Thus, to give two contrasting examples: At Ball State University in Indiana the share of degrees awarded in the arts and sciences rose between 1954 and 1970 from 2.5 percent to almost 30 percent, and then declined by 1986 to about 13 percent. At Cornell, on the other hand, the comparable figures for 1954 and 1986 were 49.3 percent and 47.1 percent—more or less stable, with no significant change between 1970 and 1986.[22] Given the fact that most of the authors of the ACLS report were teaching at leading research universities like Cornell, their puzzlement about claims of a dramatic flight from the humanities was understandable. By and large, it was not something happening (or, in the late 1980s at least, *still* happening) at their sort of institution, but rather, elsewhere in the system. In fact, if we are looking for something to worry about, perhaps we should be brooding about what seems to be a growing polarization "between [higher educational] sectors that have a strongly professional/vocational orientation and [those] sectors that give a greater emphasis to the traditional fields within the arts and sciences," including the humanities.[23]

Fourth, when Turner and Bowen checked to see if the changing composition of the American student body overall in terms of age, race, or ethnicity afforded any explanatory key to the marked instability of enrollments in the arts and sciences, they found that it did not. What *did* matter, it turned out, was the changing *gender* composition of the student body—or at least it did when taken together with the shifting curricular choices being made from the mid-1950s to the late 1980s. In fact, the changing curricular choices made by women dominated what was going on in the humanities throughout the greater part of the whole period. If you took the figures for men alone, then the share of the humanities in the total number of B.A. degrees awarded shows a gradual but more or less consistent decline from the mid-1950s onward. That is to say, numerically at least, the decline in the humanities had set in during the period which Allan Bloom portrays as the golden age of the American university. That decline was masked, however, by the fact that women undergraduates, whose numbers were steadily increasing, were also choosing to major in the arts and sciences in rapidly increasing numbers. In the early to mid-1950s, instead, they had majored heavily in education. In 1958, indeed, 50 percent of all the B.A. degrees awarded to women were still in education. In the late 1950s and throughout the 1960s, however, they had chosen to major increasingly in the humanities and to a lesser degree in the social sciences, so by 1986 that figure had fallen to 13 percent. But in the 1970s and 1980s that changed again. "Between 1970 and 1986, the declining participation of women [in the humanities] accounted for more than three times the loss in degree share attributable to reduced interest in the humanities among men."[24] Similarly, it accounted for the bulk of the increase in the overall numbers of students majoring in business. In 1970, only 2.8 percent of the B.A. degrees awarded to women were in business; by 1986 that figure had risen to no less than 21.7 percent.[25]

As a result, it does not seem unreasonable to speculate that, had the social and cultural norms that constrained women from entry into business-related careers eroded a decade or more earlier than they actually did, overall enrollments in the humanities might never have reached the heights attained in the late 1960s. And had that been the case, the subsequent decline would have been a far less precipitate one, and one less likely to have stimulated self-doubt on the part of those within the academy or, on the part of those without, the exercises in gloomy and mordant commentary to which we have become, somewhat restively, accustomed.

Moreover, there seems to be no good ground for postulating a connection, whether direct or indirect, between the decline in humanities enrollments and the phenomena which recent critics like to finger as the culprits: high tuition charges, the waning of the Western civilization approach to general education, the assault on the canon of great books of the Western tradition, the politicization of the curriculum, the ravages of deconstruction, the growth of cultural relativism, and so on. After all, to the degree to which these phenomena are present they are present most powerfully in the highly selective universities and colleges where, as the authors of the ACLS report rightly argue, the humanities are alive and well.

Of course, the note of passionate dismay which the critics tend to sound when they speak of these phenomena is generated by concerns that run far deeper than worries about the so-called flight from the humanities. These concerns focus somewhat obsessively on the (real or perceived) changes wrought in the academy by the great upheaval of the student spirit that occurred in the late 1960s. They gain added intensity from the challenge posed to traditional curricular arrangements and scholarly approaches by the insistent demands of women and members of minority groups for a heightened measure of cultural inclusion. And they deepen into a mood of strident resentment when confronted by the readiness of so many contemporary intellectuals to flirt with one or another form of cognitive or cultural relativism. In this last respect, I am reminded, above all, of the vituperative anguish expressed in the 1930s by the outraged defenders of historical objectivity in response to the relativistic stance adopted by Carl Becker and Charles Beard. It would take another essay to address those concerns, but perhaps I can at least edge up to them if I turn, by way of conclusion, to my third topic, the sounds, as it were, of silence.

The Silences of These Reports and Critiques. I choose to focus on the silences of these reports and critiques because here the lack of interest in the available data evident when critics talk about a flight from teaching or a flight from the humanities intersects with an obliviousness to the history of higher education in the recent as well as the more distant past that I find somewhat startling in people who so often cast themselves in the role of guardians of the Western cultural heritage. What I would argue, quite simply, is this: if one has the ambition to make a reasonably balanced appraisal of the nature and quality of undergraduate education today, then the indispensable point of departure should be the recognition of four fundamental sets of facts about the current situation of higher education in the world at large and the United States in particular.

First, given the nature and size of the American system of higher education, it may well be (though I have no better word to propose) that "system" is a somewhat misleading term to use. It consists of over 3,400 institutions of one sort or another, ranging from junior and community colleges to great research universities. The Carnegie Foundation for the Advancement of Teaching classifies it, indeed, into no less than nine distinct institutional sectors. It is a vast, sprawling, markedly variegated, and extremely decentralized system, embracing secular and religious, public and private institutions, with an independently supported private segment of a strength and size unparalleled anywhere else in the world. In itself, or so it seems to me, this is a remarkable thing, a cause for national pride, a great tribute, certainly, to the country's philanthropic energy.

This vast system may well include on its margins some of the world's worst institutions of higher education—I really don't know; for that designation the competition around the globe is really pretty fierce. What can be said, however—at least if we are prepared to believe opinion surveys taken overseas—is that the United States is now home to "two-thirds . . . of the best universities in the world," and it has certainly become "the country of choice for students around the world seeking to pursue their education overseas."[26] Foreign students have been flocking to our colleges and universities in unprecedented numbers—to such a degree, indeed, that in terms of foreign exchange earned, American higher education has become a highly successful "export industry," with no sign as yet of any significant competition from Germany or Japan. (If Lee Iacocca could make that claim for Chrysler we would never get him off the tube!)

Second, the current situation of higher education at large, distinguished by unprecedented increases in the numbers of students crowding into colleges and universities all over the world, has no historical parallel. I mean that quite literally—it has *no* historical parallel. The issue goes beyond the marked fluctuations in the demography of the traditional college-age group and concerns also the nature of the *response* to those fluctuations. Never before have societies attempted to make university and college educations available to so large a percentage of their populations or to increase that percentage at so headlong a pace. India, for example, in the fifteen years after independence, saw a twelvefold increase in its student population. And if the generalization holds true, in varying degree, for almost every part of the globe, it holds with particular force (whatever our justifiable worries about equity of access) for the United States itself. Here the numbers of those going on to some form of higher education, having already grown substantially during the 1950s, came close to quadrupling between 1960 and 1980, so that more than 60 percent of our high school graduates can now be expected at some point in their lives to enroll in a college course bearing credit toward a degree.

Third, in terms of their religion, social class, age, gender, race, and ethnicity, the diversity of students today has no historical parallel. In this respect, of course, there are variations and unevennesses in the many systems of higher education across the globe. Never before, however, has the world of higher education betrayed so urgent an impulse to insure equality of access for women and for those groups traditionally disadvantaged by race, religion, ethnicity, age, and social class—barriers sustained in the past by custom, prejudice, snobbery, stupidity, and age-old ingrained privilege. Again, if that generalization holds true, in varying degree, for practically every part of the contemporary world, it also holds with particular force (however understandable the severity of our self-criticism on this very score) for the United States itself. Members of minority groups and students from low-income families are to be found in significant numbers at every level in our complex system, not only at community colleges or in the state college systems, but also in the great state universities and the highly selective colleges and universities of the private sector. In 1980 the last of a series of reports issued by the Carnegie council on higher education concluded that "roughly one half of the students in the classroom of [the year] 2000 would not have been there if the composition of [the national student body as it stood as recently as] 1960 had been continued." [27] And given the results of the 1990 national census just published, I would judge that that prediction will turn out to have been unduly conservative.

Fourth, in responding to these seismic demographic shocks, the American system of higher education—with its decentralization, its extraordinary combination of public and private, its great variety of institutional forms, its pluralism of standards and educational aspiration, and its tradition of responsiveness to shifting social needs— has proved to be remarkably effective, especially if one measures its performance against that of other well-established systems in the industrialized world abroad, such as the Italian, the German, and the French. Unlike so many of the European systems, it has made something more than a mere beginning in the process of shifting its commitment from the training of professional elites to the more taxing endeavor of mass higher education. It could hardly have done so without the willingness to respond to local needs, the ability to adapt to variegated challenges, and the disposition to encourage innovation, qualities that go along with the dispersion of initiative and power among an array of autonomous or quasi-autonomous universities and colleges—institutions engaged of necessity in the effort to compete for capable students and faculty. That among the corollaries of so rapid a response to the demographic shifts of the past thirty years have been difficulty in maintaining equivalence of standards, the growth in some sectors of confusion about institutional mission, a drift in the admissions field into an unhealthy preoccupation with "marketing," an unambiguous lurch in the direction of heightened vocationalism, and a certain amount of curricular disarray, no one, I assume, would be disposed to contest. New populations of students, teachers, and scholars tend understandably to bring forth new issues, raise new questions, introduce new perspectives, feel their way toward new configurations of knowledge—and to do so, often, with a degree of angry and peremptory confusion. As a result, even apart from the intense "postmodern" debates about the nature and grounding of knowledge currently roiling the waters of the humanities and social sciences (and making consensus on matters curricular so very hard to achieve), demographic shifts of the dimensions we have experienced would themselves have imposed enormous strains upon traditional curricular formations and generated powerful currents tugging even the most conservative of institutions reluctantly in the direction of change.

===

Although threatening to some and certain to destabilize traditional assumptions, the process of adapting to change shows as much promise of revitalizing education as it does of being a destructive force. Liberal learning has gone through comparable upheavals in the past and emerged from them renewed. The infiltration of the work of Aristotle and his Muslim commentators into the arts curriculum of the University of Paris during the thirteenth century understandably provoked condemnation from the ecclesiastical authorities, dismay among the theologians, and anguished debate in the university at large. But it was not to be halted by nostalgia for an "Augustinian" or prescholastic past, and the prolonged dialectic of assimilation and critique that it generated proved to be one of the great turning points in European intellectual history. And given the intensity of our contemporary battle of the books and the degree to which the humanities have become the focus of so much intellectual excitement, I really find it hard to believe that there is little or nothing to celebrate in all of this.

Indeed, I see the great clash we are currently witnessing as being much more obviously and universally the deliverance of the Western intellectual and educational tradition, which has always been a highly conflicted one, than is the solution so many critics are pressing: namely, the core-curricular approach to general education, with its reverential canonization of selected ancient classics and other "great books of the Western tradition." About that approach there is really nothing age-old. It is a specifically American creation, and one of comparatively recent vintage. It came to the fore during the years between the world wars by way of reaction to the more egregious excesses of the free-elective system, which had left many of our leading colleges and universities on the eve of World War I with fewer curricular requirements than they have today. Even in its heyday its appeal was fairly limited, and, whatever its virtues (and they are real), I cannot ascribe to the view that the only way forward today lies via a retreat into *its* particular past.

In saying this I am not suggesting that any of us can afford to be satisfied with our curricular efforts. We cannot. But I conclude that in a higher educational system as complex and pluralistic as the American, the appropriate form of dissatisfaction is likely to vary from one type of institution to another. For some of us, I would suggest—and I have in mind our leading research universities and liberal arts colleges—that dissatisfaction should properly focus less on increasing attention to any particular body of subject matter than on recognizing our failure to make the most in our teaching of the great intellectual disagreements of the day and to exploit them for their undoubted educational value. In the course of any given week, as they move in a liberal arts setting from courses in the natural sciences to classes in religion, the behavioral sciences, literature, and history, I have the uneasy sense that many of our students are fated to traverse epistemological centuries and to maneuver among radically divergent theories of knowledge without being fully conscious of so doing. They deserve better of us than that. Ideas have consequences. So, too, does intellectual confusion.

Speaking of literature and literary criticism in particular, Gerald Graff has urged us to direct our teaching toward the unresolved intellectual conflicts of the day.[28] What he has especially in mind are the conflicts between differing schools of literary theory. But such issues resonate beyond the study of literature and Graff's interesting if obsessive message has a more general import. The great interpretative disputes that currently agitate and energize the humanities and social sciences are no more to be wished away today than were the truly subversive novelties of Aristotelian metaphysics in the thirteenth century. (And, despite Thomistic attempts via the scholastic method to render compatible the contradictory and harmonious the dissonant, those novelties really were, in traditional Christian terms, highly subversive.) Nor will we serve our students well if, in constructing our curricula, we attempt to sidle around contemporary disputes and dilemmas. For some of us, I believe, the great pedagogic challenge for the immediate future will be that of inserting those disputes, instead, into the very heart of our teaching endeavor.

Notes

This essay was originally a public lecture delivered on 9 April 1991 at the National Humanities Center in Research Triangle Park, North Carolina. Some paragraphs in this essay appeared previously in two journal articles: "Apocalypse Now in U.S. Higher Education," *America* 160 (1 April 1989), and "Point of View," *The Chronicle of Higher Education* (14 March 1990). Permission to reprint is gratefully acknowledged.

1   I would divide these publications into two groups. The first is a series of reports and analyses, all of them somewhat discouraging in tone but lacking the harder edge that characterizes the second group, which includes some works of markedly punitive and vituperative bent. The first group includes the following works: William J. Bennett, *To Reclaim a Legacy: A Report on the Humanities in Higher Education* (Washington, D.C.: The National Endowment for the Humanities, 1984); Ernest L. Boyer, *College: The Undergraduate Experience in America* (New York, 1987); Lynne V. Cheney, *Humanities in America: A Report to the President, the Congress, and the American People* (Washington, D.C.: The National Endowment for the Humanities, 1988); idem, *Tyrannical Machines: A Report on Educational Practices Gone Wrong and Our Best Hopes for Setting Them Right* (Washington, D.C.: The National Endowment for the Humanities, 1990); Mark H. Curtis et al., *Integrity in the College Curriculum: A Report to the Academic Community* (Washington, D.C.: Association of American Colleges, 1985). In the second group I would place the following works: Allan Bloom, *The Closing of the American Mind: How Higher Education Has Failed Democracy and Impoverished the Souls of Today's Students* (New York, 1987); Dinesh D'Souza, *Illiberal Education: The Politics of Race and Sex on Campus* (New York, 1991); Roger Kimball, *Tenured Radicals: How Politics Has Corrupted Our Higher Education* (New York, 1990); Page Smith, *Killing the Spirit: Higher Education in America* (New York, 1990); Charles T. Sykes, *ProfScam: Professors and the Demise of Higher Education* (New York, 1990). The gloomy phrases quoted below are drawn from works in both groups.

2   I draw this lugubrious list from Clark Kerr, "The Moods of Academia," in *Education and the State*, ed. John F. Hughes (Washington, D.C., 1975), 267–75.

3   Roger Kimball's claim (*Tenured Radicals*, 4) that former Secretary of Education

William J. Bennett's report *To Reclaim a Legacy* "occasioned paroxysms of rage" within the academy comes depressingly close to the mark.

4 Sykes, *ProfScam*, 4.
5 Anthony Grafton and Lisa Jardine, *From Humanism to the Humanities: Education in the Liberal Arts in Fifteenth- and Sixteenth-Century Europe* (Cambridge, Mass., 1986).
6 Thus Sykes, *ProfScam*, 54 (italics his). He adds: "In the modern university, no act of good teaching goes unpunished." This is in a chapter entitled "The Crucifixion of Teaching" following on the heels of one entitled "The Flight from Teaching."
7 Smith, *Killing the Spirit*, 199.
8 Cheney, *Tyrannical Machines*, 30. In the same place she noted an 800 percent increase in the number of books and articles published annually on Virginia Woolf, a figure that presumably reflects a shift in the focus of scholarly interest.
9 I draw these figures and those cited below from Ernest L. Boyer, *Scholarship Reconsidered: Priorities of the Professoriate* (Princeton, N.J.: Carnegie Foundation for the Advancement of Teaching, 1990), appendix A, tables A-26, A-21, A-20, A-19.
10 Thus Martin Trow and Oliver Fulton, "Research Activity in American Higher Education," in *Teachers and Students: Aspects of American Higher Education*, ed. Martin Trow (New York, 1975), 39–83, at 49 and 79.
11 Boyer, *Scholarship Reconsidered*, appendix A, tables A-39, A-40; cf. p. 56, table 12.
12 Trow and Fulton, "Research Activity in American Higher Education," 66–75, 79.
13 Ibid., 47.
14 Everett Carll Ladd, Jr., "The Work Experiences of American College Professors: Some Data and an Argument," *Current Issues in Higher Education* (1979): 3–12.
15 Boyer, *Scholarship Reconsidered*, appendix A, tables A-23 and A-32.
16 Ladd, "The Work Experience of American College Professors," 5. "It may be," he adds, "that research, properly construed—meaning scholarly activity aimed at the creation of new ideas, new knowledge, new art forms, and the like—makes demands and requires skills such as to permanently restrict participation in it to a distinct minority of faculty."
17 Cheney, *Humanities in America*, 4.
18 Ibid., 4–5; Bennett, *To Reclaim a Legacy*, 2, 6–8, 13–20.
19 Kimball, *Tenured Radicals*, xvii and 34–37, where he comments on George Levine et al., *Speaking for the Humanities*, American Council of Learned Societies Occasional Paper No. 7 (New York, 1989), esp. 21–24, 35–37.
20 See William G. Bowen and Julie Ann Sosa, *Prospects for Faculty in the Arts and Sciences: A Study of Factors Affecting Demand and Supply, 1987 to 2012* (Princeton, N.J., 1989), esp. 46–57.
21 Sarah E. Turner and William G. Bowen, "The Flight from the Arts and Sciences: Trends in Degrees Conferred," *Science* 250 (26 October 1990): 517–21.
22 Ibid., 518, table 1; Bowen and Sosa, *Prospects for Faculty in the Arts and Sciences*, 55–57.
23 Bowen and Sosa, *Prospects for Faculty in the Arts and Sciences*, 57.

24   Turner and Bowen, "The Flight from the Arts and Sciences," 520.

25   Ibid.

26   Henry Rosovsky, *The University: An Owner's Manual* (New York and London, 1990), 29–30, where he adds, "By two thirds (perhaps three quarters) of the best, I mean that surveys of world universities rank a majority of American *public and private* institutions at the top." See also Derek Bok, *The President's Report 1988–89: Harvard University* (Cambridge, Mass., 1989), 2.

27   *Three Thousand Futures: The Next Twenty Years for Higher Education*, Final Report of the Carnegie Council on Policy Studies in Higher Education (San Francisco and London, 1980), 54. It continues: "This is a fundamental, almost radical change in higher education."

28   Gerald Graff, *Professing Literature: An Institutional History* (Chicago, 1987), and his "Teach the Conflicts: An Alternative to Educational Fundamentalism," in *Literature, Language, and Politics*, ed. Betty J. Craige (Athens, Georgia, 1988), 99–109. See also his contribution to the present volume on pp. 57–74.

Notes on Contributors

STANLEY FISH is Arts and Sciences Professor of English and Professor of Law at Duke University. He is the author of *Doing What Comes Naturally: Change, Rhetoric, and the Practice of Theory in Literary and Legal Studies* (Duke, 1989) and is currently working on a book-length study of the domestic quarrel.

PHYLLIS FRANKLIN is Executive Director of the Modern Language Association. She has published work on American literary realism and the history of English studies in the United States.

HENRY LOUIS GATES, JR., is W. E. B. DuBois Professor of Literature at Harvard University. The author of *Figures in Black: Words, Signs and the Racial Self* and *The Signifying Monkey*, which won the 1989 American Book Award, he is also the general editor of *The Norton Anthology of African-American Literature*.

HENRY A. GIROUX is Professor and Renowned Scholar in Residence at Miami University. His most recent books are *Schooling and the Struggle for Public Life* (1988), *Postmodern Education* (with Stanley Aronowitz, 1991), and *Border Crossings: Cultural Workers and the Politics of Education* (forthcoming).

DARRYL J. GLESS is Associate Professor of English, Associate Dean of General Education, and a recipient of the Tanner Award for Excellence in Undergraduate Teaching at the University of North Carolina at Chapel Hill. He is the author of books and articles on William Shakespeare and Edmund Spenser.

GERALD GRAFF is George M. Pullman Professor of Humanities, English and Education at the University of Chicago. He is the author of *Professing Literature: An Institutional History* (Chicago, 1987) and is completing a book on the curriculum controversy.

GEORGE A. KENNEDY is Paddison Professor of Classics and Chair of the Curriculum of Comparative Literature at the University of North Carolina at Chapel Hill. He is the author of six books on the history of rhetoric and the editor of volume 1 of the *Cambridge History of Literary Criticism* (1989).

BRUCE KUKLICK is Mellon Professor of the Humanities at the University of Pennsylvania. He is most recently the author of *To Every Thing A Season: Shibe Park and Urban Philadelphia, 1909–1976* (Princeton, 1991).

RICHARD A. LANHAM, Professor of English at UCLA, is the author of *A Handlist of Rhetorical Terms, Tristram Shandy: The Games of Pleasure, Analyzing Prose, The Motives of Eloquence, Literacy and the Survival of Humanism*, and other books. He is currently writing a book on the electronic text.

ELIZABETH KAMARCK MINNICH is Professor of Philosophy and Women's Studies at the Graduate School of the Union Institute, Cincinnati. Her book *Transforming Knowledge* was awarded the 1990 Frederic W. Ness Prize.

ALEXANDER NEHAMAS is Edmund Carpenter II Class of 1943 Professor of the Humanities, Professor of Philosophy, and Professor of Comparative Literature at Princeton University. He is the author of *Nietzsche: Life as Literature*, cotranslator of Plato's *Symposium* and *Phaedrus*, and is working on aesthetic and moral issues raised by television.

FRANCIS OAKLEY is Professor of History at Williams College and its president. He is the author of *Omnipotence, Covenant, and Order*, among other works.

MARY LOUISE PRATT is Professor of Spanish and Portuguese and Comparative Literature at Stanford University and Chair of the Program in Modern Thought and Literature. She is coauthor of *Women, Culture and Politics in Latin America* (1990) and author of *Imperial Eyes: Studies in Travel Writing and Transculturation* (forthcoming, 1991).

RICHARD RORTY is University Professor of Humanities at the University of Virginia. His most recent books are *Objectivity, Relativism and Truth* and *Essays on Heidegger and Others*, both published in 1991.

EVE KOSOFSKY SEDGWICK, Professor of English at Duke University, is the author of *Between Men: English Literature and Male Homosocial Desire* (1985) and *Epistemology of the Closet* (1990).

BARBARA HERRNSTEIN SMITH is Braxton Craven Professor of Comparative Literature and English at Duke University and author of *Contingencies of Value: Alternative Perspectives for Critical Theory* (1988), among other works.

Index

inquiry, 219, 220; sovereignty and, 196; thinking and, 197
Freire, Paulo, 70
French verse, Black, 101–2
Freshman composition programs, 49, 50
Fundamentalism, educational. *See* Neoconservatism
Futurists, 43

Gangbusters (television drama), 168
Gans, Herbert, 174
Gardiner, Anne Barbeau, 255–56
Garrison, William Lloyd, 106
Gates, Henry Louis, Jr., 233
Gay literature, 148–51, 161
Gay studies, 149, 151
Gender, 146–48, 190, 199, 280. *See also* Women
"General Motors Rule," 36
Genovese, Elizabeth Fox-. *See* Fox-Genovese, Elizabeth
Gerbner, George, 173
German scholarship, 207
Gilman, Charlotte Perkins, 8, 9, 131
Giroux, Henry A., 70, 236
Gitlin, Todd, 169
Godwyn, Morgan, 101
Goetz, George. *See* Calverton, V. F.
Governing elites, 131, 193, 197. *See also* Leadership
Graff, Gerald, 53, 247–48, 264, 286
Grafton, Anthony, 271
Gramsci, Antonio, 139
The Grapes of Wrath (Steinbeck), 242–43, 252
Great Books, 27, 34, 38–40, 65–67
Gross, Larry, 173
"The Growth of Negro Literature" (Calverton), 103–4

Haraway, Donna, 112
Harlem Renaissance, 103
Harper, Frances E. W.: *Iola Leroy*, 105

Harvard University, 261
"Havelock Compact," 37, 38
Hegelianism, 194
Herder, Johann, 101
High culture: formulaic literature and, 166; popular entertainment and, 174–75, 240 n.10; in Stanford core reading list, 19; television and, 178. *See also* Literary canons
Higher education: criticism of, 266–89; democracy and, 119–44, 189; democratization of, 34–36, 58, 71, 283–84; Eliot and, 207; history of, 204–6; "Killer Bs'" contempt for, 15–16; public interest in, 213–21; purposes of, 120–21, 127–28; social change through, 138–40; state of, 282–85
Hill Street Blues (television drama), 169, 171
Himmelfarb, Gertrude, 163
Hirsch, E. D., Jr., 34, 240 n.3; *Cultural Literacy*, 75–94, 123, 124–25, 236–37
Hispanic culture, 22
History, 208, 264–65
Holmes, Oliver Wendell, 220
Homer, 6, 7
Homeric poems, 224–25, 230
Homophobia, 30, 113, 145–62
Hook, Sidney, 260
Horkheimer, Max, 134
Horton, George Moses, 102
Howard University Honors Seminar, 97–98
Hull, Gloria T., 191
Humanism: experimental, 46, 47; Renaissance, 209
Humanities: emergence of, 201–12; at Stanford University, 21; student interest in, 277–82; teaching of, 7–8; unworldliness of, 209. *See also* Liberal arts
Humanities in America (Cheney), 258–60
Hume, David, 185

Library of Congress Cataloging-in-Publication Data

The politics of liberal education / Darryl J. Gless and Barbara
Herrnstein Smith, editors.
Revised papers originally presented at a conference held in 1988
at Duke University and the University of North Carolina.
All but two essays previously published as vol. 89, no. 1 (winter
1990) of the South Atlantic quarterly.
Includes index.
ISBN 0-8223-1183-6 (alk. paper).—ISBN 0-8223-1199-2 (pbk.: alk. paper)
1. Education, Humanistic—United States—Congresses.   I. Gless,
Darryl J., 1945–   .   II. Smith, Barbara Herrnstein.
LC1023.P65   1992
370.11′2—dc20   91–29303   CIP